THE BATTLE OF GLENSHIEL

The Jacobite Rising in 1719

Jonathan Worton

'This is the Century of the Soldier', Falvio Testir, Poet, 1641

Helion & Company

Helion & Company Limited
Unit 8 Amherst Business Centre
Budbrooke Road
Warwick
CV34 5WE
England
Tel. 01926 499 619
Fax 0121 711 4075
Email: info@helion.co.uk
Website: www.helion.co.uk
Twitter: @helionbooks
Visit our blog at http://blog.helion.co.uk/

Published by Helion & Company 2018
Designed and typeset by Serena Jones
Cover designed by Paul Hewitt, Battlefield Design (www.battlefield-design.co.uk)
Printed by Henry Ling Limited, Dorchester, Dorset

Cover image, 'The Battle of Glenshiel', by Peter Tillemans, c.1719, © Scottish National Portrait Gallery.

Text © Jonathan Worton 2018. Jonathan Worton has asserted his right under the Copyright, Designs and
Patents Act 1988 to be identified as the author of this work.
Images 21, 33, 36, 40, 41, 49, 54 and 57 photographed by Georgina Worton-Boughen; 25, 31, 46, 50 drawn
by Ed Dovey, © Helion and Company Limited. Colour plate B © Ed Walker. Other images from the author's
collection unless otherwise noted.
Maps © Jonathan Worton 2018

ISBN 978-1-912174-97-3

British Library Cataloguing-in-Publication Data.
A catalogue record for this book is available from the British Library.

For details of other military history titles published by Helion & Company
Limited, contact the above address, or visit our website: http://www.helion.co.uk

We always welcome receiving book proposals from prospective authors.

Contents

List of Illustrations & Maps

Illustrations

Chronology

1718

November–December
The Jacobite general the Duke of Ormond meets in Madrid with Spain's first minister Cardinal Alberoni. Together they plan an invasion of England and a diversionary military expedition to Scotland.

1719

23 February
The Spanish invasion fleet sails from Cádiz with an estimated 5,000 troops aboard.

25 February
The main contingent of the diversionary Jacobite expeditionary force sails from Spain for Scotland.

8 March
The second contingent of the expeditionary force sails from France.

11, 29 March
Squadrons of the British Royal Navy set out to intercept the Spanish invasion fleet.

18–19 March
The Spanish fleet is scattered during an Atlantic storm and forced to return to port.

30 March
Both contingents of the Jacobite expeditionary force meet at Stornoway on the Isle of Lewis.

13 April
The Jacobite expeditionary force lands in Kintail on the mainland of Scotland.

Later April
The Jacobites establish a beachhead in Kintail awaiting news of the Spanish landings in England.

10 May
A Royal Navy squadron bombards and captures the Jacobite stronghold and depot at Eilean Donan Castle. A subsidiary Jacobite magazine is also destroyed.

13 May
The Jacobites withdraw inland.

24 May
Major-General Wightman arrives at Inverness as his base of operations against the Jacobites and takes command of government forces.

4 June
With a general rising announced, Jacobite forces begin to gather in the pass of Glenshiel.

5 June
Wightman's army marches from Inverness seeking battle with the Jacobites.

9 June
Wightman's army camps within short marching distance of the Jacobites positioned in Glenshiel.

10 June
The Jacobites are decisively defeated in the battle of Glenshiel, effectively ending the rising.

11 June
The remaining Jacobites disperse, while an allied Spanish contingent surrenders to Wightman.

Later June
Wightman conducts counter-insurgency reprisal actions in the region of the rising, returning to Inverness on 25 June.

Introduction

The battle of Glenshiel was fought during the long daylight hours of an early summer evening in the far north-west Highlands of Scotland on 10 June 1719. The engagement took place within the mountainous valley (or glen) across the lower slopes of ridges rising steeply from sea level to a height of approximately 3,500 feet (1,067 metres). The pass of Glenshiel has a natural grandeur surpassing any other historically identified British battlefield. Its remoteness and degree of preservation – apart from plantations of 20th century commercial forestry, the landscape is little changed since the 1700s – makes the Glenshiel battleground exceptional. Glenshiel lies within Kintail, and this part of the Highland region remains distant from large population centres. The modern A87 road running through the pass, seasonally busy with holidaymakers, makes the battlefield accessible. But for outsiders to reach Glenshiel still requires a lengthy journey. This sense of distance and of the remote expansiveness of the Highlands was heightened for 18th century incomers. Before later century notions of Romanticism reimagined the Scottish Highlands as wild but attractively picturesque, to outsiders this was an unforgiving alien land. Despite his familiarity with the region, a Lowland Scot employed on government business in the Highlands in the 1720s found it disconcerting, indeed 'most horrid', to 'look at the hills [i.e. mountains] from east to west, or vice versa, for then the eye penetrates far among them, and more particularly their stupendous bulk, frightening irregularity and horrid gloom'.[1]

Two concurrent conflicts were fought over on this extraordinary battlefield. On one hand the battle in Glenshiel was a continuation of the Jacobite risings and wars. This period of intermittent armed conflict from 1689 to 1746 was, in effect, a protracted British civil war over the succession to the throne of the Kingdom of Great Britain and Ireland. The Highland clansmen forming most of the Jacobite army at Glenshiel ostensibly fought for the exiled James Francis Edward Stuart, titular Prince of Wales. As the son and heir of the late deposed King James II of England and VII of Scotland, he was regarded by supporters – the Jacobites – as the rightful King James III and VIII. The opposing regular soldiers of the British Army – with an accompanying contingent of Highlanders, for Scots fought on both sides

---

1   R. Jamieson (ed.), *Letters from a Gentleman in the North of Scotland to His Friend in London*, 2 vols. (1822), vol. 1, p. 286.

1.. The pass of Glenshiel. Looking westward, from the vicinity of the British army's initial deployment, towards the Jacobite positions in the narrowing glen.

at Glenshiel – were in turn engaged to maintain the government and person of King George I; as a German speaker emotionally attached to his native kingdom of Hanover, an unlikely monarch of the British Isles.

An action of internecine British conflict on one hand, on the other Glenshiel had an international dimension. It was an engagement of the (now largely forgotten) War of the Quadruple Alliance. Ranging a coalition of Great Britain and France (at this time in historically unusual partnership), Imperial Austria and the Dutch Republic against the Kingdom of Spain, the war had reached Scotland as a result of Spanish support for the Jacobites. For this reason, a battalion of white-coated Spanish infantry fought at Glenshiel. There were European auxiliaries opposing them too, for Dutch infantrymen formed a contingent in the government army.

The battle of Glenshiel was the single and decisive major engagement of the 1719 Jacobite rising. Eclipsed in history by the longer-lasting and larger Jacobite risings of 1715–16 and 1745–46 (the latter still tinged with 'Bonnie Prince Charlie' romanticism), the events of 1719 have sometimes been dismissed simply as a fiasco.[2] While it was short-lived and for the Jacobites certainly inglorious, the 1719 rising should not be consigned to a footnote in the history of the period. It was in fact a watershed in Jacobitism and opposition to it. Ending in failure like the greater rising finished just three years before, the '19' caused a hiatus in armed Jacobitism for the best part of a generation until the final rising attempted in 1745–46. Furthermore, the events of 1719 are interesting in several ways: in the diplomatic and military activity leading to an attempted Spanish invasion of England and the dispatch of a Jacobite expeditionary force to Scotland; in the diversity of armed forces engaged – in their military cultures, equipment and tactics; in the biographies of the leading personalities involved; in the way rivalry between the European powers became focused in a far corner of the British Isles; and, not least, in the arresting geographical setting where the rising ran its course.

The year 2019 will bring the tercentenary of the battle of Glenshiel. This will generate further curiosity about the events of 1719, which, at the time of writing this introduction in summer 2018, have only once been treated as a single subject in book form; Dickson's *The Jacobite Attempt of 1719* dates from 1895.[3] Dickson's scholarship has stood the test of time (the many contemporary documents he included formed a valuable primary source for this present work), although *The Jacobite Attempt* is inevitably now very dated, including the brief account of the battle of Glenshiel. The burgeoning historiography of the Jacobite period since has touched on 1719 in passing to a greater or lesser extent, but Dickson's remains the only full-length study published to date.[4]

---

2 For historians dismissing the 1719 rising as farcical or fiasco-like, see: F. McLynn, *The Jacobites* (1985), p. 104; S. Reid, *1745 A Military History of the last Jacobite Rising* (1996), p. 3; B. Lenman, 'From the Union of 1707 to the Franchise Reform of 1832', in R.A. Houston and W.W.J. Knox (eds.), *The New Penguin History of Scotland: From the Earliest Times to the Present Day* (2002), p. 321; P. Kennedy, *The Rise and Fall of British Naval Mastery* (1976) 2017 rev. edn., p. 88.

3 W.K. Dickson, *The Jacobite Attempt of 1719* (1895).

4 The historiography of the 1719 rising is plentiful but patchy in coverage. A.H. Millar, in 'The Battle of Glenshiel, 10th June 1719. Note Upon an Unpublished Document in the Possession

This book therefore presents a timely fresh narrative and analysis of the background and course of events of the 1719 Jacobite rising. It includes a more detailed reconstruction of the battle of Glenshiel than has been published before. While the eventual battle is the focus and finale, wider contexts as well as the course of events are considered in depth. The opening pair and fourth chapters provide context: in considering the origins and progress of the Jacobite movement up to 1718, within the sphere of British and European political, diplomatic and military history; and in considering the leading figures and armed forces involved in the military events of 1719. Chapters three, and five through to eight form a narrative reconstructing the course of events in Scotland and elsewhere leading to the battle of Glenshiel, the subject of chapter nine. The concluding tenth chapter considers immediate and longer-term outcomes into the 1720s, in both the context of Scottish Jacobitism and the effort the British government made to strengthen its authority in the Highlands.

A Note on the Calendar

Until 1752 the British at home and in their colonies continued to use the Julian, or Old Style (O.S.) calendar, in which the legal New Year began on 25 March.[5] However, from March 1700 the Julian calendar had fallen 11 days behind the Gregorian calendar then in use across the continent of Europe, referred to as New Style (N.S.). Dates in this book have been reconciled and given in Old Style, as would have been understood across the British Isles in the early 18th century – although the New Year is taken as beginning on 1 January.

---

of His Grace The Duke of Marlborough', *Proceedings of the Society of Antiquaries of Scotland,* 27 (1882–3), pp. 57–69, making reference to a contemporary battlefield map attempted to reconstruct the battle of Glenshiel for the first time in detail – preceding Dickson's lengthy overview of events. J. J. Galbraith's 'The Battle of Glenshiel, 1719', *Transactions of the Gaelic Society of Inverness,* 34 (1927–8), pp. 280–93, revised Millar's interpretation with the benefit of primary sources published by Dickson. D. Sharp's 'The Battle of Glenshiel', *Military History Magazine* (June 2006), unknown pagination, is a more recent but rather unsatisfactory revision. The current (June 2018) entry in Historic Environment Scotland's *Inventory of Historic Battlefields,* under 'Inventory Battlefield, Battle of Glenshiel, Reference: BTL10, Date of Battle 10 June 1719', available at http://portal.historic-scotland.gov.uk, provides an informative description of the battle and battleground. The battle of Glenshiel and the rising are widely mentioned in general studies of the Jacobite period: in passing, for example by H. Kemp, *The Jacobite Rebellion* (1971), p. 77, by McLynn, *Jacobites,* pp. 102–4, and by D. Szechi, *The Jacobites: Britain and Europe, 1688-1788* (1994), pp. 109–10; in summary, for example by B. Lenman, *The Jacobite Risings in Britain, 1689-1746* (2004), pp. 189–94, and by C. Duffy, 'The Jacobite Wars, 1708-46' in *A Military History of Scotland,* (eds.) E.M. Spiers, J.A. Crane, M.J. Strickland (2012), pp. 356–8; and in greater depth by C. Sinclair-Stevenson, *Inglorious Rebellion: The Jacobite Risings of 1708, 1715 and 1719* (1971), pp. 172–87.

5   Although in Scotland since 1600 the New Year had begun on 1 January, otherwise the Julian calendar was retained there.

1

The Jacobite Cause, 1688–1718: Monarchies, Risings and Wider Wars

'In a country where nine of ten are rebels [...] we can want [for] nothing.'

The Glorious Revolution and Rise of Jacobitism

The reasons for the Jacobite rising in 1719 originated in events almost 30 years earlier. Around Christmas 1688, King James II of England and VII of Scotland, sovereign of Great Britain and Ireland, was compelled to seek refuge in France. As a Roman-Catholic king of the predominantly Protestant Three Kingdoms of the British Isles, James's rule since 1685 had caused increasing disquiet among the religious and political establishment. His preoccupation with religious toleration seemed a disguise to reintroduce Catholicism by the back door, and his autocratic approach to kingship appeared to emulate the absolutist monarchy of the Catholic King Louis XIV of France. James also increased the land forces in England, Scotland and Ireland to approximately 34,000 men; a number unknown in peacetime since the military-backed rule of the republican governments of the 1650s.[1] Fears of a Catholic dynasty on the throne of England seemed justified when in June 1688 Queen Mary delivered James Francis Edward, Prince of Wales.

The birth of a son and heir coupled to the King's apparent unconstitutional behaviour finally compelled a party in England, represented by seven peers of the realm (the so-called 'Immortal Seven'), to invite the Dutch Protestant Prince William of Orange to intervene militarily to preserve Protestantism and a free parliament. As stadtholder William was de facto head of state of the United Provinces, and was also James's son-in-law. On 5 November William's fleet made landfall at Torbay, Devon, bringing 14,000 mainly Dutch troops. While William gradually gained support, King James lost his

---

1   C. Barnett, *Britain and Her Army: A Military, Political and Social History of the British Army, 1509–1970* (1970), 2013 reprint, p. 120.

nerve and abandoned his army mobilised to oppose the invaders in the West Country. James's daughter Anne, senior army officers and close political supporters deserted him, and William did not obstruct his eventual flight to France; a convenient turn of events for William's backers they presented as James's self-abdication.

In London in the New Year, a transitional Convention parliament enabled the joint accession of William and his wife Mary – James II's eldest daughter. Acting on the basis that James had de facto abdicated, and that this so-called 'Glorious Revolution' was saving the kingdom from popish and arbitrary rule, the Convention issued a Declaration of Rights, later enacted in the Bill (and Act) of Rights. This was designed to bind William to a constitutional arrangement founded on the primacy of parliamentary government that barred the crown to Catholics. Under this arrangement, on 13 February 1689 the joint sovereignty of King William III and Queen Mary II over England and Ireland came into effect.

Scotland, however, was not bound to this settlement. Although England and Scotland had been jointly ruled since the accession in 1603 of King James I of England and VI of Scotland, the northern kingdom retained its own parliament and a considerable degree of autonomy. Scotland in fact was religiously, economically and legally largely self-determining. Therefore, in March 1689 a Convention of the Scottish political nation met to decide the future of the Scottish crown. The divisive debate over testimonials from both William III and James VII was marked by fierce exchanges between declared 'Williamites' and James's supporters. However, William's tactfully worded assurances gained sway, and on 4 April the Convention declared James was a despot who had forfeited his right to the crown. It was instead offered jointly to King William III and Queen Mary II as joint monarchs of Scotland, in accordance with the Convention's condition that the monarchy must uphold Protestantism.[2]

The acceptance, in the meantime since he landed on French soil on Christmas Day 1688, by King Louis XIV of James II as the rightful sovereign laid the foundation for Jacobitism. The movement's purpose was to restore the direct Stuart line to the throne of Great Britain and Ireland, and from later 1714 to overturn the Hanoverian succession. King James's supporters became known as Jacobites – from the Latin form of James, 'Jacobus'. Louis granted James the chateaux of St. Germain-en-Laye to be his court and had it suitably refurbished. Situated near to Paris, this was a royal residence second in importance only to Louis's magnificent new palace at Versailles. At once, the court at St. Germain became the hub of the Jacobite movement.

The backing of Louis XIV, monarch of the most powerful nation in Europe, for the deposed James was an unequal alliance that usefully accommodated

---

2   T. Claydon, 'William III and II (1650–1702)', in (eds.) C.G. Matthew and B. Harrison, *Oxford Dictionary of National Biography* – hereafter *ODNB* – (2004), online edn., accessed 5 Aug. 2017; M. Magnusson, *Scotland: The Story of a Nation* (2000), pp. 511–14; W. Ferguson, *Scotland 1689 to the Present. The Edinburgh History of Scotland, Volume 4* (1978), pp. 4–5; K. M. Brown, 'Reformation to Union, 1560–1707', in R.A. Houston and W.W. J. Knox (eds.), *The New Penguin History of Scotland: From the Earliest Times to the Present Day* (2002), p. 259.

the French king's hostility to William of Orange's United Provinces. The relationship established the twin, interconnected courses of Jacobitism: as a complex phenomenon native to the British Isles with an international dimension. Firstly, the exiled presence of the legitimate king and his heirs would remain a cause of intermittent political instability and civil war in the British Isles for more than two generations. Fears of Jacobite uprisings and supportive invasions became an overbearing concern shaping British governmental policy.[3] At the same time, the second course of Jacobitism was to attract the intervention of European powers hostile to the incumbent British government. Due to increasing governmental authority and shifts in society away from the private ownership of weapons (with the notable exception of the clans of Highland Scotland), Jacobites at home had little opportunity to acquire arms. This made the backing of foreign powers, with money, armaments, and, in particular, regular troops, vital to any attempted uprising or coup. The difficulty for the Jacobites, however, was that such opportunities arose only in time of European war. Even then, gaining the element of surprise and coordinating action in Britain with an invading force would always remain extremely difficult to achieve.[4]

2. James II of England & VII of Scotland, monarch of the Kingdom of Great Britain and Ireland from 1685 to 1688. Jacobites sought to bring about James's restoration after his deposition and exile during the so-called 'Glorious Revolution' of 1688.

Jacobitism was foremost an armed movement. Apart from during the Tory ministry of 1710–14, when Jacobites hoped a peaceful transition from Queen Anne to her half-brother James might be brokered, political action alone would not restore James II and his line without an at least convincing show of armed force. Leading Jacobites in exile therefore always favoured a military solution.[5] Nonetheless, Jacobitism was shaped by politics and religion. It was a divisive force in the fractious relationship between Whigs and Tories. Known at often sharply contested constituency level as the 'Whig interest' and the 'Tory interest', they formed the two opposing groupings of late 17th and early 18th century British politics.[6]

Whigs, Tories and Jacobites
The title Whig labelled English politicians campaigning in the parliaments between 1679 and 1681 to exclude the Catholic Duke of York (later King

---

3   P. S. Fritz, *The English Ministers and Jacobitism between the Rebellions of 1715 and 1745* (1975), p. 137.

4   A.I. Macinnes, 'Jacobitism', *History Today,* 34 (1984), *passim*; Szechi, *Jacobites*, pp. 41–3; D. Szechi, *1715: The Great Jacobite Rebellion* (2000), pp. 46–7, 61.

5   D. Szechi, *Jacobitism and Tory Politics, 1710–1714* (2003), pp. 18–19, 196.

6   W.A. Speck, *Tory & Whig, The Struggle in the Constituencies 1701–1715* (1970), p. 7.

James II) from succeeding his brother King Charles II. From 1688 the Whig party assumed political prominence as the leading backers of the Protestant Glorious Revolution. The Whigs kept intermittent power during the reigns of William and Mary and their successor Queen Anne, and became the dominant political party and oligarchy from 1714 under the Georgian dynasty. In their self-image Whigs were defenders of all shades of Protestantism and stout opponents of popery. This wariness of High-Church practice meant that Scots Whigs adhered strongly to Presbyterianism. Alongside religious toleration, Whigs professed to stand for parliamentary rights and freedoms in a balanced constitution. These proto-liberal views (and the Whigs were the forerunners of the 19th century Liberal Party) were shared by a combination of landowners, new-moneyed businessmen and the professional class. In foreign affairs, Whigs favoured military interventionism to contain Louis XIV's France. Whigs could imagine themselves upholding the constitutional values of the Parliamentarian cause of the mid-17th century Civil Wars. However, their Tory opponents targeted holding to parliamentary ascendancy and tolerance of religious dissent as anti-monarchical and dangerous to the established Anglican Church.

For their part, the Tories have been characterised as the party of the squire and the parson. Habitually conservative (they evolved in the 19th century into the Conservative Party), in their religious self-image Tories were steadfast defenders of the primacy of Protestant Anglicanism and were known as the 'Church party'. They justified their role in the Glorious Revolution as having saved the Church of England from Catholicism.[7] Tories generally accepted the post-1688 religious settlement but were suspicious of Protestant non-conforming Dissenters, who they regarded as at least as threatening to the established Church as Catholicism. Tories also disliked the interventionism in European affairs resultant from William III's accession. Tories could picture themselves as heirs to the Royalist cause of the Civil Wars, as the party of monarchism and Church. They took their name (used insultingly against them at first) from the parliamentary grouping that during the so-called Exclusion Crisis of 1679–81 supported the right of James Duke of York to succeed to the throne. By backing the heir apparent, the Tories intended to uphold the due process of divinely-appointed monarchical succession. Most Tory MPs were country gentlemen representing the party of the landed class, but the Whigs too were led by grandee landowners.[8]

Tories mostly tolerated the revolutionary constitutional settlement of 1689, and by the second decade of the 18th century held more enlightened views of a Protestant monarchy acting through parliament. However, abiding Tory principles of hereditary kingship coupled to an established Episcopalian Church encouraged an inclination to Jacobitism. This was true of Jacobite Tories who clung to the ancient and inalienable constitutional rights of

---

7   Szechi, *Jacobitism and Tory Politics*, p. 42.
8   Speck, *Tory & Whig*, pp. 1–7, *passim*; Szechi, *Great Jacobite Rebellion*, pp. 32–3; E. Evans (ed.), *British History, A Source Book* (2006), *passim*; Anon., *The Hutchinson Illustrated Encyclopedia of British History* (1995), *passim*.

the Crown in the bloodline of James II.[9] In Scotland, most political Tories adhered to the Scottish Episcopal Church, despite its suppression since 1690 by an Act of the Scots parliament restoring Presbyterian governance and practice in the Church of Scotland. This had resulted in the expulsion of many Episcopalian ministers, known as Non-jurors, for refusing to renounce their oaths to James II in favour of William and Mary. Episcopalians hoped for a Stuart restoration as the means to reverse what they perceived to be Presbyterian ecclesiastical hegemony. Thus Episcopalian became the favoured Church of Scottish Jacobitism.[10]

In heated political disputes both north and south of the Anglo-Scottish border, Whigs could turn Tory association with High Church worship against them, tainting them as Jacobites seeking the restoration of popish absolutist monarchy.[11]

The First Jacobite Rising

While the Glorious Revolution was being settled, the first Jacobite uprising began in Highland Scotland. The rebel army consisted mostly of clansmen led by their chiefs, setting the precedent for all future risings. In March 1689, John Graham, Viscount Dundee, an army officer devoted to King James, rejecting the Scottish Convention parliament's acceptance of William of Orange headed for the Highlands. There was much support for the Stuarts among the Highland clans, but Dundee's was not an isolated effort. On 12 March James II, with French backing, had landed in Ireland. James was encouraged by Louis XIV to make Ireland a springboard to regain the kingdoms of England and Scotland. Dundee, meanwhile, raised an army mostly from the western clans but also including some Lowland gentry and cavalry, and a few hundred Irish Foot. The Convention parliament in turn mobilised an opposing army under the command of General Hugh Mackay to crush the rising. The armies engaged on 27 July just north of the Pass of Killiecrankie in Highland Perthshire. Mackay's army of approximately 5,000 men, English and Lowland Scots regulars, and regiments from the Scots Brigade of the Dutch Army, outnumbered Dundee's by two to one, but was overwhelmed and mostly routed by the Highlanders in a short, bloody action. Dundee was killed, however, and without his charismatic leadership the Jacobites were beaten by government infantry in street fighting at Dunkeld on 21 August. Dispirited, the Highlanders dispersed northward and this first phase of the rising petered out in sporadic guerilla activity.

The rebellion lay dormant over winter. But in early 1690 Thomas Buchan, a major-general in James's army in Ireland, brought military supplies and a few troops to encourage the clans to take up arms again in the spring. In April, Buchan was joined by about 1,500 clansmen, including MacDonalds, Camerons and MacPhersons. Most chiefs, however, hedged their bets by staying at home. General Mackay deputised Sir Thomas Livingstone,

---

9   Szechi, *Jacobitism and Tory Politics,* pp. 49, 51, 54.
10 Brown, 'Reformation to Union', pp. 260, 312; Ferguson, *Scotland,* pp. 103, 127.
11 Szechi, *Great Jacobite Rebellion,* pp. 32–3; McLynn, *Jacobites,* pp. 64–5; Magnusson, *Scotland,* pp. 520–1;

3. William III, king of Great Britain and Ireland from 1689 to 1702. As the Dutch Prince of Orange, William gained the throne from King James II and VII during the Glorious Revolution of 1688. (New York Picture Library Digital Collection)

leading 1,200 government Horse and Foot with several hundred Whig Grant and MacKay militia, to stamp out the rising. Around dawn on 1 May Livingstone, making decisive use of his horsemen, took by surprise and routed Buchan's Jacobites encamped at Cromdale in Strathspey, south-east of Inverness. Several hundred Highlanders were killed or captured. The rising was broken, and in summer Mackay marched 6,000 troops from Perth north-west through the Highlands to Loch Linnhe, where he ordered a stronghold named Fort William built and garrisoned. Mackay's show of force set the pattern for future governmental action against Jacobitism in the Highlands.[12]

King William was advised to show clemency, and in August 1691 offered an amnesty to rebel chiefs who swore allegiance to him by the New Year. Nearly all did so, once they had received King James's grudging permission. But Alasdair MacIan, chief of the Jacobite MacDonalds of Glencoe, unintentionally missed the deadline. The Earl of Stair, secretary of state for Scotland, used this as a pretext to make a punitive example of MacIan's troublesome clan and to cow Jacobitism in the Highlands. The outcome was the notorious massacre by government troops of MacIan and 37 other Glencoe MacDonalds in mid-February 1692.[13]

The Jacobite War in Ireland and the Nine Years' War

In Ireland, in the meantime since James II's arrival in March 1689, a far greater Jacobite war had been fought out. The standing forces in Ireland were an army of occupation of the English government, maintained on a separate military establishment to England and Scotland. However, from 1685 to 1688 James's commander-in-chief in Ireland and lord deputy Richard Talbot, Earl of Tyrconnell, had shaped the 10,000-strong army there into a predominantly Catholic force.[14] Remaining loyal to James, Tyrconnell's army opposed the Protestant Glorious Revolution in Ireland and backed a Catholic rebellion. In spring 1689 Jacobites invaded Protestant Ulster, which if taken would enable communications with Dundee's forces in Scotland. However, the key strongholds of Enniskillen and Londonderry, summoned to surrender by James in April, held out until relieved in late July. English and Dutch-Huguenot reinforcements arrived under the command of the

12 Magnusson, *Scotland*, pp. 514–20; M. Barthorp, *The Jacobite Rebellions, 1689–1745* (1982), pp. 3–6; J. Prebble, *Glencoe: The Story of the Massacre* (1987), pp. 68–74, 90–4, *passim*.
13 Brown, 'Reformation to Union', p. 260.
14 Barnett, *Britain and Her Army*, p. 120; J. Childs, 'The Restoration Army 1660–1702', in D. Chandler and I. Beckett (eds.), *The Oxford History of the British Army* (1994), p. 58.

pedestrian veteran Dutch general Schomberg, and they slowly regained lost ground as the Jacobites withdrew from Ulster.

The war in Ireland was by now also a front of the wider European War of the Grand Alliance (or Nine Years' War). This coalition had been fashioned by William III to align Great Britain, the United Provinces, Spain, and Imperial Austria against Louis XIV's France.

The reinforcement for the Irish Jacobites of 6,000 French regulars landed in March 1690 was countered in June by the arrival of King William with 15,000 English, Danish and Dutch troops. On 1 July William's army, grown to around 35,000 men, defeated the 25,000-strong Jacobite field army at the battle of the Boyne, the turning point of the war. Although most of his army remained intact, James lost his nerve and returned to France. Dublin surrendered without resistance on 4 July, the day that James sailed, although Williamite hopes of a Jacobite collapse proved unfounded. Sieges of their strongholds of Athlone and Limerick had to be abandoned in July and August respectively, the latter with heavy losses for William's forces. However, Franco-Jacobite forces were now on the defensive and in retreat.

From spring 1691 Tyrconnell upheld the Jacobite war effort with the benefit of French military supplies. However, the fall in June of Athlone on the defensive line of the River Shannon was the precursor to the decisive Anglo-Dutch victory over the Jacobite field army at Aughrim the following 12 July. Aughrim heralded the end of the war in Ireland, and Galway surrendered at the end of the month. In August William's troops laid siege to Limerick, the last major Jacobite stronghold. The terms of the city's surrender in October formed part of the wider Treaty of Limerick concluding the war.[15] The lenient conditions for disbandment allowed most Jacobite troops to seek exile in France. By 1693 there were more than 16,000 Irish infantry in French service. At first reorganised under the patronage of James II and his court at St. Germain, after the 1697 peace this semi-autonomous force was fully integrated into the French Army and thus cut off from James's control.[16]

James had lost Ireland but retained Louis XIV's support. The French king next backed a plan for James's restoration in England by a cross-channel invasion. Planned for spring 1692, this would also serve Louis's purpose as a diversion to draw William III's forces from Flanders, the seat of the war. It was intended that combined French squadrons from the Mediterranean and Atlantic stations would achieve superiority in the English Channel before the Anglo-Dutch fleets united, thus enabling landings in the English West Country. A powerful expeditionary army 24,000 strong assembled in Normandy, joined in April by James. However, in early May Admiral Tourville on the Atlantic coast felt compelled to put to sea with his ships alone. On the

15 McLynn, *Jacobites*, pp. 13–18; Barnett, *Britain and Her Army*, pp. 149–51; R. Dunlop, rev. H. Murtagh, 'Schomberg, Frederick Herman de, first duke of Schomberg (1615–1690)', in *ODNB* (2004), online edn., accessed 6 Aug. 2017; Claydon, 'William III and II'. This summary of the war in Ireland also draws on: J. Barratt, *Battles for the Three Kingdoms: The Campaigns for England, Scotland and Ireland 1689–92* (2007); J. Childs, *The Williamite Wars in Ireland 1688–1691* (2007).

16 G. Rowlands, 'Foreign Service in the Age of Absolute Monarchy: Louis XIV and His *Forces Étrangères*', *War in History*, 17 (2010), pp. 145, 147–8, 163–4.

4. Louis XIV, king of France from 1643 to 1715. Louis sponsored the Jacobite court in exile and used the Jacobites as a fifth column against Great Britain during his European wars.

19th Tourville's 44 warships engaged an Anglo-Dutch fleet they found outnumbered them by almost two to one, and were duly outfought by nightfall. The French fleet scattered or was beached, and over following days English raiding parties operating inshore burnt 12 ships of the line and some transports. The battle of Cape Barfleur-La Hogue was a notable Allied victory celebrated in England as a great deliverance from invasion. James's immediate hopes of regaining his crown were scuppered with the French fleet. Nonetheless, in 1696–97 Louis XIV again kept an invasion army on standby, this time at Calais. The French, however, were discouraged by the lack of enthusiasm for the enterprise shown by James and his English supporters. Coupled with the Anglo-Dutch blockade of French Channel ports, this meant an invasion never got underway. Jacobite plots to effect the assassination of King William proved equally unsuccessful.[17]

The War of the Grand Alliance ended in 1697 with the Treaty of Ryswick. Its terms compelled Louis XIV to recognise William III's sovereignty over Great Britain and Ireland. While James II kept his court at St. Germain-en-Laye, subsidised by Louis's generous pension, he had to resign himself to permanent exile. While his religious piety sustained him in adversity, James grew frail and died on 5 September 1701. Louis, as he had promised the late king, immediately proclaimed his thirteen-year-old son Prince James Francis Edward Stuart as King James III of England and VIII of Scotland. His supporters would come to know Prince James by the romantic pseudonym the 'Chevalier de St. George'. To his opponents, however, he was always simply the 'Pretender'; and in later years, once his son Charles Edward Stuart was the leading light of Jacobitism, the 'Old Pretender'. Before then, his gloomy disposition had earned James the soubriquet 'Old Mr Melancholy'.

Louis's acknowledgment of James II's heir breathed life into the Jacobite movement, but was tantamount to a declaration of war on Williamite England. The English Parliament was also uncomfortably only too aware that the exiled Prince of Wales endangered the hard-won Protestant succession.

Upholding the Protestant Succession

Queen Mary had died childless in 1694, and William III showed no inclination to remarry. Mary's sister Anne, James II's younger daughter, was heir to the throne, but her only surviving child, the Duke of Gloucester, died in 1700. The 17 other children borne by Anne had died in infancy, so it seemed unlikely

---

17 N.A.M. Rodger, *The Command of the Ocean: A Naval History of Britain, 1649–1815* (2006), pp. 148–51; B. Wilson, *Empire of the Deep: The Rise and Fall of the British Navy* (2014), pp 268–70; McLynn, *Jacobites*, pp. 22–4.

that at the age of 36 she and her husband, Prince George of Denmark, would have a long-living offspring. Anne was the last direct Protestant Stuart descendant of James I and VI, and so was generally accepted by the British establishment as William's successor. In the event of her death, however, there was no obvious Protestant heir, and the 1689 Bill of Rights blocked a Catholic candidate. This impasse had the potential to provoke civil war if the restoration of the male Stuart line in the person of Prince James Francis Edward was attempted.

To forestall this nightmarish eventuality as it perceived it, the English Parliament in June 1701, without involving its Scots equivalent, passed the Act of Settlement. This reaffirmed the provision of the Bill of Rights denying the English crown to Catholics. Moreover, to guarantee a Protestant succession the Act legislated that Anne (or William, if he outlived her) would be succeeded by a German Protestant of Stuart descent and her line. She was Sophia, dowager Electress of the north-German state of Hanover. A seemingly

5. Anne, queen of Great Britain and Ireland from 1702 until 1714. In the event last of the Stuart monarchs, Jacobites hoped childless Anne would be succeeded by her half-brother James Francis Edward Stuart. (New York Picture Library Digital Collection)

unlikely candidate, Sophia's qualification for the English crown, in addition to her Lutheran Protestantism, was that she was on her mother's side the grand-daughter of King James I and VI. Sophia was then aged 70, and so it was likely it would be her son, the forty-one-year-old Georg Ludwig, the Elector of Hanover, who would succeed Anne.

The Act of Settlement, however, applied only to the English crown. As it had in respect of William and Mary, the Scots Parliament reserved power of choice over its monarch. Early in Anne's reign, in August 1703 Scots parliamentarians asserted this autonomy by an Act of Security. This legislated that the next sovereign of Scotland would be a Protestant, but not necessarily the English parliament's choice.[18] This raised the possibility that if James Francis Edward Stuart converted to Protestantism, Scots might consider him an acceptable king.

William III had died in March 1702. Queen Anne's succession was peacefully proclaimed and generally popularly accepted across the Three Kingdoms. However, the continued reluctance of the Scots Parliament to guarantee the Hanoverian succession threatened the monarchical union. This uncertainty was a prime motive for its backers on both sides of the border for the incorporating political and economic union of Scotland with England. After a polarising debate in Scotland, the resultant Treaty and Act of Union came into force on 1 May 1707. The Scots Parliament was dissolved, and a single unitary parliament established at Westminster committed to

18 H. Kemp, *The Jacobite Rebellion* (1975), p. 6; Magnusson, *Scotland*, pp. 533–4, 541–2; Ferguson, *Scotland*, p. 40.

6. James Francis Edward Stuart (*b*. 1688, *d*. 1766), exiled Prince of Wales. Following the death in 1701 of his father King James II and VII, Jacobites regarded James Francis as the rightful King James III & VIII. Opponents ridiculed him as 'The Pretender'.

the Hanoverian succession. Apart from leading figures benefitting personally, and those able to foresee the likelihood of long-term economic benefits, Scots gave the Union at best grudging acceptance. Many openly expressed hostility and warmed to Jacobitism to express their national identity. Previously easily tainted as a traitorous extension of French foreign policy, Jacobitism now achieved respectability as a Scottish nationalist movement.[19]

The Franco-Jacobite Expedition of 1708

Since 1702, the British nations had renewed conflict with France in the War of the Spanish Succession. Great Britain was the cornerstone of the Second Grand Alliance, recreated by the late King William III to check the hegemony of Louis XIV's France and prevent unification of the French and Spanish crowns; given that since 1700 Spain had been ruled by King Phillip V, who was the French-born Duke of Anjou and Louis XIV's grandson.

In 1708, Louis once more turned to the Jacobites as a fifth column to destabilise the British war effort, then being successfully prosecuted by the Duke of Marlborough in Flanders. James Francis Edward Stuart was to accompany a French expeditionary force to Scotland to convert discontent over the Act of Union into open rebellion. The French were encouraged by convincing reports from Scotland by the Jacobite agent Colonel Nathaniel Hooke, that once ashore James would have widespread support. The Jacobite Duke of Hamilton also reckoned that 30,000 Scots would rise for James given French backing. There were at most 2,000 government troops in Scotland and their fortifications were obsolescent, so part of Marlborough's army would have to be recalled as reinforcements. This could give France the advantage in the war in Flanders, and if Scotland rose for James Britain's capacity to continue the Continental war would be diminished.[20]

Six thousand French troops assembled at Dunkirk, but inter-service cooperation was poor and the naval commander Admiral Forbin disliked the enterprise. Suspicious of optimistic Jacobite claims that Scotland was ripe for rebellion, Forbin worried now to establish a beachhead on the east coast. In doing so he overlooked the strategic possibilities a successful landing might bring. The fleet, 15 transports and five escorting men-of-war, sailed in early March 1708, later than planned, with James aboard recovering from measles. The British were by then alert to the danger, and the Royal Navy's

19   McLynn, *Jacobites,* pp. 74–6; Szechi, *Great Jacobite Rebellion,* p. 61.
20   Sinclair-Stevenson, *Inglorious Rebellion,* pp. 44–6; Duffy, 'Jacobite Wars', pp. 349–50; J. Childs, 'Marlborough's Wars and the Act of Union, 1702–14', in *A Military History of Scotland,* p. 338; Ferguson, *Scotland,* p. 55.

North Sea squadron commanded by Admiral George Byng gave pursuit to Forbin, albeit at a distance. The French reached the Firth of Forth, but could not establish firm contact with Jacobites on shore. With Byng closing from the south, Forbin headed further northward, ignoring James's requests to be put ashore. A plan to land the French troops at Inverness was abandoned because of bad weather that also hampered Byng's pursuit. Forbin brought the fleet and the despondent James back to Dunkirk at the end of March, with the loss of one ship captured.[21]

The expedition seemed to have been a fiasco, but 10 veteran British battalions (including two Scots regiments) were kept at sea for a month, shipped to Scotland in March and back to Flanders in April. Not a single soldier landed in Scotland, and the units were for some time rendered ineffective by sickness.[22] The invasion scare compelled the British government, belatedly recognising that things could have turned out very differently, to hurriedly improve the defences of its garrisons in Scotland. Historians accept that James's landing with French troops could well have encouraged a successful rising. But Daniel Defoe, a contemporary, found most ordinary Scots ambivalent. While working in Scotland to promote the Union, Defoe became an informed commentator on the national mood. He returned there as a government correspondent in 1708, shortly after the failed French expedition. He later commented: 'It began to be said at the time of the invasion: "It lay between the English and the French, let them fight it out". There was nothing for the honest people, as they call themselves, to do in it.'[23]

The remainder of the War of the Spanish Succession provided the Jacobites with no further strategic opportunities. James Francis Edward Stuart gained some practical experience of soldiering, serving with distinction in King Louis's household corps at the battles of Oudenarde (1708) and Malplaquet (1709).

The Hanoverian Succession and 1715 Jacobite Rising

The British wartime general election in summer 1710 produced a Tory ministry inclined to disengage from the war. However, peace with France was conditional on the expulsion of James Francis Edward Stuart. Sympathetic English ministers therefore acquiesced when in early 1713 Louis had James relocated to Bar-le-Duc, capital of the Duchy of Lorraine, a nominally autonomous territory within the French border.[24] The dowager Queen Mother, Mary of Modena, was allowed to maintain a separate court at St. Germain-en-Laye, to which a shrinking number of older Jacobites remained attached. The Hanoverian succession was written into the treaties of Utrecht (1713) and Rastatt (1714) agreed by Louis XIV, which together formed the European peace settlement ending the War of the Spanish Succession.

---

21 Sinclair-Stevenson, *Inglorious Rebellion*, pp. 47–53; Rodger, *Command of the Ocean,* pp. 173–4.

22 D. Chandler, 'The Great Captain-General, 1702–1714', in *Oxford History of the British Army*, p. 74; Childs, 'Marlborough's Wars', pp. 338–9.

23 P.R. Backscheider, 'Defoe, Daniel (1660?–1731)', in *ODNB* (2004), online edn., accessed 24 July 2017; Quotation cited by Sinclair-Stevenson, *Inglorious Rebellion*, p. 53.

24 E. Gregg, 'James Francis Edward (1688–1766)', in *ODNB* (2004), online edn., accessed 24 July 2017.

The death of Queen Anne on 1 August 1714 finally put to the test the carefully laid plans for the Hanoverian succession. There was no Jacobite coup, and the predominantly Tory parliament stuck to arrangements made during Anne's reign for an orderly transition that brought the Elector Georg Ludwig to London as King George I on 20 September.[25] However, Whig politicians had actively managed George's succession, and the Whig party had championed the Hanoverian settlement. Whigs rewarded by him for their loyalty therefore came to dominate the new king's ministry. They did so at the expense of leading Tories, who were either shunned by George or else refused to serve alongside Whig rivals. Some leading Tories associated with Jacobite plots (that collapsed because the aspirant James III and VIII would not abjure Catholicism) fled to join him in France for their personal safety. In the prevailing antagonistic political climate Whigs discredited Tories for being closet Jacobites.

In autumn 1715, the Georgian regime was endangered by a rebellion that generated the most armed support of all the Jacobite risings.[26] It was triggered by the Earl of Mar, an alienated Tory grandee turned Jacobite, the former secretary of state for Scotland. On his estates in Highland Deeside in early September, Mar and a gathering of clan chiefs and landed aristocrats proclaimed James III and VIII rightful king of Scotland and Great Britain. Jacobites quickly occupied Inverness, Aberdeen and Perth, but failed to seize Edinburgh Castle, the British Army's headquarters in Scotland. By October Mar had about 7,000 Horse and Foot based at Perth. They greatly outnumbered the British army blocking the way south at Stirling led by the Scot Lieutenant-General John Campbell, Duke of Argyll, commander-in-chief in Scotland. Mar also awaited reinforcements equivalent to another Jacobite army numbering as many as 6,000 men, formed of Highland clansmen and followers of north-eastern Jacobite landlords. But these were delayed in sideshow campaigns in the north and western Highlands against pro-government Whig clan militias. Nonetheless, by early November much of Scotland north of the central Lowland belt looked to be under Jacobite control.

Mar's best strategy would be quickly to take Argyll's outnumbered regulars at Stirling head on, to force the way to the Lowlands and Edinburgh. Instead, in early October 2,000 Jacobite troops detached from Perth were ferried across the Firth of Forth to outflank Edinburgh. Failing to endanger the capital, they instead shifted southward to join Scots and English border Jacobites at Kelso. The commanders of the conjoined forces committed to an impromptu invasion of England, hopeful of recruiting support along the way. This southern Jacobite army advanced unopposed as far as Preston in Lancashire, where outnumbering government forces converged on them. In street fighting on 12 November the remaining 1,400 or so Jacobites successfully beat off British attacks, but they had no hope of reinforcement or retreat. Their morale and leadership were spent, and they surrendered unconditionally two days later.

---

25 G.C. Gibbs, 'George I (1660–1727)', in *ODNB* (2004), online edn., accessed 7 Aug. 2017.

26 Summaries of the 1715–16 rising, of varying length, include: Barthorp, *Jacobite Rebellions*, pp. 6–9; Ferguson, *Scotland,* pp. 66–9; Duffy, 'Jacobite Wars', pp. 350–6; Sinclair-Stevenson, *Inglorious Rebellion*, pp. 84–137; Kemp, *Jacobite Rebellion*, pp. 12–74. Szechi's *Great Jacobite Rebellion* is a comprehensive and detailed full-length study.

In Scotland meanwhile, the standoff by the armies between Perth and Stirling had continued to Argyll's advantage. It was not until 11 November that Mar, his army swelled to probably 9,000 men by the arrival of contingents from the north, advanced towards Stirling. Two days later the Jacobites encountered and engaged Argyll's army, about two-fifths their number, on high moorland at Sheriffmuir, north-east of Dunblane. The battle was hard-fought and confused. The left centre and wing of each army was beaten and driven off by its opposing number, but parts of both armies held their ground or rallied. The reformed remainder of the Jacobite army outnumbered the remaining British units but did not resume the attack, and nightfall ended the stalemate. The battle of Sheriffmuir was indecisive, with heavy casualties on both sides. But it was the strategic turning point of the rising in the government's favour. The Jacobites had been stopped from breaking into the Lowlands, and their post-battle withdrawal to Perth presaged a long retreat further northward.

James Francis Edward Stuart finally landed in north-east Scotland just before Christmas. He brought a few followers, but no French troops, and lacked a masterplan to revitalise the rising. His backer King Louis XIV had died in August, before Mar's Highland uprising was underway. Louis's nephew, Phillip, Duke of Orléans, became regent of France in the minority of the five-year old Louis XV. Orléans was committed to the Peace of Utrecht, and would not risk war with Britain by giving the Jacobites material aid. A dozen ships readied to sail from French ports with troops and military supplies therefore stayed put.[27] The Regent did however, overlook James's journey (made in disguise) to the coast. He eventually took passage to Scotland aboard a Dunkirk privateer.[28]

James made a show of setting up court at Perth, but his military situation seemed hopeless. As the Jacobite army dwindled by desertion, Argyll's grew by reinforcements from England and the arrival of Dutch auxiliaries. James was melancholic and temperamentally ill-equipped to inspire his followers. With his army having abandoned Perth at the end of January 1716 retreating northward, in early February James gave up his cause as lost and sailed for France. He left his army demoralised and his popularity in Scotland permanently damaged; a reputation sullied before his departure when, in an act of scorched earth meant to impede Argyll's pursuing army, the Jacobite rearguard torched several Perthshire villages.

The remaining 4,000 or so men of the Jacobite army fell back on Aberdeen and disbanded in mid-February. In the spring, columns of government troops directed by General William Cadogan, new commander-in-chief in Scotland in place of Argyll (replaced for allegedly not having prosecuted the campaign more vengefully) probed the Highlands to discourage further resistance. Most clans pragmatically submitted peacefully, making a show of surrendering some weapons. However, it was operationally very difficult for Cadogan's subordinates to root out rebels in hiding. The leading figures and many lower ranking officers of the Jacobite army therefore eventually escaped to the Continent, after lying low in the Highlands and Islands waiting for

---

27 Kemp, *Jacobite Rebellion*, p. 11.
28 Gregg, 'James Francis Edward Stuart'.

French rescue ships. It has been estimated that the Jacobite diaspora from the failed rising may have numbered as many as 2,000 individuals.[29]

Outcomes of the '15 in Scotland and Abroad

The rebellion in Scotland was over by May 1716. In its aftermath, the victorious Georgian regime acted leniently. There was little appetite in Scotland (where sympathy for Jacobitism remained strong among the upper and middling classes) to worsen social wounds of civil war by pursuing rebels, and so most went unpunished. Most of the approximately 100 Jacobite prisoners held in Scotland were freed, or tried and released without sentence. In Scotland, the London government had more to gain by showing magnanimity. It instead focussed its vengeance in England, upon the leaders and unfortunate lower ranks of the Jacobite southern army captured at Preston.[30] However, noble Scots rebels who during the course of the rising had been made subject to parliamentary Acts of Attainder for high treason were punished *in absentia*, their estates and revenues being made forfeit of the Crown. In June 1716 an Act was passed, 'For appointing commissioners to enquire of the estates of certain traitors […] in order to raise money out of them severally for the use of the publick [sic]'.[31] From September the government's Forfeited Estates Commission operated out of Edinburgh, but found its work of land confiscation and resale and rent collection increasingly difficult the further north it reached. Well-wishers reclaiming property on their behalf coupled with grassroots support from obedient rent collectors and tenants enabled dispossessed Jacobites to maintain an interest in their estates and income. The confiscations and work of the Commission and associated York Buildings Company, a private venture in land speculation, was contested in law and rendered financially unprofitable by what has been described as a campaign of 'legal guerilla warfare', conducted in the courts by the families and associates of attainted Jacobites.[32] A further Act, enforceable from November 1716, 'for the more effectual securing the peace of the Highlands in Scotland', was intended to demilitarise the Jacobite clans. It proscribed carrying arms in public and encouraged the surrender of weapons.[33] But like the measures for forfeiture of property, this so-called Disarming Act was enforced patchily and with difficulty. Belligerent Highlanders also exploited a loophole allowing them to be reimbursed for trading-in old and worn out weapons.

By summer 1717, the situation in Scotland had normalised to the extent that the London government considered the time right to extend an offer of royal pardon to ex-rebels. In July, parliament passed the 'Act

---

29 D. Szechi, ' "Cam Ye O'er Frae France?" Exile and the Mind of Scottish Jacobitism, 1716–1727', *Journal of British Studies*, 37 (1998), p. 363.

30 Sinclair-Stevenson, *Inglorious Rebellion*, pp. 134–7; Kemp, *Jacobite Rebellion*, pp. 72, 74; Macinnes, 'Jacobitism', p. 28.

31 D. Pickering (ed.), *The Statutes at Large from the Twelfth Year of Queen Anne to the Fifth Year of King George I* (1764), p. 299.

32 M. Sankey and D. Szechi, 'Elite Culture and the Decline of Scottish Jacobitism 1716–1745', *Past & Present*, 173 (2001), pp. 90–128, quotation from p. 110.

33 Pickering, *Statutes at Large from the Twelfth Year of Queen Anne to the Fifth Year of King George I*, pp. 306–310.

for the King's Most Gracious, General and Free Pardon', imparting clemency for King George's British subjects 'artfully misled into treasonable practices against his person and government'. The main consideration was to reassure low-ranking individuals associated with active Jacobitism that the Act allowed a fresh start and cleaning of the slate. Promising full pardon, acquittal, and release and discharge from detention, this was intended as an inclusive measure, 'to quiet the minds of all'. The Act was on one hand conciliatory, on the other unyielding. It included many grounds for exception. Clauses excluded 'such persons […] any ways employed by or in the service of the person who, since the death of the late King James, hath taken upon himself the style and title of King of England, or King of Great Britain', and individuals active in 1715–16 who had since clandestinely visited or permanently returned to Scotland. Public officials who had 'committed high treason in levying war against his majesty in the rebellion which began in the year 1715' might still face legal prosecution, and penalties against property remained in effect.

The Free Pardon was specifically denied to the outlawed Clan MacGregor.[34]

When James Francis Edward Stuart had returned to France in February 1716, he found it no longer a supportive safe haven. With his authority as regent strengthened, the Duke of Orléans set about reversing the late king's policy by encouraging peaceful relations with Great Britain. Orléans and his Anglophile foreign minister, Cardinal Guillaume Dubois, could present rapprochement as good for France. It also served the Regent's interest as heir to the throne. France badly needed a breathing space to recover economically, financially and militarily from Louis XIV's protracted and costly wars. Because the territorial settlement of the Peace of Utrecht had not been unkind to France, the Orléanist government was not preoccupied with regaining lost possessions, unlike King Phillip V's Spain. France, like Britain, also hoped to reap the commercial peace dividend offered by greater access to Spanish-American trade.[35]

Still detectable French sympathy for Jacobitism aside, King George I's government was content with Orléans as France's de facto ruler. Indeed, France's acceptance of the Hanoverian succession under the Peace of Utrecht accorded with the Regent's situation. As the late king's nephew, Orléans was heir apparent if the sickly young Louis XV died. But Phillip V of Spain, as

---

34 Anon., *The Political State of Great Britain, Volume XIV* (1717), pp. 59–72.
35 R. Harding, *Seapower and Naval Warfare, 1650–1830* (1999), p. 183.

Louis XIV's grandson, could endanger the succession. Phillip's renunciation of the French crown was a cornerstone of the Peace of Utrecht, but he might choose to repudiate it and assert his counter-claim. While Great Britain could never tolerate the unification of the crowns of France and Spain, Orléans's succession would have British acquiescence.[36]

The stumbling block in the path to closer Anglo-French relations was of course the presence on French soil of the claimant to the British throne. But in March 1716 the Regent compelled the Duke of Lorraine to refuse James Francis Edward Stuart's return to Bar-le-Duc. This forced James and his court to seek refuge in far south-east France, in the Papal enclave of Avignon. James's ejection was not, however, followed by expulsion of the numerous exiled Scots and Irish Jacobites resident in France. Nonetheless, in distant Avignon James and his close followers seemed much less of a threat to the Georgian government.

The Regent's decision to expel James had been encouraged by the British ambassador to Paris, John Dalrymple, 2nd Earl of Stair, a Scots peer and former soldier. Before Louis XIV's death Stair had deliberately befriended the Duke of Orléans, and, although wary of French motives, worked assiduously to further Anglo-French relations. To combat Jacobitism, Stair pressed the French to abide by the terms of the Peace of Utrecht. He also established what seems to have been the largest of the British government's ministerial intelligence agencies.[37] Stair and fellow ministers were mindful of the Jacobite refugees in those parts of the Continent closest to England, gathered in small numbers in the Austrian Netherlands but mostly in France. As well as the court at Avignon, the exiles clustered around Paris, Toulouse and Bordeaux. For his part, the Earl of Mar, now first minister to the titular King James III and VIII, advised James's followers to disperse to avoid surveillance and infiltration by Stair's numerous spies. Nonetheless, benefitting from increasing co-operation with the French authorities, Stair's agents and informants kept the British and Orléanist governments well informed about Jacobite whereabouts and intrigue.[38]

Stair's operation in France was but one branch of the Georgian government's increasingly effective, well-organised and funded anti-Jacobite ministerial intelligence system, operating at home and abroad. This involved the interception of mail across the British Isles and the Continent, the decryption of Jacobite codes and ciphers, and the employment of spies and informants in a network of counter-espionage. Such was the scale of the operation by 1718 that a Secret Department and a Deciphering Branch, tasked respectively with monitoring foreign correspondence and with code-breaking, were established.[39]

---

36 Szechi, *Jacobites*, pp. 90–1; Sinclair-Stevenson, *Inglorious Rebellion*, pp. 164–5.

37 Fritz, *English Ministers and Jacobitism*, p. 53.

38 H.M. Stephens, rev. W.C. Lowe, 'Dalrymple, John, second earl of Stair (1673–1747)', in *ODNB* (2004) online edn., accessed 21 July 2017; W. Michael, *England under George I: The Quadruple Alliance* (1939), pp. 146–9, *passim*.

39 Fritz, *English Ministers and Jacobitism*, p. 52–3. See also Fritz's, 'The Anti-Jacobite Intelligence System of the English Ministers, 1715–1745', *The Historical Journal*, 16 (1973), pp. 265–89, *passim*.

The Orléanist rejection of active Jacobitism was cemented by the conclusion at The Hague on 4 January 1717 of a treaty of defensive alliance between Great Britain, France and the United Provinces. This pragmatic realignment in Anglo-French relations in particular, lasting until 1731, guaranteed the succession to the crowns of France and Great Britain recognized under the Peace of Utrecht.[40]

The immediate and necessary casualty of this so-called Triple Alliance was James Francis Edwards Stuart's stay in France. In early February 1717, James and his court decamped from Avignon for the Italian Papal States. Pope Clement XI grudgingly allowed James sanctuary with the trappings of kingship. He provided James with a town house in Rome, the Palazzo Muti; an ageing, but imposing, ducal palace in Urbino as a country residence; and a generous life-long papal pension.[41]

Notwithstanding Anglo-French intergovernmental cooperation, in Regency France attitudes to Jacobite exiles remained equivocal. They were never treated generally by the authorities as *personae non-grata* or systematically harassed.[42] Nevertheless, selective pressure was applied to certain individuals, and the British government was satisfied by the detachment of James Francis Edward Stuart from the bulk of his followers, making it far more difficult to develop schemes for his restoration. Furthermore, the Italian-based Catholic Pretender could now be convincingly characterised as nothing more than a dependent cats-paw of the Pope.

The Jacobites and the Northern Powers

Denied the mainstay of French support, Jacobite diplomacy under the Earl of Mar's direction cast about for backing in the wider sphere of European diplomacy. Attention shifted to the northern powers. They remained locked in the Great Northern War, in which Sweden was engaged against a coalition involving Russia, Poland-Saxony, Denmark and Prussia. For some time, Jacobite emissaries misled themselves by attempting to court an agreement with Tsar Peter I, including promoting an unlikely three-way alliance requiring the reconciliation of Russia and Sweden. From April 1715, however, they developed promising contacts with officials of Charles XII, the warrior-king of Sweden, because of his animosity to King George I's Hanover.

During the course of the Great Northern War, Denmark and Prussia had overrun Swedish territory in north Germany. Denmark conquered the duchies of Bremen and Verden, and in May 1715 King Frederick IV sold them by treaty to Hanover in a deal involving the Electorate's backing in the war with Sweden. Bremen gave Hanover access to the Baltic Sea, and Jacobite propagandists seized upon this. In October 1715, the titular King James III & VIII issued a proclamation warning that the expansionist Usurper King George would use German troops and migrants to turn Britain into

---

40 Anon., *A Collection of all the Treaties of Peace, Alliance and Commerce, between Great-Britain and other Powers, from the Revolution in 1688, to the Present Time*, 2 vols. (1772), vol. 1, p. 287.

41 Gregg, 'James Francis Edward Stuart'.

42 Szechi, "Cam Ye O'er Frae France?", p. 371.

8. Likenesses of, left, King Charles XII of Sweden (*b.* 1682, *d.* 1718) and his first minister Baron Georg Heinrich von Görtz. Charles remained lukewarm about Görtz's scheme to in 1717 land Swedish troops in Britain in support of the Jacobites.

a Hanoverian province. Sweden's view of Britain as, de facto, an enemy appeared clear in summer 1715, when George I promoted a show of naval strength. Largely at his behest, a powerful Royal Navy fleet commanded by Admiral Sir John Norris patrolled the Baltic – the first of seven such major deployments there continuing into the 1720s. The pretext was the threat to the international Baltic trade from Swedish privateers active against Russian and Danish shipping. Norris's orders from the Admiralty were therefore to convoy and protect British and Dutch merchantmen. But Norris also had King George's authority and encouragement to take action alongside the Danes and Prussians against Swedish forces if necessary.[43]

Charles XII was furious with Hanover, and imagined the Jacobites as a means of revenge on King George I. But Charles was unable to convert his anger into military action because Swedish troops could not be spared for Scotland. However, in 1716 James Francis Edward Stuart welcomed a Swedish plan to bring 10,000 troops to Britain to overthrow George the Usurper. The scheme was the brainchild of four diplomats: Lieutenant-General Count (viscount in the Jacobite peerage) Arthur Dillon, an Irish exile and respected senior officer in the French Army's Irish Brigade, who was also James's representative in Paris; Baron Sparre, the Swedish ambassador in the French capital; Count Gyllenborg, Swedish ambassador to Britain; and

43 Harding, *Seapower and Naval Warfare,* p. 188; Rodger, *Command of the Ocean,* pp. 229–30; Szechi, *Jacobites,* pp. 104–5; N. Harding, *Hanover and the British Empire, 1700–1837* (2007), pp. 53–4; Fritz, *English Ministers and Jacobitism,* pp. 29 30.

their superior, Charles XII's first minister Baron Georg Heinrich von Görtz, then acting also as Sweden's envoy to The Hague. Because Charles XII was cash-strapped, James's followers were required to contribute to finance the expedition – and some English Jacobites raised quite significant sums. Spain also pitched in from the sidelines by promising a subsidy.[44]

Despite Charles XII giving no clear commitment, the plan gained momentum. Swedish troops would land in Scotland or England in spring 1717, bringing armaments for as many as 15,000 Jacobite recruits. In October 1716, Count Gyllenborg enthusiastically reckoned, that 'in a country [i.e. Scotland] where nine or ten are rebels, and where everything abounds, we can want [for] nothing'.[45] For his part, the alliance would enable King James III and VIII to project the backing of Protestant Sweden as a powerful signal that he would not foist Catholicism on his subjects. After all, three generations earlier during the Thirty Years' War had not Sweden, under the leadership of Charles XII's predecessor King Gustav Adolf, the so-called 'Lion of the North', been regarded as the military saviour of northern-European Protestantism against the forces of Catholicism?

However, the scheme was exposed and collapsed in January 1717 when British intelligence intercepted Gyllenborg's correspondence. Government ministers considered the evidence sufficiently damning to justify violating diplomatic immunity. A detachment of Foot Guards led by Major-General George Wade surrounded and entered Gyllenborg's house in London, seizing further incriminating documents and arresting Gyllenborg himself. Görtz was later detained in the Netherlands.[46] While both were eventually repatriated, Charles XII overlooked the diplomatic scandal. He probably never had much confidence in the over-optimistic plotting of his officials with excitable Jacobites, who between them overlooked the problem of shipping a Swedish army to Britain past the powerful and vigilant Royal Navy. Moreover, Sweden remained too embattled in the Great Northern War to mount powerful operations in the British Isles. While the Jacobites optimistically continued to entertain hopes of Swedish backing well into summer 1717, they gained firm support from a more likely quarter – Spain.[47]

Spanish Expansionism and the Jacobite Alliance

Bourbon Spain had lost both territory and prestige by the Peace of Utrecht. King Phillip V had to accede to the loss of Spain's Italian possessions, including the kingdoms of Naples and Milan to Imperial Austria, and to the transfer to Austria of the Spanish Netherlands (territories approximating to present Belgium and Luxembourg). The British kept Gibraltar and Minorca (the latter including the strategically important Port Mahon), captured

---

44 E. Lord, *The Stuarts' Secret Army, English Jacobites, 1689–1752* (2004), pp. 122–3; Fritz, *English Ministers and Jacobitism*, pp. 12–16, *passim*.

45 Cited in C. S. Terry, *The Chevalier St. George and the Jacobite Movements in His Favour, 1701–1720* (1901), p. 451.

46 Sinclair-Stevenson, *Inglorious Rebellion*, pp. 166–7; Terry, *Chevalier St. George*, pp. 446–54, *passim*.

47 F.H.B. Daniell (ed.), *Calendar of the Stuart Papers belonging to His Majesty The King Preserved at Windsor Castle*, 7 vols. (1902–23), vol. 4, pp. 232, 247.

from Spain in 1704 and 1708 respectively. In 1713 Spain had also to assign to Britain for 30 years the *Asiento de Negros*, the monopoly contract with the Spanish crown to supply slaves to Spain's American empire, and to allow some trade in goods with those colonies. This gave British merchants and smugglers inroads to the traditionally closed markets of the Spanish Americas. Mindful of these unwelcome commercial concessions but wary

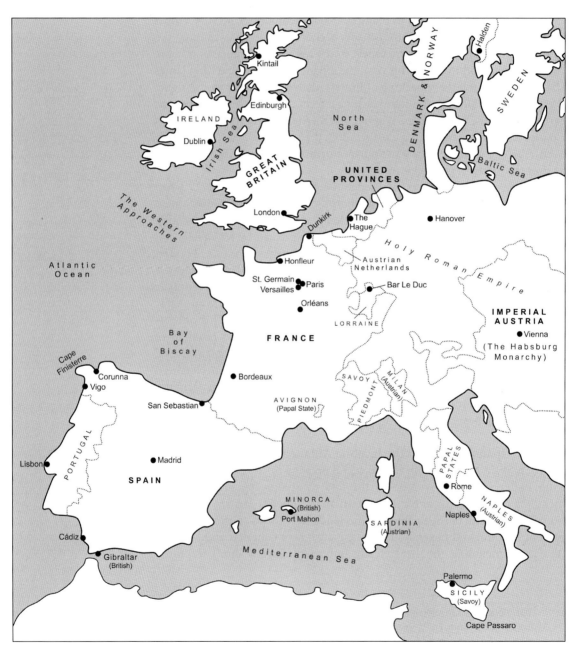

Map 1. Western Europe *c.*1716, following the Peace of Utrecht settlement. Selected state boundaries and places mentioned in the text are shown.

of British naval supremacy, Spain acted to regulate trade with the British by commercial treaties in December 1715 and July 1716. This appeasement was intended also to distract British naval attention from the Mediterranean, where Spain intended to regain its Italian empire. It also suited Spain to encourage the Jacobites. From 1716 Phillip V secretly allowed James Francis Edward Stuart a small pension, while Spanish officials engaged with Jacobite diplomacy with Sweden and Russia.[48]

Phillip was determined to restore Spanish power curtailed by the Peace of Utrecht. To that end, he promoted governmental fiscal and administrative reform. This enabled a programme of rearmament, including warship building. King Phillip was influenced both by his domineering queen, the strong-willed Italian princess Elizabeth Farnese of Parma, and his able and ambitious Italian-born first minister, Cardinal Giulio Alberoni, who together drove Spanish foreign policy. Alberoni had risen from the priesthood to political influence. He was secretary to Louis XIV's illegitimate son the Duc de Vendome, and later consul to Spain of the ruling house of Farnese of Parma. In 1714 Alberoni had arranged the marriage of Elizabeth Farnese to King Phillip, and she in turn promoted his advancement to Phillip's ruling council. By 1717 Alberoni was in effect the Spanish premier.

Alberoni pursued a robust foreign policy. He encouraged King Phillip, grandson of the late Louis XIV, to entertain hopes of uniting the Bourbon crowns of France and Spain, while engaging with Queen Elizabeth's military ambitions in Italy – in the national interest of Spain and to the benefit of the Farnese dynasty. The Anglo-Austrian and Anglo-French treaties of defensive alliance, of May 1716 and January 1717 respectively, partly intended to maintain curbs imposed on Spain by the Peace of Utrecht, galvanized Spanish opposition. Rejuvenated militarily, Spain intended to regain control in the Italian Mediterranean. In August 1717 Spanish forces invaded Sardinia, ceded to Imperial Austria in 1714. Within two months they had captured the capital Cagliari and overrun the island.[49]

With the navy further strengthened, in summer 1718 Spain acted to regain Sicily. Under the Peace of Utrecht, the island had been handed to Victor Amadeus II, jointly the Duke of Savoy and Prince of Piedmont. In July, in a much larger amphibious operation, a Spanish expeditionary army numbering 35,000 men landed on Sicily. They took the capital Palermo and besieged the remaining Piedmontese garrison in Messina.

In response, on 22 July Great Britain agreed with France and Imperial Austria a treaty already under negotiation. It became known as the Quadruple Alliance, albeit a term that in time became a misnomer; the fourth allied power was the United Provinces, but in order to protect Dutch international trade the States-General never fully adhered to the military conventions of the alliance. This 'Treaty of Alliance for Settling the Public Peace',[50] joined by Victor Amadeus II in October, was promoted by the British to maintain

48 Szechi, *Jacobites* pp. 107–9; D. McKay and H.M. Scott, *The Rise of the Great Powers, 1648–1815*, (2014), p. 107.

49 Szechi, *Jacobites* pp. 107–9; B. Lenman, *Britain's Colonial Wars, 1688–1783* (2001), p. 189.

50 *A Collection of all the Treaties*, vol. 1, p. 301.

by collective security the balance of power in western Europe established under the Peace of Utrecht; an arrangement presently endangered by Spain's actions in the Mediterranean. The Quadruple Alliance stipulated that Phillip V must renounce his territorial ambitions, and the Emperor Charles VI abandon lingering aspirations of Austrian Habsburg reunification with Spain. All powers were to respect the established succession of the British and French monarchies. Allied governments saw the international status quo threatened by the ambition of Cardinal Alberoni. He was no doubt seen as 'the embodiment of European unrest and they considered his fall an essential condition of peace'.[51]

While the provisions of the Quadruple Alliance envisaged the co-operative peaceful inclusion of Spain, the only force readily able to impose allied demands was the British Royal Navy. Already on 3 June a fleet, including 17 ships of the line, commanded by Admiral George Byng had sailed from England for the Mediterranean to counter Spanish expansionism. With war not declared, Byng was to engineer a cessation of hostilities in Sicily pending a diplomatic settlement. But he also had discretion to use actual force. Sailing *en route* off Spain's Atlantic coast, Byng relayed his orders to the British consul in Madrid. These were made known to King Phillip, but he refused to back down. On 4 July Cardinal Alberoni wrote advising the consul, 'His Majesty has done me the honour to tell me that the Chevalier Byng may execute the orders which he has from the king his master'.[52]

Byng's fleet sailed on, and joined by British warships already on station in the Mediterranean anchored in the Bay of Naples around 20 July. The admiral sent his senior captain to negotiate with the Spanish commander in Sicily, the Marquis de Lede. But de Lede would not agree to a cease-fire. Therefore, when the Spanish fleet set sail from the Roads of Messina, apparently seeking sea room to manoeuvre, Byng launched a pre-emptive attack. During a running fight off the east coast of Sicily on 31 July to be known as the battle of Cape Passaro, Byng's more heavily armed and better handled 24 men-of-war achieved a decisive victory, chasing and sinking three and capturing 11 of 21 Spanish warships engaged. A few days afterwards, the commander of a squadron Byng sent to pursue surviving Spanish ships inshore laconically reported: 'We have taken and destroyed all the Spanish ships and vessels [that] were on the coast'.[53] A further dozen Spanish craft had been captured or burnt. The British victory at Cape Passaro dealt a crippling blow to Spain's Mediterranean strategy. The Spanish army on Sicily was left isolated, but it would require the landing of Austrian troops shipped under the protection of Byng's fleet to dislodge it. Byng's ships in the meantime maintained a close blockade of Sicilian and Sardinian ports.[54]

---

51 McKay and Scott, *Rise of the Great Powers*, pp. 114–15; Michael, *England under George I*, p. 70. Quotation from the latter.
52 Cited in Dickson, *Jacobite Attempt*, pp. xxv–xxvi.
53 Daniell, *Calendar of the Stuart Papers,* vol. 7, p. 226.
54 P. S. Mahon, *History of England from The Peace of Utrecht to the Peace of Aix-la-Chapelle*, 3 vols. (1839), vol. 1, pp. 205–28, *passim*; Rodger, *Command of the Ocean*, pp. 227–8; J. Black, *Politics and Foreign Policy in the Age of George I, 1714–1727* (2014), pp. 108–9; Dickson, *Jacobite Attempt*, pp. xxv–xxvi.

Lord Sunderland, King George's leading minister, confidently expected that by Byng's victory, 'there is an end put to the Cardinal's projects'.[55] However, while war remained undeclared, Spain disregarded the Quadruple Alliance and threatened British mercantile interests. The Spanish ambassador to London was recalled, and British officials dismissed from Spanish territory. The commercial treaties of 1715 and 1716 were rescinded. British goods and vessels in Spanish ports were impounded, and British merchants harassed. Phillip V authorised letters of marque licensing Spanish privateers to prey on British merchantmen either side of the Atlantic. But the weakness of Spanish naval power limited the options to do more than harry British maritime trade. However, Alberoni recognised the opportunity for retaliation against British intervention in the Mediterranean by playing the Jacobite card. Spain had remained receptive but in practice lukewarm to Jacobite advances, Alberoni having blocked a request for the titular James III & VIII to establish his court there. However, James had adeptly influenced Pope Clement XI to appoint Alberoni to the cardinalate in July 1717.[56] James remained a pensioner of King Phillip, and Spain maintained covert relations with his court in Italy. Therefore, in October 1718 Alberoni invited the Duke of Ormond, an Irish-born Jacobite general and one-time commander of British land forces, then living in semi-retired exile near Paris, to join him at Madrid to mastermind an invasion of the British Isles.[57]

---

55 Cited by Fritz, *English Ministers and Jacobitism*, p. 48.
56 *Ibid.*, pp. 46–7.
57 Szechi, *Jacobites*, p. 109; Dickson, *Jacobite Attempt*, pp. xxvi–xxvii.

2

Leading Personalities of the 1719 Rising

'He did not think it for the King's honour, nor that of the nation, to give up the game without putting it to a trial.'

Those leading Jacobites who in 1719 acted to attempt a rising in Scotland and a Spanish invasion of England were a disparate group. Among them, neither the Duke of Ormond nor the Earl of Mar, two of the principal followers of the titular King James III and VIII, reached Scotland, while James himself was also unable to get there.

James Butler, 2nd Duke of Ormond (*b*. 1665, *d*. 1745) was born in Ireland at Dublin Castle.[1] He was the son of Thomas Butler, 6th Earl of Ossory, soldier and politician, and his Dutch wife Aemelia van Nassau, daughter of an aristocratic army officer. His paternal grandfather James Butler, 1st Duke of Ormond (1610–1688), was the leading political and military figure of royal authority in Ireland throughout the Civil Wars of the 1640s, and again after the Stuart restoration in 1660.

As Lord James Butler, in July 1680 he succeeded his father as Baron Butler of Moore Oak in the English peerage, but went by his superior Irish title Earl of Ossory. In 1685 Ossory entered the court of King James II as a gentleman of the royal bedchamber. His military career had begun in Ireland in 1683 with a regiment of Horse, and continued the following year with the French army in the Low Countries.[2] In 1688 Ossory succeeded his grandfather as Duke of Ormond. During the Glorious Revolution he sided with William of Orange, although as a Tory probably had sympathy for King James II. Nonetheless, Ormond's Dutch familial connections encouraged his integration into the new regime. Enjoying the patronage of King William III, Ormond in 1689 was appointed a gentleman of the royal bedchamber, and commissioned into the

---

1   For a recent succinct biography of Ormond, see S. Handley, 'Butler, James, second duke of Ormond (1665–1745)', in *ODNB* (2004) online edn. (available June 2018).

2   *Ibid.*, accessed 21 Apr. 2015.

household cavalry as captain of the second Troop of Lifeguards (equivalent in rank to a colonelcy in a line regiment of Horse).

During the Nine Years' War against France, in 1689 Ormond campaigned in the Netherlands; in 1690 with William's army in Ireland when on 12 July, after the battle of the Boyne, he took formal possession of Dublin Castle; and for much of 1692 to 1696 in the Low Countries. Ormond's distinguished conduct at the battle of Neerwinden/ Landen fought on 29 July 1693 was magnified in a later panegyric: 'He performed wonders at the battle of Landen; he often rallied his scattered troops, and fought in the front, equally exposing himself to the fury of the enemy's fire [...] he gave there a testament of his abilities in war, by his conduct and personal bravery.'[3] Wounded during the fighting and taken prisoner of war, Ormond was later exchanged for the French Marshal James FitzJames, Duke of Berwick, the illegitimate son of King James II and Arabella Churchill, sister of the Duke of Marlborough (making Berwick the half-brother of James Francis Edward Stuart). Ormond was promoted major-general in 1692, and to lieutenant-general in 1694.[4]

9. James Butler, 2nd Duke of Ormond. Jacobite general and former British Army commander-in-chief, in 1719 Ormond planned to lead a Spanish invasion of England. Portrait by or after Michael Dahl. Oil on canvas, 1713. (© National Portrait Gallery, London)

Early in the War of the Spanish Succession, in 1702 Ormond had joint command of the Anglo-Dutch land forces transported with Admiral Sir George Rooke's fleet against the Spanish naval base at Cádiz. The army ashore from mid-August to mid-September failed to attack Cádiz, but Ormond gained reflected credit from the returning fleet's victory over a Franco-Spanish naval force in Vigo Bay on 12 October.[5] In 1703 his political career was boosted by being made Queen Anne's lord lieutenant of Ireland; in effect, her viceroy there. This was a popular appointment, given his grandfather's reputation and because Ormond was the first native to hold the office since the Glorious Revolution. Four years later, the Whig-dominated wartime ministry had Ormond replaced as lord lieutenant of Ireland, but he was reappointed in October 1710 when the Tories gained power.

When the Tory ministry dismissed the Duke of Marlborough from his military offices on 1 January 1712 Ormond was the beneficiary, appointed the same day as captain-general and commander-in-chief of British land forces.[6] Ormond thus had the inglorious task of executing government policy

---

3   Anon., *The Life and Character of James Butler, late Duke, Marquis and Earl of Ormond* (1739), pp. 23–4.
4   C. Dalton (ed.), *English Army Lists and Commission Registers, 1661–1714*, 6 vols. (1892–1904), vol. 3, p. 283, vol. 4, p. 49.
5   Harding, *Seapower and Naval Warfare*, p. 169.
6   Handley, 'Ormond'; Dalton, *Army Lists and Commission Registers*, vol. 6, p. 19.

of disengaging the British army in Flanders, whilst their erstwhile Dutch and Imperial Austrian allies continued the war against France. Acting under the secret 'restraining orders' issued in mid-May and with the benefit of an armistice with France, by July 1712 Ormond had withdrawn the remaining British troops to the Channel coast at Dunkirk.[7]

When sitting in the House of Lords Ormond supported the Tory ministry. He received further honorific offices, as Warden of the Cinque Ports, and lord lieutenant of Norfolk, although in September 1713 was again replaced as lord lieutenant of Ireland. From that time Ormond developed clandestine contacts with the Jacobite court in exile. By spring 1714 he was prepared to back a Jacobite restoration upon Queen Anne's death. As captain-general he was expected to engage the support of the British Army for James III and VIII, or to at least ensure its neutrality when James returned to England. However, a contemporary noted that Ormond was 'himself not sure of the army', having 'much more credit with the people than he had with the troops'.[8] Ormond dismissed some politically unreliable officers, but it was recognised that the army's commissioned ranks largely remained 'composed of the same Whig officers who had served under the Duke of Marlborough'.[9] Like other Tory grandees Ormond was left flat-footed when upon Queen Anne's death on 1 August their Whig political opponents (with allied Tories) quickly acted to ensure the accession of the Elector of Hanover. Ormond was, however, a signatory to the proclamation of King George I.

Among the first state papers signed by the new monarch was the commission reappointing the Duke of Marlborough captain-general in place of Ormond, who under the Whig ministry lost his other appointments.[10] Deprived of office, in 1715 Ormond associated with a small handful of Tory peers, including the Earl of Mar, contemplating instigating pro-Jacobite uprisings in England. However, in July the Whig-dominated parliament initiated proceedings against the late Tory ministry; already on 21 June Secretary of State James Earl Stanhope had demanded Ormond's impeachment. Under this threat, on or about 21 July Ormond set out to flee to France. On 8 August he was impeached *in absentia* for high treason, accused of having as captain-general in 1712 betrayed Britain's allies and connived with the French. On 20 August Ormond was attainted by parliament and his English and Scottish honours and estates made forfeit. The parliament in Ireland similarly acted against his estates there. Ormond's private secretary was also arrested and disclosed plans for a rising in the English West Country.[11]

---

7   C.T. Atkinson, *Marlborough and the Rise of the British Army* (1921), pp. 470–2.

8   J. Keith, *A Fragment of a Memoir of Field-Marshal James Keith, Written by Himself,* (ed.) T. Constable (1863), p. 4.

9   *Ibid.*

10 Atkinson, *Marlborough*, p. 482.

11 G.E. Cockayne (ed.), *Complete Peerage of England, Scotland, Ireland, Great Britain and The United Kingdom,* 8 vols. (1887–98), vol. 6, pp. 151–2; G.V. Bennett, 'English Jacobitism, 1710–1715; Myth and Reality', *Transactions of the Royal Historical Society,* 32 (1982), pp. 145, 148–9; P. Rae, *The History of the Rebellion raised against His Majesty King George I By the Friends of the Popish Pretender* (1746), pp. 154, 162–5; Dickson, *Jacobite Attempt*, xx.

In exile in France, Ormond intended to rekindle the western rebellion in support of the Earl of Mar's Highland rising. Accordingly, on 10 October he was commissioned by the titular James III and VIII captain-general and commander-in-chief in England and Ireland. In later October, and perhaps again in early November, Ormond sailed off south-west England but returned to France on news that the rising had been nipped in the bud. Consequently James Francis Edward Stuart resolved instead to land in Scotland.[12] Ormond thus played no further part in the 1715–16 rising, and in spring 1716 accompanied the Jacobite court in exile to its new refuge in Avignon. Based in Paris in 1717, Ormond was involved in attempts to gain support from the northern powers, in pursuit of which in the autumn he embarked on an ultimately fruitless diplomatic mission to the Swedish and Russian courts.[13] In June 1718 Ormond returned to Paris. In October he was sumoned to Madrid to lead an assumed Hispano-Swedish invasion of Britain to restore the Stuart dynasty.

After involvement in the events of 1719, Ormond for the next few years continued in the service of Spain. He remained engaged with schemes to bring about the Stuart restoration, including in 1721–22 planning a Spanish-backed military expedition to southern England. However, this was abandoned when the so-called Atterbury Plot, intended to orchestrate risings in support, was exposed.[14] In 1732 Ormond left Spain for Avignon, where he spent his remaining years in comfortable retirement. 'To say the truth', wrote Lady Mary Wortley Montagu, after meeting Ormond at Avignon in 1743, 'nobody can be more insignificant. He keeps an assembly where all the best company go twice in the week, lives here in great magnificence, is quite inoffensive, and seems to have forgotten every part of his past life and to be of no party'.[15] Ormond died there two years later.

The Duke of Ormond never fulfilled the leading military role assigned to him in the Jacobite cause. Contemporaries remarked on his bravery and affability, but recognised his shortcomings for high leadership. John Macky, a contemporary Scots journalist and spy for the British government, saw Ormond as: 'Certainly one of the most generous, princely brave men that ever was, but good natured to a fault; loves glory and is consequently crowded with flatterers; hath all the qualities of a great man except that of a statesman, hating business'.[16] The sometime Jacobite soldier James Keith penned a fuller portrait of his superior:

> The Duke of Ormond had been bred from his youth to arms [...] with the reputation of a very brave officer, tho' [sic] he never had that of a very able one. He was a man of a very easy temper, and an ordinary understanding, so diffident of himself that he often followed the advice of those who had a smaller share of sense than himself; he

---

12 R. Patten, *The History of the Rebellion in the Year 1715* (1745), p. 216; Daniell, *Calendar of the Stuart Papers*, vols. 1 & 2 combined, p. 456.

13 Dickson, *Jacobite Attempt*, xxii.

14 Lenman, *Jacobite Risings*, pp. 196–202, *passim*; Lord, *Stuarts' Secret Army*, pp. 133–5.

15 Cited in Dickson, *Jacobite Attempt*, lviii.

16 Cited in Cockayne, *Complete Peerage*, vol. 6, p. 152.

was as irresolute and timorous in affairs as he was brave in his person, and was apt to lose good opportunities by waiting to remove difficulties which naturally attend great designs, and of which a part must always be left to fortune in the execution; he was a man of entire honour, a good friend, and a strict observer of his word.[17]

John Erskine, 6th Earl of Mar (*b.* 1675, *d.* 1732) was born at Alloa, on the Lowland estates of his father Charles Erskine, 5th Earl and chief of Clan Erskine.[18] The family pedigree was considered among the oldest in Scotland and habitually loyal to the House of Stuart. However, the effects of civil war coupled to financial mismanagement of the family estates during the 17th century left the Erskines heavily in debt. Thus when in 1689 John succeeded his father as 6th Earl he probably inherited, as a critical fellow Jacobite later put it, 'more debt than estate'.[19] Intending to restore the family fortune and aspiring for power Mar pursued a political career, entering the Scottish parliament in 1696.[20] A talent for bureaucracy underpinned his ambition; 'He was bred up to the pen', a contemporary remarked, 'and was early brought into business'.[21] Mar advanced under the patronage of the court magnate James Douglas, Duke of Queensberry, and in 1697 was appointed to the Scottish Privy Council. After Queensberry's governmental departure in 1704, Mar associated with Jacobite-inclined Scots Tories. However, with his patron's return to power Mar became a leading figure in Scottish politics, from autumn 1705 as a secretary of state. He was a principal proponent and agent of the Anglo-Scottish Union of 1707. The Jacobite MP George Lockhart of Carnwath reckoned that Mar 'promoted all the court of England's measures with the greatest zeal imaginable'.[22] In the unified Westminster parliament Mar sat in the House of Lords as one of 16 representative peers of Scotland. While advancing his political career, Mar meanwhile developed a reputation as a talented garden designer and amateur architect, advising wealthy Scots landowners on improving their estates.

As a negotiator of the Treaty of Union, Mar had associated with English court politicians. He gained the patronage of Robert Harley, 1st Earl of Oxford, who by the Tory election victory in 1710 became Queen Anne's chief minister. Mar was the most prominent Scots courtier, notwithstanding from 1712 his publicly expressed reservations about the Union. Now at the pinnacle of his political career Mar lived fashionably in London, and in autumn 1713 became the first post-Union secretary of state for Scotland.

Mar strove to maintain a political balancing act, securing his interests and employment. Accordingly, in 1714 before Queen Anne's death he more closely

---

17 Keith, *Fragment of a Memoir*, p. 3.
18 For a recent succinct biography of Mar, see C. v. Ehrenstein, 'Erskine, John, styled twenty-second or sixth earl of Mar and Jacobite duke of Mar (*bap.* 1675, *d.* 1732)', in *ODNB* (2004), online edn. (available June 2018).
19 J. Sinclair, *Memoirs of the Insurrection in Scotland in 1715. By John, Master of Sinclair,* (ed.) Anon (1858), p. 58.
20 Ehrenstein, 'Mar', accessed 4 Jan. 2017.
21 Keith, *Fragment of a Memoir*, p. 3.
22 A. Aufnere (ed.), *The Lockhart Papers: Containing a Memoir and Commentaries upon the Affairs in Scotland from 1702–1715 by George Lockhart*, 2 vols. (1817), vol. 1, p. 114.

associated with Whig politicians. However, King George I quickly dispensed with Mar's services as a mistrusted figure of the former Tory ministry. His ambitions thwarted and livelihood overturned, Mar's Jacobitism grew out of personal animosity to the new monarch, rather than ideological attachment to the House of Stuart. 'Observing one thing previous to the rebellion', a fellow Jacobite remarked, recognising similarities between the leading figures, 'many of the gentlemen concerned, but even the Earl of Mar himself, who was the first mover and head of the rebellion itself, had not only offered their services to the King [i.e. George I], but had taken oaths to continue faithful to him, and had in particular abjured the interest of the Pretender'.[23]

By early July 1715, Mar and the Duke of Ormond jointly had prepared for James Francis Edward Stuart an invasion plan. The memorandum pragmatically presented 'the extreme difficulties of such an attempt', given that there was 'no hope of succeeding in it without the assistance of regular forces, or a general rising of the people in all parts of England'.

10. John Erskine, 22nd or 6th Earl of Mar. An ex-Tory secretary of state for Scotland turned Jacobite, Mar in 1719 was first minster in exile to the titular King James III and VIII. Likeness by John Smith, after Sir Godfrey Kneller, Bt. Mezzotint and engraving, 1703. (© National Portrait Gallery, London)

Their additional prerequisites were 10,000 firearms, artillery, and plenty of cash. Mar and Ormond advised that to allow time for such preconditions to be met, an attempt to overthrow the Georgian regime should not be made before October.[24] In the event, however, Mar, like Ormond, recognised that intrigue exposed him to likely impeachment. Therefore, on 2 August he left London for Scotland intending to trigger a rising there. Although Mar acted precipitately, contrary to his own recommendation, and upsetting the plans of Jacobites in France headed by the exiled Viscount Bolingbroke, another Tory grandee estranged from the Georgian government, he was the first notable Jacobite to take up arms.

The Jacobite rising of 1715–16 began during 26/27 August, when Mar on his estates near Braemar held a Jacobite gathering under the guise of a traditional Highland hunting party.[25] A council of war followed on 3 September at Aboyne in Aberdeenshire. While Mar was at Braemar instigating the rising, in France the would-be King James III and VIII at his court at Bar-le-Duc made him general and commander-in-chief in Scotland.[26] Mar was a politician not a soldier, but he had some military credentials. Inspired with martial ambition, in 1702 he gained the captaincy of the garrison company at Stirling Castle, and

23 Patten, *History of the Rebellion*, p. 2.
24 Daniell, *Calendar of the Stuart Papers*, vols. 1 & 2 combined, pp. 520–5.
25 Rae, *History of the Rebellion*, pp. 188–90.
26 Daniell, *Calendar of the Stuart Papers*, vols. 1 & 2 combined, p. 415.

the same year patriotically recruited a regiment of Foot.[27] Mar, however, was never inclined to go on active service.

Notwithstanding this experience and his administrative ability, Mar, out of his depth, struggled with the generalship of the disparate Jacobite army. Commentators ever since have heaped criticism on Mar's leadership for having resulted in the failure of the 1715–16 rising. He did, however, acknowledge his limitations and did not expect to hold command for long. In early October, James Francis Edward Stuart appointed the Duke of Berwick captain-general and commander-in-chief in Scotland as Mar's successor, under instructions to travel there to take charge.[28] That he expected Berwick to take over and saw his own as a stopgap command may account for Mar's strategic procrastination prior to the battle of Sheriffmuir. However, Berwick as an officer of the French army instead obeyed the Regent Duke of Orléans and remained in France. Mar also lacked talented subordinates. Major-General George Hamilton, for example, who had served stolidly with the Dutch army, and accompanied Mar from London as his military advisor, was reckoned 'tho' [sic] an old officer […] not in the least equal to the affair he was to undertake […] being a man whom only experience, not natural genius, had made an officer'.[29]

Due to the strategic defeats at Sheriffmuir and Preston, by the time the titular James III and VIII landed in Scotland at Peterhead on 22 December Mar probably saw little hope in continuing the rising.[30] His clandestine abandonment of the army by sailing for France accompanying James on 4 February 1716 therefore exposed Mar to the derision and future mistrust of fellow Jacobites.

Nonetheless, at Paris in March Mar returned to more familiar ground as a politician, replacing Bolingbroke as secretary of state to King James III and VIII. James held Mar in high esteem, as an experienced statesman and for being first to take up arms on his behalf the previous year. That October, James had bestowed upon him the titles Duke of Mar and Marquis of Erskine in the rival so-called Jacobite Peerage (titles that were repudiated by the Georgian government).[31] However, Mar's disposition to intrigue clouded attempts to form alliances with the European powers, and fostered infighting within the Jacobite movement. As James's first minister Mar was a divisive figure, mistrusted by contemporaries including the Duke of Ormond and the Earl Marischal. Mar's 'great talent', concluded George Lockhart, 'lay in the cunning management of his designs and projects, in which it was hard to find him out, when he aimed to be incognito; and thus he showed himself to be a man of good sense, but bad morals'.[32]

Sidelined by Ormond in the planned invasion and rising of 1719, Mar sought to renew contacts with the British authorities. In March 1719 he resigned as Jacobite secretary of state, and probably connived in his

---

27 Dalton, *Army Lists and Commission Registers*, vol. 5, pp. 212, 226.
28 *Ibid.*, p. 532.
29 Keith, *Fragment of a Memoir*, p. 10.
30 Kemp, *Jacobite Rebellion*, p. 65.
31 Ehrenstein, 'Mar'.
32 Aufnere, *Lockhart Papers*, vol. 1, p. 114.

own arrest in May by the authorities in Geneva acting for the Georgian government.[33] Detained during 1720 at Geneva at British behest, Mar before being permitted to travel to Paris with his family negotiated some financial concessions from King George's officials. Living in the French capital Mar acted duplicitously, as, in effect, a double agent. He hoped on one hand for a pardon from London, whilst on the other to maintain influence in the Jacobite movement. Mar's double-dealing was exposed in the aftermath of the stillborn Atterbury Plot of 1722 intended to otherthrow King George I. In August 1724 James Francis Edward Stuart dismissed Mar from his service. A year later, James found it necessary to encourage supporters in Scotland to distance themselves from his ex-first minister:

> I have endeavoured to spare Mar hitherto as much as my service would allow, so it is not like to require me to mention him any more; I am persuaded in a very little time I shall not have a sincere well-wisher whose eyes will not be opened in that respect, or who will have any dealings with him or any of his adherents.[34]

Mar became a political non-entity distrusted by Jacobites and British officials alike, and lived in increasingly straightened financial circumstances. Although granted a limited pardon, he was never allowed to return to Scotland. Mar therefore could not execute the elaborate improvements planned for his home estate at Alloa that were the centrepiece of his architectural and literary works in exile. In his later years Mar's health declined markedly, and he died in May 1732 at the fashionable spa town of Aix-la-Chapelle (the present city of Aachen).

The Jacobite expedition to Scotland in 1719 was first led by Mar's antagonist, **George Keith** (*b.* 1692/3, *d.* 1778), **styled the tenth** (and last) **Earl Marischal of Scotland**.[35] However, it was not long before Keith had to relinquish command to his rival, the Marquess of Tullibardine; a handover that exacerbated the disunity of the expedition's leadership.

George Keith was the eldest son of William Keith, 9th Earl Marischal, who for opposing the Act of Union had in 1708 been imprisoned as a Jacobite. The Earls Marischal had long been the hereditary keepers of the royal regalia, known as the Honours of Scotland. While by the early 18th century the family's wealth had diminished along with its honorific duties, from their principal seat at Fetteresso Castle in Aberdeenshire the Keiths remained influential in north-east Scotland. John, Master of Sinclair, in 1715 a fellow Jacobite officer, and in his memoirs an outspoken critic of the army's leadership, characterised Keith as having 'little or no estate, was a young man of ambition; and 'tho [*sic*] his family was sunk, yet the name of ıt had an influence in the country, which he'd readily make use of'.[36]

---

33 Ehrenstein, 'Mar'.

34 Lenman, *Jacobite Risings,* pp. 202–3; Quotation from Aufnere, *Lockhart Papers*, vol. 2, p. 200.

35 For a recent succinct biography of Keith, see E.M. Furgol, 'Keith, George, styled tenth Earl Marischal (1692/3?–1778)', in *ODNB* (2004), online edn. (available June 2018).

36 Sinclair, *Memoirs of the Insurrection,* p. 68.

Keith was commissioned into the British Army in March 1711 as a captain in the Earl of Hyndford's Regiment of Dragoons.[37] Upon the death of his father, in May 1712 he succeeded to the earldom. In January 1714 he was commissioned as captain of the second, Scottish, Troop of Horse Grenadier Guards, a prestigious command.

Because of his Jacobite sympathies, however, Keith by May 1715 had resigned or, more probably been deprived of his commission during a purge instigated by the Duke of Marlborough of officers suspected of disloyalty to the Georgian regime. Returned to Scotland, George persuaded his younger brother **James Francis Edward Keith** (*b.* 1696, *d.* 1758) to join him at the Earl of Mar's gathering at Braemar. During the Jacobite council of war at Aboyne, Marischal expressed firm support for a rising and was received by Mar as a leading ally. It was said, that 'no man [at Aboyne] was more forward for what was agreed to than the Earl Marischal'.[38] When in September it was hoped the Duke of Atholl would commit to the Jacobite cause as commander-in-chief, Marischal with Mar were expected to become his close advisors.[39]

Marischal entered Aberdeen on 20 September and had King James III and VIII proclaimed at the market cross.[40] He raised a body of 80 horsemen, in which his brother James also served, and later had command of a second squadron. In Perthshire, Marischal tried to use his familial influence to encourage a recruitment drive for his brother's own regiment. Instead, he found that few enlisted, apparently for the reason that: 'nobody can prove then by history that ever Marischal's family had a Highland following'.[41] Given his experience as a regular cavalry officer, in November just before the battle of Sheriffmuir Mar appointed Marischal major-general of Horse. At the battle he commanded the Jacobite squadrons jointly with James Drummond, Duke of Perth; as lieutenant-general of Horse his immediate superior.

The would-be King James III and VIII slept the second night after landing in Scotland at Peterhead at Marischal's house at Newburgh, and he joined the Jacobite inner circle tending upon him. James rewarded Marischal on New Year's Day 1716 by making him a gentleman of the royal bedchamber.

As the Jacobite army retreated from Perth to Montrose in later January, Marischal was invited to join Mar and other notables in accompanying James back to France. Instead, by his brother James's recollection, Marischal wished to fight on. He told Mar that 'tho' [*sic*] we were in a bad situation he did not think the case so desperate as he [Mar] represented; that the troops we had in the north would […] make us very near equal to the enemy'. Furthermore, 'he did not think it for the king's honour, nor that of the nation, to give up the game without putting it to a trial [i.e. battle]'.[42] It seems Marischal chose to remain with the army when James's party sailed from Montrose for France

---

37 Dalton, *Army Lists and Commission Registers*, vol. 5, p. 208.
38 E.E. Cuthell, *The Scottish Friend of Frederick the Great, the last Earl Marischal,* 2 vols. (1915), vol. 1, p. 31.
39 Daniell, *Calendar of the Stuart Papers,* vols. 1 & 2 combined, p. 415.
40 Cuthell, *Scottish Friend of Frederick the Great*, vol. 1, p. 34.
41 Sinclair, *Memoirs of the Insurrection*, p. 101.
42 Keith, *Fragment of a Memoir,* p. 28.

on the night of 4 February. On the other hand, another contemporary account mentioned that Marischal actually intended to join them, but arriving late was left stranded because there was no small boat to carry him to the rescue ship.[43]

Whether remaining by choice or mischance, Marischal voiced the army's sense of abandonment by the lack-lustre James, and moreover of its betrayal by Mar. When James's apologetic letter of departure was read to the soldiers at Aberdeen, Marischal reportedly 'could not contain himself from the most injurious expressions'. He was outspoken among fellow officers. 'His prejudice […] increased', one of them later informed Mar, 'and he took all manner of ways to lessen your character, even at the expense of the king's'. When the army disbanded at Ruthven in Badenoch on 15 February 1716, Marischal was said to have declared that 'he did not desire any capitulation'.[44]

Marischal with his brother dispersed with the army into the Highlands, keeping company with other Jacobite fugitives in the Western

11. George Keith, 10th Earl Marischal. Keith led the Jacobite expeditionary force to Scotland in 1719, but had to relinquish command to his rival the Marquess of Tullibardine. Portrait attributed to Placido Costanzi. Oil on copper, *c*.1733. (© National Portrait Gallery, London)

Isles. In April, the Keiths along with other Jacobite officers were lifted from the island of South Uist by the *Marie Therese*; the same French vessel that had rescued James Francis Edward's party in February. During the voyage to Brittany Marischal resumed his condemnation of Mar, for his conduct of the campaign and cowardice in deserting the army. A fellow evacuee reported how 'the Earl Marischal whom they thought particular friends with Mar, encouraged the clamour against him'.[45]

Basing himself in exile in Paris, Marischal remained a staunch Jacobite but continued to censure Mar. By May 1716, factionalism had already spread between adherents of Mar and Marischal among the Jacobite exiles arrived in France.[46] Marischal steadfastly bore a grudge; as the philosopher Jean-Jacques Rousseau remarked, who befriended Marischal years later at the court of King Frederick II of Prussia: 'misled he sometimes was by his prejudices, and can never be disabled of them'. Stung by Marischal's attacks, Mar in later 1716 plaintively confided to the Duke of Perth: 'You can bear witness how little I deserved this usage (which all my accounts confirm) from that person since my coming to France […]. Had my own brother or son rose up against me it could not have surprised me more'.[47] Like Mar,

43 Patten, *History of the Rebellion*, p. 208.
44 Cuthell, *Scottish Friend of Frederick the Great*, vol. 1, pp. 57, 60–1.
45 *Ibid.*, p. 65.
46 Szechi, 'Cam Ye O'er Frae France?', p. 373.
47 Cuthell, *Scottish Friend of Frederick the Great*, vol. 1, pp. 102, 67.

Marischal was subject to a British governmental Act of Attainder, declaring him treasonous and his estates forfeit of the crown.

After playing a leading role in the 1719 rising Marischal returned to Spain. It was a country to which, as his brother put it, 'Lord Marischal was much attached [...] where, as he used to say, he had many good friends, not to mention the sun'.[48] He represented James Francis Edward Stuart at the Spanish court, and occasionally soldiered with the Spanish Army. In 1744, Marischal was the designated Jacobite commander-in-chief for Scotland of a planned French invasion of Britain. The French, however, abandoned the scheme and Marischal fell out of favour with both James Francis Edward and his son Prince Charles. He therefore played no part in the 1745–46 rising.

James Keith had pursued a successful military career in the Spanish and then Russian service. In 1747 the brothers reunited in Prussia. James went on to serve King Frederick II as a field marshal in the Prussian Army until his death in battle in 1758. George embarked on a political career, as Frederick's envoy to France and later as Prussian ambassador to Spain. Up until his death at Potsdam in May 1778, the Earl Marischal remained a close associate of King Frederick the Great.[49]

Successor to the Earl Marischal in command of Jacobite forces in Scotland in 1719 was **William Murray** (*b.* 1689, *d.* 1746), 3rd **Marquess of Tullibardine**.[50] He was the second son of John Murray, 1st Duke of Atholl, at the time Scotland's leading magnate.[51] In February 1708, as Lord William Murray he joined the British Royal Navy. In 1710 he served with the Mediterranean fleet. Murray inherited the title Marquess of Tullibardine after the death in August 1709 of his elder brother John at the battle of Malplaquet while serving with Marlborough's army. After leaving the navy in 1712 Tullibardine lived in London. Falling into debt, he came into contact with Jacobite circles and with the Earl of Mar. The Jacobite Sinclair described Tullibardine as a 'modest, good-natured young gentleman who he [Mar] had gained by paying his debts at London'. As one of 'Mar's friends', Tullibardine in 1715 was said to have been 'soon engaged by him in a cause he loved by paying his debts with the king's money [...] and [was] sent to Scotland before his Lordship of Mar, in hopes he'd [*sic*], with the assistance of his uncle and brothers, secure his father's vassals who were naturally well inclined'.[52]

Because the Duke of Atholl had opposed the Act of Union, in 1708 Jacobites optimistically assumed his support for James Francis Edward Stuart had the French expeditionary force landed – notwithstanding the Duke giving little indication of being prepared to do so.[53] In 1715, Jacobites remained hopeful that Atholl would play a leading role, despite his expressed intent to remain

---

48   Keith, *Fragment of a Memoir*, x.
49   Furgol, 'Keith', accessed 20 Apr. 2015.
50   For a recent succinct biography of Tullibardine, see M.G.H. Pittock, 'Murray, William, styled second duke of Atholl and marquess of Tullibardine (1689–1746)', in *ODNB* (2004), online edn. (available June 2018).
51   Tullibardine House in Perthshire was the Duke of Atholl's second seat.
52   Sinclair, *Memoirs of the Insurrection*, pp. 34, 67–8.
53   J.R. Young, 'Murray, John, first duke of Atholl (1660–1724)', in *ODNB* (2004) online edn., accessed 28 Nov. 2016.

loyal to King George I – as in the event he resolutely did. Thus when Tullibardine paused at the family seat at Blair Castle in Perthshire in mid-August and declared before his father his principled opposition to King George, that 'he [instead] owed a duty in the first place to the king [i.e. James III and VIII]', it was little wonder that the Duke furiously wrote after him: 'If you continue in disobedience to your father you will neither prosper in this world, nor be happy in the next, and your days will be short. If you obey not my commands in this, it shall be the last letter you shall receive from your father'.[54] The Duke's rage grew when he found out that Tullibardine's younger brother Lord George Murray had joined him. George was a subaltern in the Earl of Orkney's Regiment of Foot, but instead of returning from leave to his unit accompanied his brother at Mar's Jacobite gathering at Aboyne. In due course Atholl ensured that Tullibardine's lands were forfeited, and, by parliamentary Act in 1716, that his title passed to his loyalist younger son, Lord James Murray, then also a serving British Army officer.

12. William Murray, Marquess Tullibardine. In 1719 Tullibardine took command of the Jacobite expeditionary force from his rival George Keith, the Earl Marischal. Contemporary likeness by an unknown artist. (Reproduced courtesy of Roy Precious Fine Art)

Tullibardine, Lord George Murray, another brother Lord Charles Murray, and their uncle William, Lord Nairn, the Duke of Atholl's brother (described by a contemporary as 'a mighty stickler against the Union'), each raised a battalion from their familial Perthshire estates; 'some stronger, some weaker, as they could get those men to follow them'. The Duke himself angrily described this substantial body of rebel recruits as 'men he [i.e. Tullibardine] has robbed me of'.[55]

In October, the Atholl Brigade joined the Jacobite field army mustering at Perth. Before the battle of Sheriffmuir Mar, probably partly for flattery, partly to counterpoise his appointment of the Earl Marischal to similar rank with the Horse, made Tullibardine a major-general of Foot – notwithstanding his total lack of experience leading infantry in battle. As his fellow-officer Sinclair reflected:

> I can't but think that Tullibardine would have been of more us at the head of the Atholl-men than a major-general of the Foot; which, had not Mar put upon him, I am sure his natural modesty would never allowed him to ask, having said to myself and several others, that morning of our skirmish [i.e. on the day of the battle of Sheriffmuir], after it was determined to fight, that had it been in affairs of

---

54 John, 7th duke of Atholl (ed.), *Chronicles of the Atholl and Tullibardine Families*, 5 vols. (1908), vol. 2, pp. 185, 188.
55 Patten, *History of the Rebellion*, p. 44; Sinclair, *Memoirs of the Insurrection*, p. 34; Atholl, *Chronicles*, vol. 2, p. 196.

sea, having served in that element, he would [have] given his judgement, but being entirely ignorant of the land service, he was glad to acquiesce to whatever any who had the least experience or knowledge should advise him.

In an uncharacteristically charitable remark about one of the Jacobite army's senior officers, Sinclair reckoned that 'no man in all our business had more good will and less affectation' than Tullibardine. Not necessarily as a result of his own military inexperience, at Sheriffmuir the left wing of Jacobite infantry where Tullibardine was positioned was defeated. In the post-battle recriminations Tullibardine, according to Sinclair, an ever-critical eye-witness, was shielded by his patron from accusations about his conduct: 'Tullibardine had more favour showed him than any; and here Mar distinguished his own friends, by covering the shame of some whose easy temper, or whose necessities, rendered useful to him to carry on his wicked project to the last'.[56] In early February 1716 Tullibardine was based at Brechin when James Francis Edward Stuart's party sailed for France. Later with brother George he joined the flight of the officer corps of the Jacobite army into the Highlands, and in early summer was evacuated to France.

Tullibardine remained loyal to Mar, and was also rewarded by the titular King James III and VIII with a lieutenant-generalship. In January 1717 at Avignon, James favoured Tullibardine with the command-in-chief 'of all our forces in Scotland', in readiness to lead the anticipated Swedish-backed invasion upon which Jacobite hopes were then focused. Soon after, James also elevated Tullibardine with a dukedom and additional titles. In name only, therefore, Tullibardine became 'Duke of Rannoch, Marquess of Blair, Earl of Glen Tilt, Viscount of Glenshee and Lord Straith-Bran'.[57] In Scotland meanwhile, at his father's behest his estates had been made forfeit.

Returning to exile in France after the 1719 rising, Tullibardine withdrew from public life. When his father died in November 1724, Jacobites recognised him as the legitimate Duke of Atholl. During the 1720s and 1730s Tullibardine once again fell heavily into debt and relied upon associates for support. His most recent biographer has indicated that this vulnerability resulted from a marked decline in both his mental and physical health.[58]

But in 1745 Tullibardine rallied to the Jacobite cause. In July he was one of the so-called 'Seven Men of Moidart' accompanying Prince Charles Edward Stuart to Scotland. Notwithstanding his precarious health, Tullibardine played a leading part in the resultant rising, early on encouraging recruitment from the Atholl estates where he was popularly regarded as the legitimate duke. He fought with the Atholl Brigade at the battle of Culloden on 16 April 1746, but fleeing from the defeat was betrayed and taken into captivity. He died imprisoned at the Tower of London in July 1746, exhausted by privation and his lengthy exile.[59]

---

56 Sinclair, *Memoirs of the Insurrection*, p. 234.
57 Atholl, *Chronicles*, vol. 2, pp. 257–9.
58 Pittock, 'Tullibardine', accessed 26 Nov. 2016.
59 *Ibid.*

As mentioned previously, Tullibardine's younger brother **Lord George Murray** (*b*. 1694, *d*. 1760), deserted the British Army for the Jacobite cause. In Flanders in 1712, probably the Duke of Ormond himself commissioned the seventeen-year-old George as an ensign in the Earl of Orkney's Regiment of Foot.[60] While serving with the Dunkirk garrison Murray became sickly and indebted. In January 1713, his commanding officer notified his father the Duke of Atholl, that: 'He is extremely headstrong, and thinks himself more capable of giving advice than taking; he is given extremely to gaming [...]; in a word, he wants one to look over him, and that has authority, else I doubt in the way he is in he won't do well.' In Scotland in August 1715 Lord George's wayward inclination was to follow the lead of his older brother in joining the Jacobite rising. Murray held command in the family-led Atholl Brigade, but his battalion did not fight at Sheriffmuir because at the time it was based in Fife.[61]

When Murray arrived with Tullibardine in France in June 1716 he based himself with other Scots refugees at Avignon. By summer 1717 he had again fallen in debt, writing apologetically to the Earl of Mar for having done so, 'when on all accounts he ought to have been saving'.[62] Like most fellow exiles of the 1716 Jacobite diaspora, Murray's finances were fragile and reliant on a small pension from the Jacobite court. By 1718 he had joined the exile community in Bordeaux, the majority of whom by then were living more or less in poverty.[63]

Murray would play an active role in the 1719 rising, holding independent command at the battle of Glenshiel. Returning to exile in France, his education benefitted from a spell at the Paris Academy paid for by James Francis Edward Stuart himself (in 1713 the Earl of Orkney had remarked, 'how much he [Murray] needs to learn both to write and spell').[64] In 1725 Murray gained King George I's pardon, a result of his late father's intervention and James Francis Edward Stuart's consent. Murray married in 1728, and having settled down to life as a country gentleman not far from Tullibardine House, under the sufferance of his elder brother James, 2nd Duke of Atholl, appeared to have abandoned Jacobitism for good.[65] In 1745, however, when he was expected to back the Georgian government Murray instead joined

13. Lord George Murray. Better known to history for his generalship during the 1745–46 Jacobite rising, Murray at the battle of Glenshiel commanded the right of the Jacobite position. Portrait in ink as a young man, attributed to Sir Robert Strange. (© Scottish National Portrait Gallery)

---

60 For a recent succinct biography of Murray, see M.G.H. Pittock, 'Murray, Lord George (1694–1760)', in *ODNB* (2004), online edn. (available June 2018).

61 Quotation from Atholl, *Chronicles*, vol. 2, p. 149; Sinclair, *Memoirs of the Insurrection*, p. 233.

62 Daniell, *Calendar of the Stuart Papers*, vol. 4, p. 505.

63 For an overview of the Scottish Jacobite refugee experience, see Szechi, 'Cam Ye O'er Frae France?', *passim*.

64 Atholl, *Chronicles*, vol. 2, p. 148.

65 Pittock, 'Murray', accessed 28 Nov. 2016.

Prince Charles's rising with his elder brother Tullibardine. Murray served as lieutenant-general, and although some of his actions remain controversial, was the ablest commander of the Jacobite army.

After Marischal and Tullibardine, the third most significant leading Jacobite of the 1719 rising was the Roman-Catholic magnate **William MacKenzie, 5th Earl of Seaforth** (*d.* 1740).[66] The Earldom of Seaforth covered huge tracts of the north-west Highlands and Islands of Scotland. As chief of Clan MacKenzie and smaller aligned clans, William MacKenzie wielded considerable regional power. After his father, Kenneth MacKenzie, the 4th Earl, died in 1701 young William as a minor became subject to the wardship of the British government. For that reason, it seems that in 1708 at the time of the aborted French invasion he was warded in Edinburgh Castle, and in 1714 at the time of the accession of King George I detained at his family seat at Brahan Castle.[67]

Having by then attained his majority, in 1715 Seaforth could be held under no such restraint, and in later August joined the Jacobites rallying to the Earl of Mar. He assumed leadership in northerly Scotland, confirmed by his appointment under Mar as lieutenant-general and commander-in-chief of the northern counties. There he opposed pro-government Whig clan forces headed by John Gordon, Earl of Sutherland. By October Seaforth commanded a clan army of MacKenzies, MacDonalds, MacLeods, MacKinnons, Frasers and Chisholms, 3,000–4,000 strong; when confronted by which Sutherland's own clan host fled.[68] After plundering Whig territory, Seaforth negotiated a local truce to safeguard his estates, and at the end of October marched south to join Mar's field army. At the battle of Sheriffmuir, Seaforth instead of heading his clansmen joined a body of horsemen from the northern forces. This attracted the critical attention of Sinclair (with the Jacobite cavalry at the battle). 'What contributed not a little to our misfortune', he alleged:

> Was such as my Lord Seaforth did not throw themselves on foot at the head of their own clans; for it's taken for granted, that the best half of a Highlandman's courage consists in his love to his chief and master, and him he will not easily desert, and methinks the reciprocal love I ought to have for my clan, were I a Highland chief, would make me take my chance with them.

Sinclair's condemnation of Seaforth in person ran deeper:

> But of all engaged, Seaforth acted a scandalous part; who, in place of putting himself at the head of his clan, as all agreed, stood off in the rear, on some little rising ground, with forty scoundrels, all on horseback, with him [...] a cool spectator of the fate of his country; and when, as it was generally reported, my Lord Duffus [Kenneth Sutherland, third Lord Duffus, a cousin of Seaforth] went to him, and those about

---

66 For a recent succinct biography of Seaforth, see D. Horsburgh, 'Mackenzie, William, fifth earl of Seaforth (d. 1740)', in *ODNB* (2004), online edn. (available June 2018).

67 *Ibid.*, accessed 20 Apr. 2015.

68 Szechi, *Great Jacobite Rebellion*, p. 171

him, to entreat them to join in some one squadron or other, his lordship took not notice of it.

Carried along in or joining the retreat of the left of the Jacobite army, Duffus and Seaforth, according to Sinclair, were among the first to reach Perth. 'These are the effects', Sinclair reflected, 'of making a Highland chief a lord, and the thanks the royal family [i.e. the Stuarts] has got for dignifying Seaforth with the title of marquess [...] nor would I pursue a misfortune [i.e. allegations] of that kind so far, if we had not been deceived with the noise of the great feats he was to perform, both before and after'.[69] Although we lack a contemporary counter-balancing view, Sinclair's characterisation sheds some light on Seaforth's equivocal commitment in 1719. Nonetheless, he would lead the MacKenzies at the battle of Glenshiel and be wounded there. Seaforth was, understandably, always mindful of how his actions as a prominent Jacobite would affect his landed estates.

For that reason, by December 1715 Seaforth with some troops had returned north to secure his interests. Into the New Year he kept a truce in northerly Scotland, while clandestinely attempting to reach personal terms with the British government. However, when these contacts broke down, into spring 1716 Seaforth joined in the far north-west those chiefs in one way or another contemplating further resistance.[70] Together with other Jacobite notables, including John Cameron of Lochiel, Coll MacDonald of Keppoch and Major-General Alexander Gordon, Seaforth in mid-summer was evacuated from the Outer Hebrides by a French rescue ship.

In exile in France Seaforth joined the Earl of Mar's party. In May 1716 Seaforth was attainted by Act of parliament and his estates made forfeit, although loyal tenants would make it difficult for government officials to gather rents. His consolation from the would-be King James III and VIII was elevation to a marquisate in the Jacobite peerage. Returned to exile after the 1719 rising, Seaforth sought reconciliation with the British government. A significant step to this in 1725 was instructing his people to comply with the latest Disarming Act. His attainder was repealed in June 1726 and Seaforth returned home with the benefit an allowance from his forfeit rents. Having abandoned the Jacobite cause, Seaforth thereafter seems to have lived quietly. He died in 1740 on the Isle of Lewis.[71]

The Camerons inhabiting Lochaber – the Highland region to the west and around Fort William – were like the Earl of Seaforth's MacKenzies regarded by the Georgian government as being among 'the clans in the Highlands most addicted to rapine and plunder'.[72] Their chief for much of the 17th and into the 18th century was Sir Ewen Cameron of Lochiel. In 1689 he led his clansmen to victory with heavy casualties at the battle of Killiekrankie. Sir Ewen since was

---

69 Quotations from Sinclair, *Memoirs of the Insurrection*, pp. 231–3.
70 Szechi, *Great Jacobite Rebellion*, p. 188.
71 Horsburgh, 'Seaforth'.
72 As reported by General Wade to King George I in 1724: J. Allardyce (ed.), *Historical Papers relating to the Jacobite Period 1699-1750* 2 vols. (1895), vol. 1, p. 134.

regarded as reliably Jacobite, but along with other western-Highland chiefs in 1714 had also expressed loyalty to King George I.[73]

While the elderly Sir Ewen was by then reckoned 'tho' [*sic*] old, of a sound judgement and yet very healthful and strong in condition', his son **John Cameron of Lochiel** (*b.* 1663, *d.* 1748) was the effective head of the Camerons. In 1715 John Cameron engaged his clan, at the time reckoned to have an armed strength of 800 or upward of 1,000 men, to the Jacobite cause. However, because Cameron lands were threatened both by the garrison at Fort William and by the Whig Clan Campbell to the south, some clan gentry were reluctant to commit their people. Lochiel eventually united his clan regiment with the Earl of Mar's army in time to fight at Sheriffmuir on 13 November. However, when they returned home to Lochaber old Sir Ewan was said to have criticised his son for the Camerons not having fought more bravely.[74]

Into spring 1716 Lochiel actively encouraged those fellow western chiefs, including Coll MacDonald of Keppoch, Alexander Dubh MacDonnell of Glengarry and Ranald MacDonald of Clanranald, contemplating further resistance, until inroads by government forces into the western Highland and Islands made that impossible.[75] In July, Lochiel with Seaforth and others was evacuated to France to begin what became, apart from his return to Scotland in 1719, life-long exile. His elevation in January 1717 as Lord Lochiel in the Jacobite peerage was little recompense for being attainted as a traitor by the British government. With the death of the ninety-year-old Sir Ewen and the return of his father to exile, in later 1719 John's son Donald assumed the leadership of Clan Cameron. During the 1745–46 rising Donald would in turn lead the Camerons in the Jacobite cause in support of Prince Charles Edward Stuart.[76]

The eldest of the leading Jacobites involved with the 1719 rising was Brigadier **William Mackintosh** (*b. c.*1657, *d.* 1743), of Borlum, Inverness-shire. He was known at the time rather uncharitably as 'Old Borlum'. However, Mackintosh's military career before 1715 remains shadowy. A biographer thought it 'obvious that his foreign military service could not have been other than slight and intermittent'. He probably served occasionally as an officer in the French service during the 1670s, 1680s and early 1700s.[77] Borlum is another prominent figure of the period whose reputation is coloured by fellow-Jacobite opinion. Sinclair disparaged him for having 'no pretensions to know anything of [military] service, who the world had no better opinion of at that time [1715] than they have at present, who had nothing to recommend him but that his chief, the laird of Mackintosh, imagined him wiser than himself, and delivered himself and clan up to his disposal'. Patten, in 1715 a chaplain with the northern English Jacobites, acknowledged 'the Brigadier has got the character of brave and bold: he has given signal instances thereof beyond the seas;' but added, 'we saw very little of

---

73 E.M. Furgol, 'Cameron, Sir Ewen, of Lochiel (1629–1719)', in *ODNB* (2004), online edn., accessed 28 Nov. 2016.

74 Patten, *History of the Rebellion,* p. 196.

75 Szechi, *Great Jacobite Rebellion,* p. 258.

76 J.S. Gibson, 'Cameron, Donald, of Lochiel (*c.*1700–1748)', in *ODNB* (2004), online edn., accessed 28 Nov. 2016.

77 A.M. Mackintosh, *Brigadier Mackintosh of Borlum: Jacobite Hero and Martyr* (1918), unpaginated.

it at Preston' (the Lancastrian town the southern Jacobite army held and then surrendered during 12–14 November 1715).[78]

Whatever his military experience, by 1711 Borlum was residing in Scotland as a landowner. However, before the accession of King George I he seems to have acted as a Jacobite agent and travelled to the court at St. Germain. In this guise he adopted the titular rank of colonel. At the onset of the 1715 rising Borlum encouraged his young kinsman and chief Lachlan Mackintosh to raise the clan. In mid-September the Mackintosh's took the lead in occupying Inverness, and Borlum had King James III and VIII proclaimed at the market cross. Having 'regulated them very well, being no less than 500 stout men', Borlum together with their chieftain colonel led the Mackintosh regiment south to join the Earl of Mar's army at Perth.[79]

Sinclair reckoned that 'Mackintosh was less qualified for the command, for he had neither rank or distinguishing thing about him'. Borlum nonetheless had sufficient martial repute for Mar to appoint him brigadier, in charge of a strategic flanking manoeuvre intended to threaten the blocking position held by the British army about Stirling.[80] In mid-October Borlum led 2,000 Highlanders, including the Mackintosh regiment, across the Firth of Forth in a well-executed amphibious operation to threaten Edinburgh from the east. While this had the desired effect of drawing enemy reinforcements from Stirling, Borlum decided not to march upon the Scottish capital. He instead led his force southward, intending to unite with Scots Borderer and northern English Jacobites, but with no more definite plan.

Lacking clear orders from Mar, into November Borlum kept together a disparate force of reluctant clansmen, Lowland Scots, and English volunteers, while acting under the titular command of the wholly militarily inexperienced Scots peer William Gordon, sixth Viscount Kenmure, and the English Northumbrian politician and landowner Thomas Forster, as this southern Jacobite army progressed south-westward from the Borders, into Cumbria and finally to Lancashire. Dwindling to about 1,500 men and forced into fighting a two-day defensive action holding out at Preston, on 14 November the Jacobites capitulated and Borlum went into captivity.

In London in early April 1716, Borlum with other leading Jacobites taken at Preston was indicted for treason. However, on 4 May he and several other inmates broke out of Newgate Prison.[81] Borlum made his way to Shoreham in Essex and took ship to safety in France. This bold escapade made Borlum for a while something of a folk-hero among ordinary Londoners holding Jacobite sympathies. A popular ballad celebrating his exploits, *An Excellent New Song of the Rebellion*, ran:

---

78 Sinclair, *Memoirs of the Insurrection*, p. 156; Patten, *History of the Rebellion*, p. 98.
79 Patten, *History of the Rebellion*, p. 133.
80 Sinclair, *Memoirs of the Insurrection*, p. 255.
81 *The Weekly Packet*, 5–12 May 1716.

14. George Carpenter, Baron Carpenter. Lieutenant-General Carpenter was commander-in-chief of British land forces in Scotland at the time of the 1719 Jacobite rising. Portrait by John Faber Jr, after Johan van Diest. Mezzotint, 1719 or after. (© National Portrait Gallery, London)

Mackintosh is a soldier brave,
And did most gallantly behave
When into Northumberland he came,
With gallant men of his own name.[82]

Borlum probably spent his first period of exile in France in Paris. In 1719 he was recruited to join the expedition to Scotland and fought at Glenshiel. Afterwards he returned to exile, at first in Brittany, but from time to time during the 1720s made covert journeys to Scotland, where notwithstanding the threat of capture he spent increasing time. In probably November 1727 Borlum was seized by the authorities (or perhaps gave himself up to them) and was committed to Edinburgh Castle. Due to his age and infirmity Borlum was never tried for treason, but remained incarcerated at Edinburgh until his death in 1743.[83]

Opposing the Jacobites in 1719 in overall command of British government land forces in Scotland was Lieutenant-General **George Carpenter** (*b.* 1657, *d.* 1732). Like most of his fellow senior officers in the British Army Carpenter was a career soldier.[84] The youngest of seven children, he was born at Ocle Pychar, Herefordshire, into a local landed gentry family.[85] Grammar school educated, in 1671 the teenage George went to London as a page to Ralph, Earl of Montagu on his embassy to France, the Carpenters having secured Montagu's patronage. Returned to England, in 1672 George's military career began as a gentleman trooper in the third Troop of Horse Guards. Lacking means to purchase a commission in the household cavalry, Carpenter in 1685 joined the Earl of Peterborough's Regiment of Horse as a quartermaster. He was commissioned as a cornet in 1687, then became a captain, was made major in 1691, and in 1692 lieutenant-colonel and regimental second in command. During active service in Ireland and Flanders Carpenter was said to have 'distinguished himself to great advantage, by his courage, conduct and humanity'.[86]

In December 1703 Carpenter purchased the colonelcy of the Queen's Regiment of Dragoons. Promoted major-general in December 1705, during the War of the Spanish Succession he served with the British expeditionary

---

82 Cited in Mackintosh, *Brigadier Mackintosh of Borlum*.
83 *Ibid.*
84 For a recent succinct biography of Carpenter, see H.M. Stephens, rev. T.H. Place, 'Carpenter, George, first Baron Carpenter of Killaghy (1657–1732)', in *ODNB* (2004), online edn. (available June 2018).
85 *Ibid.*, accessed 3 Dec. 2016.
86 Anon., *Biographica Britannica, or the lives of the most eminent persons who have flourished in Great Britain and Ireland*, 6 vols. (1847), vol. 2, p. 1177.

force in Spain as quartermaster-general and general of cavalry.[87] At the Allied defeat at Almanza in April 1707, Carpenter led the cavalry rearguard covering the army's retreat, thereby safeguarding the British baggage train. In January 1710 he was promoted lieutenant-general, and in July wounded directing the cavalry during the Allied victory at Almenar. Early that December Carpenter was more seriously wounded and taken prisoner of war when a Franco-Spanish army stormed Brihuega. A musket ball broke Carpenter's jaw and caused severe dental damage, and until the ball was removed a year later he was unable to eat solid food.[88]

Upon returning to England from captivity Carpenter, like the majority of British Army officers, loyally backed the Hanoverian succession. In 1715 he began a political career, as MP (until 1722) for Whitchurch, Hampshire, and was preparing to travel to the Imperial court at Vienna as British ambassador when the rising in Scotland began. Acting in command of government forces in northern England, Carpenter first secured Newcastle-upon-Tyne against the southern Jacobite army, and then marched to intercept it in Lancashire. Arriving at Preston on 13 November he assumed command from Major-General Charles Wills, tightening the blockade of the Jacobite defenders and dictating their terms of capitulation next day. A pre-existing quarrel, however, caused both generals to dispute credit for the victory. This led in February 1716 to Carpenter challenging Wills to a duel – 'the motives reported for this were some words which had passed between then in Spain and were revived again at Preston'[89] – although the timely intervention of the Duke of Marlborough prevented actual confrontation.

In July 1716 Carpenter was appointed to the geographically very exclusive commands of commander-in-chief for Scotland, and governor of the Mediterranean island of Minorca and of the garrison there at Port Mahon.[90] In 1719 he deputised command of operations in northern Scotland to his subordinate Major-General Joseph Wightman, and that Maywas elevated to the Irish peerage as Baron Killaghy in the county of Kilkenny. The appointing letter patent endorsed Carpenter as 'a person who having applied himself early to the profession of arms, has passed through all military employs, to the rank he now bears, by slow and gradual promotions, his services always preceding his advancement'.[91] In military retirement, Carpenter from 1722–27 was MP for the city of Westminster. He was probably already quite infirm when a fall in late 1731 worsened his chronic dental condition. It seems that malnutrition hastened Carpenter's death in February 1732.

In effective command of British forces in Scotland in 1719 and of the army at the battle of Glenshiel was Major-General **Joseph Wightman** (*b.* c. 1670?, *d.* 1722).[92] His origins remain obscure; Dalton suggested he came

87 Dalton references Carpenter's military career in: *Army Lists and Commission Registers,* vol. 2, pp. 46–7, 104, 122; vol. 3, pp. 179, 225; vol. 5, pp. 17, 28, 37, 231; vol. 6, pp. 17, 385–6.
88 Stephens, 'Carpenter'.
89 *Biographica Britannica*, vol. 2, p. 1177.
90 C. Dalton, *George The First's Army, 1714–1727*, 2 vols. (1910), vol. 1, p. 248.
91 Cited in *The Weekly Journal or British Gazetteer*, 13 June 1719.
92 For a recent succinct biography of Wightman, see J. Falkner, 'Wightman, Joseph (d. 1722)', in *ODNB* (2004), online edn. (available June 2018).

from a Leicestershire gentry family.[93] Wightman began his military career in December 1690 as an ensign in the First Regiment of Foot Guards. It must be assumed that during the Nine Years' War he served with the regiment in Flanders. In August 1693 Wightman was promoted lieutenant and acting company captain. His advancement was probably a result of officer casualties at the battle of Neerwinden/Landen in July, where the brigade of Foot Guards suffered heavy losses. In December 1696 he was promoted senior captain, so ranking as lieutenant-colonel. After the Guards returned home in 1697 Wightman seems to have transferred as lieutenant-colonel to a line battalion, Colonel Sir Matthew Bridge's Regiment of Foot.[94]

At the beginning of the War of the Spanish Succession Bridge's regiment served in Flanders under the Duke of Marlborough. In August 1703 the colonelcy passed to Brigadier-General Holcroft Blood. That autumn Blood's Regiment was listed in the expeditionary force to be led by the Earl of Galway to Portugal. Blood's concurrent responsibility for the artillery train with the army in Flanders, however, prevented him accompanying the regiment to Portugal. Wightman therefore assumed command, having already been promoted brevet-colonel in August. 'I dare say the service will not suffer by Colonel Blood's absence', Marlborough noted in a dispatch from Flanders that October, 'Colonel Wightman, who is at the head of it [i.e. Blood's Regiment] with a commission of colonel, being a very careful, diligent officer'.[95]

Wightman led Blood's Regiment through the campaigns in Portugal and Spain, including in April 1707 at the battle of Almanza, where it suffered heavy casualties. In January that year Wightman had been promoted brigadier-general, and after the death of Brigadier-General Blood in August secured the colonelcy of the regiment. In Spain in January 1710 he was promoted major-general, and was posted to Scotland later that year. In June 1712 Wightman became acting commander-in-chief in Scotland, in the absence of his superiors, the Duke of Argyll and Major-General Thomas Wetham.[96]

Upon the death of Queen Anne, in August 1714 Wightman dutifully upheld the Hanoverian succession. He acted to gauge the loyalty of the Highlands, and ensured army officers in Scotland swore allegiance to King George I.[97] Wightman took effective action at the beginning of the 1715–16 rising before the arrival of his superior Argyll. He deployed the few regular troops in Scotland to secure strategically important Stirling and organised the defence of Edinburgh. At the battle of Sheriffmuir Wightman commanded the infantry centre of Argyll's army. After the collapse of the army's left he creditably deployed the remaining intact battalions to hold the British position. Into spring 1716 Wightman conducted counter-insurgency operations in the Highlands under the direction of the new commander-in-chief in Scotland Lieutenant-General William Cadogan. It was reported

93 Dalton, *George The First's Army*, vol. 1, p. 48.
94 Dalton, *Army Lists and Commission Registers*, vol. 3, pp. 136, 306, vol. 4, p. 123.
95 G. Murray (ed.), *The Letters and Dispatches of John Churchill, first Duke of Marlborough, from 1702 to 1712*, 5 vols. (1845), vol. 1, p. 192.
96 Dalton, *Army Lists and Commission Registers*, vol. 5, pp. 111, 159, vol. 6, pp. 18, 89, 220.
97 Dalton, *George The First's Army*, vol. 1, p. 50.

from Edinburgh on 3 April, that 'We have an account from Inverness, that General Wightman with all the troops quartered thereabouts is marched to Riven [Ruthven] in Badenoch [in Speyside, south of Inverness]'. While operating from Inverness Wightman caused his superior some short-term discomfort by seizing the Earl of Seaforth's coach and six horses from his seat at Brahan Castle. Seaforth's mother, the dowager Countess Seaforth, complained vociferously about the loss to Cadogan, but to no effect.[98]

Wightman subsequently resumed his role as acting commander-in-chief in Scotland. His last engagement was the battle of Glenshiel. In reward for his service in Scotland he was later appointed to the governorship of Kinsale in Ireland. But before he could take up his post Wightman died suddenly, probably of a stroke, at Bath in September 1722.[99]

---

98 *The Exeter Mercury, or Weekly Intelligencer*, 10–13 April 1716; Dalton, *George The First's Army*, vol. 1, p. 51.
99 Falkner, 'Wightman', accessed 20 Apr. 2016.

3

The Cardinal, the Duke, and the Exiles

'It would be necessary to have a diversion made in Scotland'.

An Invasion of England and a Rising in Scotland

By December 1718, clandestine diplomacy conducted between officials of the Spanish and Swedish monarchies promised fresh military backing for the Jacobite cause. In October, a plenipotentiary of Charles XII meeting in Paris with the Spanish ambassador, the Prince Cellamare, expressed the King of Sweden's intent to ally with King Phillip V of Spain in order to bring about the downfall of King George I. The proposal chimed with Spanish foreign policy under Cardinal Alberoni's direction, following the humiliating defeat at Cape Passaro and subsequent rupture in Anglo-Spanish relations. Accordingly, Alberoni sent Sir Patrick Lawless, an Irish soldier in the Spanish service and trusted Jacobite agent, to secure Charles XII's commitment to a proposed alliance in which Spanish subsidy would fund Swedish military effort.

Alberoni understood that James Butler, Duke of Ormond, with his martial repute and perceived popularity in England, was the leading soldier among the Jacobite exiles. He seems to have been prepared to overlook Ormond's command in 1702 of British land forces sent to take Cádiz. Ormond was at Paris when he received via Prince Cellamare the cardinal's invitation to come to Madrid. With a few staff officers and servants Ormond surreptitiously left Paris towards the end of October. Their departure was known to British and French intelligence, but because the French government preferred to believe Ormond was seeking asylum in Spain his party went there unhindered. They arrived at Madrid probably on 22 November. Warmly welcomed by Alberoni, Ormond straightaway entered into discussion with the first minister. While the favoured means to sponsor the restoration of King James III and VIII was a Spanish-financed Swedish invasion of Scotland or England, direct Spanish military intervention was considered. Ormond reckoned that an invasion army seven or eight thousand strong was necessary, bringing 15,000 muskets with ammunition to arm the British Jacobites. King Phillip looked favourably on this strategy, but was unwilling to commit any troops. This was because of Spanish military commitments in the Mediterranean, and moreover because political tension with France meant that Spain might soon have to defend her northern frontiers. Phillip nonetheless acceded to the armaments, and reiterated Spain's commitment to financial backing for Swedish operations in the British Isles.[1]

As discussions continued into December, governmental opinion in Madrid shifted in favour of an invasion of England by a Spanish expeditionary force. Ormond was appointed commander-in-chief, jointly commissioned captain-general of King James III and VIII and generalissimo of the army and vice admiral of the invasion fleet in the service of King Phillip V of Spain. The landing would take place in south-western England, as Ormond had intended in 1715. It was over-optimistically envisaged that in the West Country civilian Jacobites joined by British troops disaffected with the Georgian regime would flock to Ormond and advance on London, led or joined soon afterwards by James Francis Edward Stuart himself. King Phillip was

15. Likeness of Cardinal and statesman Giulio Alberoni (*b.* 1664, *d.* 1752). As first minister to King Phillip V of Spain, Alberoni allied Spanish foreign policy to the Jacobite cause.

willing to commit a 5,000-strong army, of 4,000 infantry and 1,000 cavalry (of whom 300 would be mounted, the remaining horseflesh being obtained in England). It would have 10 field guns, ample munitions, including 1,000 barrels of gunpowder and the 15,000 small arms, to be shipped in the necessary transports with naval escort. Now that Spanish forces were involved, Ormond's aide-de-camp, George Bagenal, was put under orders to follow Lawless to Sweden to press Charles XII to commit to the alliance and to landings in Britain before the spring.

Ormond had already advised Alberoni to the effect, 'that it would be necessary to have a diversion made in Scotland'.[2] The Cardinal agreed to this secondary operation, which Ormond optimistically reckoned could be sustained with the infusion of two or three thousand small arms and by the leadership of his nominated commander George Keith, the Earl Marischal. Alberoni therefore instructed Ormond to summon Marischal from Paris as quickly as possible. The Duke also sought out to assist Marischal another trusted subordinate among the Jacobite exiles in France, Brigadier Colin Campbell of Ormidale. He had served as a soldier of fortune in the Russian Army, and joined the rising in Scotland in January 1716. In early May, on South Uist in the Western Isles Ormidale attempted to rally the islanders against a British amphibious force sent to disarm them. A report of the incident described how Ormidale 'being summoned to surrender, answered that he would never without honourable terms, but fight to the last drop of his blood'. The 150 or

---

1   Dickson, *Jacobite Attempt*, pp. xxvii–xxix, 15–17; Michael, *England under George I*, pp. 188–90.
2   Dickson, *Jacobite Attempt*, p. 289.

so locals with him lacked Ormidale's resolve, however, and upon '200 of the king's troops being sent against them, they all deserted upon their approach, leaving the brigadier alone, and still standing in his arms, in which posture he was taken'.[3] Later imprisoned with other Jacobites in England in Carlisle Castle, in December 1716 Ormidale had managed to escape to France.

But international events now threatened to overturn Ormond and Alberoni's plans. On 3 December 1718, the British government authorised the Royal Navy and British privateers to attack Spanish merchant shipping. On 16 December, King George formally declared war on Spain. France did so before the end of the month, thereby bringing into play the terms of both the Anglo-French Treaty of Defensive Alliance of 1717 and the Quadruple Alliance of July 1718.[4] French governmental opinion hardened against Spain as a result of the revelation earlier in December of the so-called Cellamare plot. Given encouragement from Madrid by both King Phillip and Cardinal Alberoni and directed in Paris by their ambassador Cellamare, the scheme intended to encourage Hispanophile French courtiers headed by the Duke of Maine to overthrow the Regent Duke of Orléans. With the plot exposed and the resultant arrest and expulsion of Cellamare, it was likely that in retaliation French forces would soon threaten northern Spain.

Of more immediate concern to Jacobites, however, was news of the death of the King of Sweden. Returning again to the offensive in the long-lasting Great Northern War, in autumn 1718 Charles XII invaded Norway. He led the southern division of his army that by December was besieging the fortress of Fredriksten commanding the strategically important border town of Frederikshald (the present city of Halden). There, while directing operations in the Swedish entrenchments, on 30 November Charles XII was killed by a shot to the head. His death ended any hope of Swedish military support for Spain and the Jacobites. Charles's self-appointed successor, his sister Ulrika Eleanora, was preoccupied with ensuring her accession to the throne. She was also married to Frederick, son of the Landgrave, or ruler, of the German principality of Hesse-Cassell, which sought cordial relations with Hanover. When Ulrika's coronation as Queen of Sweden took place in April 1719, she had already had Charles's pro-Jacobite chief minister Baron von Görtz executed and his followers removed from office. The following July Sweden and Great Britain agreed a preliminary peace accord that was fulfilled in January 1720 by an 18-year treaty of mutual assistance. Among its terms Queen Ulrica undertook to guarantee the Hanoverian succession in Great Britain.[5]

'The sad news of the death of the King of Sweden', the Duke of Ormond remarked in mid-January 1719, replying to Cardinal Alberoni's dispatch mentioning Charles XII's demise, 'in the present state of affairs, is a very great loss, but notwithstanding this misfortune we must follow out our enterprise'.[6] While Ormond for a while continued to entertain the unlikely

3   *The Post Man and The Historical Account*, 22–24 May 1716.
4   Anon., *The Political State of Great Britain, Volume XVI* (1719), pp. 539–40, 543–7, 556–8.
5   *Collection of all the Treaties*, vol. 1, pp. 345–66.
6   Dickson, *Jacobite Attempt*, p. 47.

hope that the joint or sole accession of Prince Frederick of Hesse-Cassell to the throne might resurrect Swedish support, preparations went ahead for the Spanish expedition to England. While Alberoni must have had serious misgivings about the likelihood of success he remained committed to the operation, although reducing its resources. The artillery train was scaled down from 10 field pieces to five; 12,000 instead of 15,000 stand of muskets would be supplied (a stand comprising one musket with ramrod and bayonet); and the cash subsidy to be allocated to Ormond in Spanish bullion was cut.[7] The invasion force would sail from the naval base of Cádiz on Spain's Atlantic-facing south-west coast, where preparations would be masked as making ready to reinforce Spanish forces in the Mediterranean. In order to maintain the subterfuge, Ormond and his staff would travel in the opposite direction, to the port of La Coruña (anglice Corunna) on the north-west coast of Galicia. There they would either rendezvous with or sail from to meet the armada. Having left Madrid early in January 1719, by the second week Ormond was based at Valladolid, about 100 miles (161 km) north-west of the capital.

It was not until mid-January that by Ormond's letters the Jacobite court in Rome knew fully of the invasion scheme. Alberoni's correspondence encouraged James Francis Edward Stuart to leave for Spain as quickly as possible. Both he and Ormond also expressed concern for James's safety in Italy under increasing occupation by Imperial Austrian forces.

Notwithstanding the enthusiasm of the titular James III and VIII and his entourage for this hoped-for fresh military venture, with Sweden sidelined prospects for success seemed less promising. Regardless of his commander-in-chief the Duke of Ormond's capacity for charismatic military leadership, James's hopes now rested on an invasion of England by another Spanish armada. It would bring the army of His Most Catholic Majesty the King of Spain to overthrow the recognised government and monarchy to be replaced by the Catholic Pretender. Rather than engender support for the Stuarts, this unlikely Hispano-Jacobite alliance would inflame English patriotism against the old enemy, Spain, uniting Whigs with the moderate majority of Tories. The depth of this animosity was reflected by the high sheriff, magistracy and other Yorkshire gentlemen gathered at the county assize court at York on 16 March. With the Spanish threat by then public knowledge, the Yorkshiremen issued a loyal proclamation. It stated their 'utmost indignation', resentment and abhorrence of the 'intended invasion from Spain, in favour of the pretender to your majesty's crown', and their united opposition to 'the Pretender, and all other his adherents'.[8]

The diversionary landing in Scotland now assumed greater strategic and political importance. The timely arrival there of a well-resourced military expedition would attract considerable support from among Highland clans and Jacobite Lowlanders. The effect of a successful conjunction of forces would be that much of the British Army would be committed in Scotland instead of

---

7   *Ibid.*, p. 41.
8   *The Weekly Journal or British Gazetteer,* 11 April 1719.

16. An 18th century depiction of Edinburgh Castle. As the capital's stronghold, Edinburgh Castle in 1719 was headquarters of the British Army in Scotland.

against Ormond in southern England. Scots Jacobites hoped that a successful rising would stiffen the resolve of their English counterparts to take action.

At Paris in mid-December, the Earl Marischal received Ormond's instruction to travel inconspicuously with his younger brother James to Madrid. To maintain secrecy, however, Ormond had not intimated the purpose of the summons or its urgency. The Keiths left Paris on probably 19 December. Travelling south via Avignon, they took passage from Marseilles and landed on Spain's north-east coast at Palamós in Catalunia. Adopting the guise of ex-British Army officers travelling to Madrid seeking employment as soldiers of fortune, the Keiths unhurriedly made their way to the capital, arriving there towards the end of January 1719.

The morning after they arrived the brothers had an audience with Cardinal Alberoni. After chiding them for not coming sooner, the Cardinal, according to James Keith's memoir, then disclosed the purpose of their mission: 'He told us the business pressed; that it was to execute an enterprise on England in favour of its lawful master; that the Duke of Ormond was already set out to embark at the Groyne [Corunna] for England; and it was resolved the Earl Marischal should go to Scotland'.[9] Alberoni then asked what Marischal needed for the expedition and what was his strategy. Uninformed, Marischal had made no such preparations, and 'that as he did not know the plan the Duke of Ormond had laid down, and as both parts must go in concert', it was agreed he should

---

9   Keith, *Fragment of a Memoir*, p. 40.

go after Ormond on his way to Corunna to confer with him.[10] While James Keith remained in Madrid to liaise with the Cardinal, Marischal, by riding quickly on a relay of government post-horses, by 3 February had caught up with Ormond's party at Astorga, 175 miles (282 km) north-west of the capital. In their ensuing discussions deputy and commander-in-chief agreed that as well as military supplies it would be advantageous to send to Scotland a force of 300 Spanish soldiers. As Ormond afterwards reiterated in writing to Alberoni:

> For when these few men have arrived, the talk of the country will make them 3,000, which will oblige the enemy to keep a large number of troops in that country, and the rumour of the regular troops being in that country will have a good effect. The number is inconsiderable in this country, but will be of great importance in Scotland.[11]

Returning to Madrid on probably 6 February, Marischal, according to his brother, 'immediately went to the Cardinal and settled the plan of the undertaking'.[12] He pressed Alberoni for 4,000 firearms and 10,000 pistoles in gold coin.[13] The Cardinal instead granted half the amount in firearms and cash. Six companies of Spanish infantry and plentiful munitions were, however, allocated to the expedition to Scotland, along with two frigates from the Spanish navy as transports. The force would sail from the naval base at San Sebastian (known to the British as Port Passage) on Spain's north-east Biscayan coast. Logistical arrangements would be managed by the Prince of Campo Florido, the military governor of San Sebastian. He was an experienced Sicilian naval officer in the Spanish service.

It was agreed the expedition would have a second component. As many of the militarily able notable Scots Jacobite exiles in France as could be gathered from their quarters in Bordeaux, Orleans, Paris and elsewhere would be shipped to Scotland. Earlier in January, Ormond had advised Alberoni of the importance of bringing this disparate group together, while acknowledging the problems in doing so: 'I had thought that it would be necessary to warn them, but I feared that they might reveal the project, and of the two evils we must choose the less. It will be desirable that they should be in their own country, but there will be much difficulty in getting them over'.[14] James Keith, who seems to have gained Alberoni's trust in his brother's absence, was tasked with overcoming the difficulties of getting the exiles to Scotland. Bearing a memorandum signed by Ormond of the cryptic sort typical in Jacobite circles, simply stating 'Pray have entire confidence in the bearer', and given a fighting fund of 18,000 Spanish crowns, James Keith hurriedly left Madrid on 7 February. He first went to San Sebastian. Arriving there on the 11th, he gave 12,000 crowns to the Prince of Campo Florido to finance the preparation and

---

10 *Ibid.*
11 Dickson, *Jacobite Attempt*, p. 61.
12 Keith, *Fragment of a Memoir*, p. 41.
13 A Pistole was the primary denomination of Spanish gold coinage, approximately equivalent to 16 English shillings.
14 Dickson, *Jacobite Attempt*, p. 38.

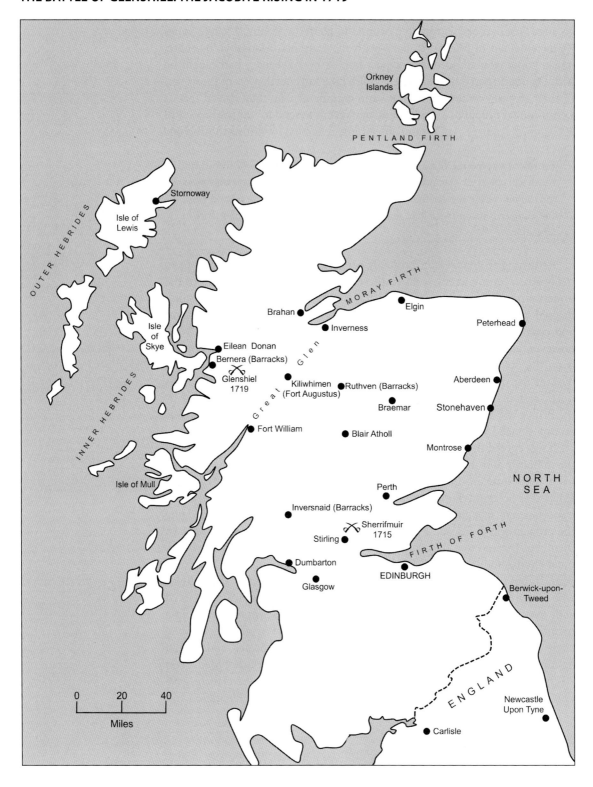

Map 2. Scotland. Selected places mentioned in the text are shown.

supplying of Marischal's force. Then, 'with the little money which remained', Keith, as he recollected, resumed his journey and 'entered France privately'.[15]

The Earl Marischal made his way later to San Sebastian to organise the expeditionary force. This involved, on or around 18 February, the embarkation aboard the frigates of 307 officers and men drafted from Colonel Don Pedro de Castro's Regiment of Foot. Also known as the Regiment of Galicia, this was a regular line infantry unit of the Spanish Army. For the expedition to Scotland, 12 rank and file were detached from each of the regiment's 26 companies (apart from the two elite companies of grenadiers) forming six 48-man companies, each officered by a captain, his lieutenant and an ensign. In command of this detached battalion was Don Pedro de Castro's deputy, Lieutenant-Colonel Don Nicolás Bolaño. In all, apart from the complements of the frigates, the expedition probably numbered 320 or so Spanish military personnel.[16] At San Sebastian Marischal was joined from Bordeaux by Brigadier Colin Campbell of Ormidale, who would remain his close associate, and by one other notable Scottish Jacobite, whose identity remains obscure; according to a Spanish officer, 'none else came in these [Spanish] frigates but three lords with their servants'.[17] Under the Prince of Campo Florido's effective supervision, Marischal's flotilla was readied and able to sail from San Sebastian on 25 February. The Spanish armada should have departed Cádiz a fortnight earlier. Given favourable weather at sea, and luck in avoiding British warships, there was a good chance that around the time Ormond landed in England Marischal's diversionary force would reach Scotland.

Objective Scotland

Alberoni, Ormond and the Keith brothers had agreed the expedition's first objective was to establish a beachhead in the Islands and Highlands of north-west Scotland. The sea passage there provided the best chance of avoiding patrolling ships of the British Royal Navy (which had prevented Jacobite landings on the east coast of Scotland in 1708, and again in 1715–16). The region was home to Jacobite-inclined clans, who were expected to provide the initial strength of a wider rising in Scotland. The mainland counties of Ross-Shire and Sutherland and much of the Western Isles were home to the MacKenzies and smaller clans and septs aligned to them – the MacRaes, MacLays, MacLennans, Murchisons and the MacLeods – under the chieftainship of William MacKenzie, Earl of Seaforth.

---

15 Keith, *Fragment of a Memoir*, p. 41.
16 The organisation of the draft battalion of the Regiment of Galicia was described to the British by one of its lieutenants, captured when the Royal Navy seized the Jacobite stronghold of Castle Donan on 10 May 1719. *The London Gazette* ran his account in the edition for 30 May–2 June. While all later writers to date have stated that Lieutenant-Colonel Bolaño's contingent numbered 306 officers and men, as will be seen between them the Royal Navy and the British Army took 317 Spanish prisoners of war during the 1719 rising. Although only one Spanish fatality seems to have been recorded – a soldier who collapsed and died of sunstroke on 4 June (Dickson, *Jacobite Attempt*, p. 296) – it seems unlikely there were no other Spanish deaths, either as a result of the battle of Glenshiel, or by accidental injury or from disease. Therefore, there were probably at least 320 Spanish soldiers with the expeditionary force.
17 *The London Gazette*, 30 May–2 June 1719.

It was agreed the expedition would rendezvous in the Isle of Lewis. Here, on the northerly main island of the Outer Hebrides, a 130-mile-long archipelago at the time known collectively as the Long Island, they could expect local support. Lewis was MacKenzie territory, the furthest extent of the Earl of Seaforth's lands. The Jacobites intended to rely on Seaforth, then in exile in Paris, and the military potential of his people. In September 1716 Colin Campbell of Glendaruel, an influential Scots Jacobite exile in France, in 'Proposals with respect to Scotland' (a feasibility study for the Earl of Mar of options for military operations there), explained that:

> It will be fit to carry the Marquess of Seaforth with you; all his command lies in the north, and he is able to raise the greatest number of Highlanders of any man in the north and is the first that can join you. You may always depend on 1,500 Foot at least from him that will continue with you, and for a brush [i.e. an engagement or campaign] in that country he may have 2,000.[18]

Glendaruel recommended Dumbarton at the mouth of the River Clyde as a suitable landing place on Scotland's west coast. From there it would be easier to advance via Glasgow against Stirling or Edinburgh. While he did not reject landing further north, Glendaruel reckoned that unless a Highland army moved quickly southward, government forces would concentrate on the key strategic position of Stirling. This was because of:

> The time it takes before you can get into England, for if the king [i.e. James Francis Edward Stuart] has not a greater force than I can foresee, he will want the Scots army to cast the balance on his side. It also gives the enemy full time to have all the troops they have in Scotland before you at Stirling and perhaps they may waft over some from Ireland, but a quick march towards Glasgow by some taking that route from Inverlochy [i.e. from the Highlands by way of Fort William] may come to prevent them.[19]

At first lodged in the far north-west, the expedition would be in largely secure territory distant from government forces. If the Spanish landing in England was delayed, this isolation would allow the Jacobites time to gather strength in preparation for Ormond's arrival. Furthermore, the garrisons in the Highlands were not an immediate threat.[20]

The British Army's key strongholds in Scotland were to the south; the permanently garrisoned royal castles at Edinburgh, Stirling, Dumbarton and Blackness. Since the attempted Franco-Jacobite invasion of 1708 and hastened by the 1715–16 rising, these had been strengthened and modernised. Despite the likelihood of further Jacobite activity, however, these were only small permanent garrisons. According to the establishment for land forces in Great Britain agreed in December 1718, the standing garrison of Edinburgh

---

18 Daniell, *Calendar of the Stuart Papers,* vol. 4, p. 82.
19 *Ibid.,* p. 84.
20 This section references mainly C. Tabraham and D. Grove, *Fortress Scotland and the Jacobites* (1995), pp. 40, 48–51, 60–5, and S. Cruden, *The Scottish Castle* (1960), pp. 234–41, *passim.*

Castle was the governor and his deputy, a 69-strong infantry company, four gunners, a chaplain and a surgeon; for Stirling Castle, 70 infantrymen and officers, four gunners, a gunsmith and a chaplain; and for Dumbarton Castle, just 15 soldiers, five officers and NCOs and a lone gunner.[21] These small garrisons if threatened could, however, be reinforced by detachments from regular marching regiments of Foot based in Scotland at the time.

The only garrison then fully operational in the Highlands proper was in Lochaber, at Fort William at the southern end of the Great Glen. This natural feature, a fault line forming a valley running coast to coast, was in effect a front line, north and west of which lay the territory of the most belligerent clans. The low-lying ramparts and projecting bastions of Fort William stood on a promontory dictating the fort's irregular pentagonal plan at the confluence of the River Nevis with Loch Linnhe. The fortification had been built, or rather, rebuilt, as an earthwork during summer 1690 under the direction of General Mackay, on the site of a similarly constructed fort dating from the English republic's military occupation of Scotland during the 1650s. The Cromwellian outpost abandoned in 1661 had been known as Inverlochy, after the nearby medieval castle. Mackay had renamed the fort site and given the name Mary Burgh to the settlement founded beside it in honour of the recently established dual monarchy. The township in the 1720s

17. Surviving length of Fort William's north rampart (left) and north-west demi-bastion (right). The arched sallyport through the rampart may date from the 1650s Cromwellian fort.

---

21 The National Archives (hereafter TNA), WO 24/92: War Office, Papers concerning Establishments, 'Establishment of His Majesty's Guards, Garrisons and Land Forces in Great Britain commencing 25 Dec. 1718'.

18. Surviving stretch of Fort William's westerly rampart, with the fort's interior at left. In the early 1720s, the Scots writer, and sometime spy for the London government, John Macky described Fort William serving 'as a bridle to keep the inhabitants in awe, who on all revolutions or emergencies of government have been very unruly'.

was described as 'originally designed as a sutlery to the garrison in so barren a country, where little can be had for the support of the troops'.[22]

Although described by Campbell of Glendaruel in 1716 as 'a place of no great strength', since 1708 Fort William had been refortified. The earthen ramparts and bastions were faced in stone, and by 1719 the rebuilding in masonry of the governor's house, barracks, magazine and storehouses was well advanced. Fort William had a transitional infantry garrison provided by marching regiments. Apart from the governor and his deputy, the only permanent personnel were three gunners, a storekeeper, a blacksmith, a carpenter and a supervising provost marshal. In January 1719 Colonel Sir Robert Pocock, a Scot and MP for Renfrewshire, had been reappointed governor. During the 1715–16 rising Pocock had held Fort William against local Jacobite forces, although his garrison had encountered little more opposition than occasional sniping from passing parties of Highlanders.

Sixty-five miles (105 km) north-east of Fort William, at the northern end of the Great Glen, lay the town of Inverness. A Cromwellian earthwork fortification, known as Oliver's Fort, constructed there in 1652 near the settlement on the east bank of the River Ness had been demolished in 1661. However, unlike the fort at Inverlochy rebuilt as Fort William in the 1690s Oliver's Fort was not reoccupied. Instead, the medieval fortifications standing on Castle Hill more closely commanding the town, comprising a tower-house with enclosing curtain walls, were strengthened by earthworks. In this form Inverness Castle was reused during the 1715–16 rising. In September 1715 Inverness was occupied by northerly Jacobite clan forces, but they abandoned

22 Jamieson, *Letters from a Gentleman*, vol. 1, p. 252.

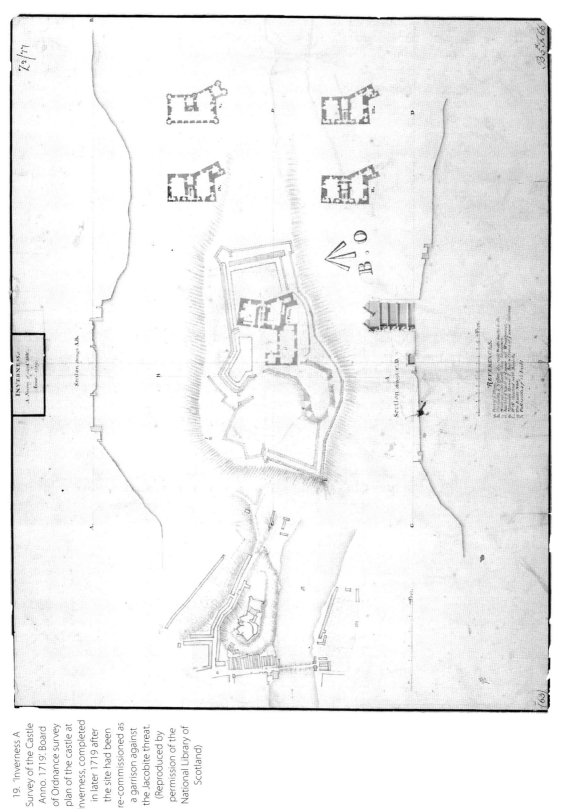

19. 'Inverness A Survey of the Castle Anno. 1719'. Board of Ordnance survey plan of the castle at Inverness, completed in later 1719 after the site had been re-commissioned as a garrison against the Jacobite threat. (Reproduced by permission of the National Library of Scotland)

the place in November when confronted by an army of Whig clansmen. Pro-government Highlanders held Inverness thereafter. Militiamen from Clan Munro garrisoned the castle and some Royal Navy cannon were emplaced there.[23] By 1719, however, Inverness Castle had no military establishment and was more or less abandoned. Despite hurried efforts that April and May to re-commission it against the Jacobite threat, a survey and resultant plan completed by army engineers later that year documented the actual state of disrepair of the old stronghold. The stone revetments of the outer defences, which had been strengthened with timber palisades, were badly built, and in places 'made up with earth, very imperfect'; the roof and floors of the five-storey barrack block converted from the earlier tower-house were 'ruinous'; the attached ground-level blockhouse, including the kitchens, was not weatherproof; and the well found to be 'choked with rubbish'.[24]

The 1715–16 rising had shown the British Army to be ill-prepared to quickly respond to an insurrection in the Highlands, where it faced particular challenges. The difficulties of policing antagonistic clans were exacerbated by the problems of billeting and concentrating forces in what for outsiders was an inhospitable region. The population was dispersed, and for a regular army communications were poor. Therefore, in August 1717 the Board of Ordnance authorised the construction of four new fort-like barracks, sited to support the existing strongpoints and to control lines of communication. 'As well for preventing the Highlanders descending in the low country in time of rebellion', the purpose of the new barracks, together with Fort William and a garrison at Inverness, would be, as General Wade explained in 1724, 'for the better quartering his majesty's troops, and keeping them in a body sufficient to prevent or subdue insurrections'.[25]

Two barracks would be positioned south of the Great Glen, each accommodating a garrison of 120 regular infantrymen. One was built to the south-eastward at Ruthven in Badenoch, in the valley of the River Spey, the second much further south, at Inversnaid, nearby the east shore of Loch Lomond. In the Great Glen itself, at the southern end of Loch Ness at Kiliwhimen (the present town of Fort Augustus, which takes its name from the much larger replacement Georgian fort begun there in 1729) the third barrack would accommodate a 360-strong garrison. It would form with Fort William and Inverness Castle a chain of strongholds spanning the Great Glen. Kiliwhimen, Wade observed in 1724, was 'the most centrical [sic] part of the Highlands, a considerable pass [i.e. way of communication], equally distant from Fort William and Inverness'.[26] The fourth and most westerly barrack would be the remote outpost at Bernera in Kintail. It would be built beside Glenelg Bay, to control the nearby drove-way route (engineered in the later 18th century as a military road) that led via Glenshiel to the narrows at

---

23 Rae, *History of the Rebellion*, p. 34.
24 The National Library of Scotland (hereafter NLS), Military Maps of Scotland (18th century): 'Inverness. A Survey of the Castle. Anno. 1719', Shelfmark MS.1647 Z.02/77.
25 Allardyce, *Historical Papers*, vol. 1, p. 134.
26 *Ibid.*, p. 141.

Kyle Reah. This was the shortest crossing point between the mainland and the Isle of Skye.

All four fort-barracks would be built to a similar rectangular plan. Two four-storey (including a garret) barrack blocks providing accommodation stood along opposing sides of a square and parade ground. The outer face of each barrack formed most of the length of two sides of the perimeter wall, which along the two other stretches had vaulted firing positions at ground level beneath a walkway and parapet. At diagonally opposing corners were two watchtowers that also provided domestic and service accommodation.

In the event, the vaunted barrack-building programme proceeded only slowly. By spring 1719 Kiliwhimen, Inversnaid and Ruthven were more or less indefensible building sites. The barrack for 240 men to be built at Bernera, within 10 miles (16 km) over loch and mountain of the Jacobite beachhead established that April, remained on the drawing board and uncompleted until 1723. It was only on 17 March 1719 that Sir Patrick Strachan, who the following May became Barrack-Master General of Scotland with oversight of the building work, had finally agreed a government contract to build the barrack at Bernera, at an estimated cost of £2,444 and 17 shillings.[27]

20. West curtain wall (incorporating arched entrance) and twin-gabled ends of both blocks of the ruinous barracks at Bernera. Incomplete until 1723, Bernera Barracks existed only on the drawing board when Jacobites landed not far away in Kintail in April 1719.

---

27   TNA, WO 47/32, folios 155–6: Ordnance Office, Board of Ordnance, Minutes, 17 Mar. 1719.

The French Connection

In France a month earlier, during the third week of February 1719, James Keith arrived at Bordeaux. There was a large community of Scots Jacobite exiles there, notwithstanding the Orléanist government's official policy to no longer tolerate them. The leading figure among the Bordeaux-based Jacobites was Major-General Alexander Gordon of Auchintoull. Gordon was a career soldier who had achieved his rank in the Russian army. During the 1715–16 rising he was one of the Earl of Mar's senior commanders and fought creditably at Sheriffmuir. Just before leaving Scotland, in early February 1716 James Francis Edward Stuart appointed Gordon commander-in-chief, in effect empowering him to negotiate terms for the surrender of the Jacobite army. Gordon himself had not submitted, however, and into spring 1716 remained in the western Highlands hopeful of reforming a clan army.

Among the other principal Jacobites sought by James Keith were Brigadier Colin Campbell of Ormidale, the Marquess of Tullibardine and his younger brother Lord George Murray, and the clan chiefs and substantial landowners John Cameron of Lochiel, Ranald Macdonald of Clanranald, John MacKenzie of Avoch, and John MacDougall of Dunollie.

The Bordeaux Jacobites had received beforehand word from the Earl of Mar, advising them to follow orders from the Duke of Ormond. But Clanranald and Major-General Gordon in particular voiced their disquiet when Keith explained what was planned. Gordon and others accordingly addressed a communiqué to Ormond, expressing 'the hazard things would be exposed to in Scotland if not better provided, and therefore by all means a larger provision should be made of what was necessary for such an undertaking'.[28] This was given to Campbell of Ormidale to deliver, who in accordance with Ormond's instructions hurriedly left Bordeaux to join the Earl Marischal at San Sebastian. After several days Gordon in turn received replies dated on or before 25 February from Ormidale and Marischal himself. Both confidently reported their understanding that Ormond had already sailed from Corunna with the Spanish fleet, and as they were about to set sail from San Sebastian for Scotland, Gordon and his compatriots at Bordeaux should waste no time in doing likewise. On the basis of this reassuring news, Clanranald, Lochiel and some others with money from James Keith's war chest chartered a vessel to take them to Scotland. However, the capable Major-General Gordon had fallen seriously ill and was unable to make the voyage.[29]

James Keith had in the meantime set out for Orléans to seek out Tullibardine. He travelled in company with a sympathetic French official, who had obtained government post-horses for them, with Keith pretending to be his servant. Arriving at Orléans on 20 February, Keith was amicably received by the marquess who readily accepted the urgency of the mission. Together

---

28 'A Distinct Abridgment of some Materiall Poynts [sic] Relating to Scotts Affairs', in T.L.K Oliphant (ed.), *The Jacobite Lairds of Gask* (1870), p. 451. Described by Oliphant as 'Lord Mar's long account of the Rising in 1719', this was a copy or paraphrasing in the Earl of Mar's hand intended for the Jacobite Lord Nairne of a lengthy dispatch from the Marquess of Tullibardine written to Mar in August 1719.

29 *Ibid.*, p. 452.

early next morning they set out for Paris. In the French capital on probably the evening of the 20th they met the Earl of Seaforth and Colin Campbell of Glendaruel. Seaforth was reluctant to take the young Keith's explanation of what was planned at face value, apparently dismissing Ormond's note as 'a credential [that] might be put to any use'. 'Glendaruel smiled at reading them', Keith recollected, 'and told me that that billet [note] would have been of little weight with them, had they not been already advertised by the Duke of Mar to obey what orders the Duke of Ormond should send. This plainly let me see', Keith concluded, 'that we had two factions amongst us, and which proved the occasion of our speedy ruin when we landed in Scotland'.[30]

Like their compatriots at Bordeaux, Tullibardine, Seaforth and Glendaruel worried about the limited objectives of the expedition to Scotland: 'by which', it was later explained, 'it appeared Scots affairs were very much disconcerted. Mr Keith said little more than an amusement was expected, for the whole stress of affairs lay on England'.[31] Nonetheless, as a group the exiles felt duty-bound to join what Tullibardine later referred to as 'my Lord Marischal's ill-conceived expedition'.[32] The exiles had only scanty prior knowledge of the enterprise, and little say in its planning. Seaforth therefore insisted that before leaving France they should seek instructions from the titular King James III and VIII himself, or at least direction from Lieutenant-General Dillon, James's emissary in Paris. Tullibardine also wanted to consult with Dillon, but Glendaruel persuaded him to accept Keith's interpretation of Ormond's orders (although both Glendaruel and Tullibardine would later write to Dillon for guidance). In his memoirs, Keith cited security as the reason for not disclosing the plan to Dillon:

21. Remains of Bernera Barracks from the east, showing shells of both piles of barracks, intervening courtyard, and stump of the south-east watchtower. The east curtain wall has been levelled to the ground.

30   Keith, *Fragment of a Memoir*, pp. 41–2.
31   Oliphant, 'Distinct Abridgment', *Jacobite Lairds of Gask*, p. 452.
32   Dickson, *Jacobite Attempt*, p. 273.

Glendaruel [later] asked me if I had seen General Dillon while I was at Paris. I told him I had not; that General Dillon being at St. Germain, I durst not venture to go there, being too well known not to be discovered; and that 'tho [sic] the interest of those that were there was the same with ours, yet their imprudence was so great that they were not to be trusted with a secret, which should it take vent, must occasion our being stopped at the instance [i.e. instigation] of the Earl of Stair, the ambassador from the court of England; that besides having no instructions to communicate anything to him, I made no doubt but he had been advertised by some other channel.[33]

Stubbornly, Seaforth remained in the capital to confer with Dillon, who, when they met, reassuringly instructed him to join the expedition. In the meantime, on 25 February Tullibardine and Glendaruel left Paris for Rouen in Normandy. There the industrious James Keith chartered a small trading vessel, of a type known as a bark or a 'pink', of about 25 tons burthen, to take the exiles to Scotland. The deal was struck with a sympathetic merchant, probably from one of the Jacobite Franco-Irish ship-owning mercantile families who had followed James II and settled in France, especially along its western seaboard.[34] The bark was soon provisioned and readied to sail. In the first week of March it passed down the River Seine to the port of Honfleur, on the south bank of the Seine estuary at its confluence with the English Channel. Meanwhile the party of exiles, including those from Bordeaux, among them Tullibardine, Lord George Murray, Seaforth, Glendaruel, Brigadier William Mackintosh of Borlum, Sir John MacKenzie of Coul (a cousin of the Earl of Seaforth), and probably also Coll MacDonald of Keppoch, chief of the MacDonalds of Keppoch of Lochaber, with servants and followers gathered at the small town of Pont-l'Évêque a few miles from Honfleur. On 7 March dispatches arrived for Tullibardine and Glendaruel from Lieutenant-General Dillon. Included was a copy of Tullibardine's commission from 1717 as commander-in-chief in waiting of James III and VIII's forces in Scotland. This would enable Tullibardine to take command of the expedition. As James Keith recollected:

The day before we embarked, the express they had sent to Paris returned with a packet from General Dillon, of which they showed a letter full of common place advices relating to the conduct we should hold in Scotland, but not a word of the commissions, which they kept to be drawn out on proper occasions.[35]

On 8 March 1719 the Jacobites boarded the pink and she headed out to sea.

---

33 Keith, *Fragment of a Memoir,* p. 43.
34 B. Lenman, 'The Jacobite Diaspora 1688–1746: From Despair to Integration', *History Today,* 30 (1980), pp. 8–9.
35 Keith, *Fragment of a Memoir,* p. 44.

4

The Opposing Armed Forces

'This savage way of fighting.'

During the 1719 rising the Jacobites deployed a force of Highland clansmen stiffened by a body of allied Spanish infantry. They were opposed by regular troops of the British state and its Dutch ally, supported by Highland militiamen loyal to the Georgian government. Warships of the British Royal Navy also operated in the region of the rising. The Jacobite Highlanders and British regulars represented very different military cultures that had clashed less than four years previously. Those differences played out in November 1715 at the battle of Sheriffmuir. British infantry trained to combat similarly organised western European Foot had instead faced the unfamiliar so-called 'Highland charge'. A generation later, a biographer of the British commander at Sheriffmuir struggled to rationalise that tactical dichotomy. The Highlanders, he wrote, attacked:

> Like furies close up to the muzzles of their muskets, pushed by the bayonets with their targets [i.e. shields], and with their broad swords spread nothing but death and terror. The three battalions of Foot on the left of the duke's centre behaved gallantly, and made all of the resistance they could make, but being unacquainted with this savage way of fighting, against which all the rules of war had no provisions, they were forced to give way […] so a total rout of that wing of the royal army ensued.[1]

The Land Forces of the British Crown and State

In 1719 the British Army was a recent and still politically contentious organisation.[2] A de facto British standing army came into being under the 1689 constitutional settlement resulting from the Glorious Revolution. This

---

1 R. Campbell, *The Life of the most illustrious Prince, John Duke of Argyll and Greenwich* (1745), cited in Terry, *Chevalier St. George*, p. 294.
2 For background to the organisation and nature of the early Georgian British Army, see: D. Chandler, *The Art of Warfare in the Age of Marlborough* (1990), *passim*; Barnett, *Britain and Her Army*, pp. 165–6, 175–8; J. Guy, 'The Army of the Georges, 1714–1783', *Oxford History of*

22. The early Georgian army and its officer corps could still bask in the reflected glory of victories achieved during the War of the Spanish Succession (1701–14), such as Blenheim (1704). This detail from one of the Marlborough Tapestries at Blenheim Palace depicting the battle, shows the fighting arms of early-18th century western European armies: artillery, or ordnance (middle distance); cavalry, or Horse (foreground, and engaged far distance right); and infantry, or Foot (grenadier foreground, and troops occupying village far distance left). (Reproduced with kind permission of his Grace the Duke of Marlborough)

shifted the army from being a royal household corps to an instrument of state of crown *and parliament*, dependent for funding on the latter. The standing land forces on the separate establishments (pay-rolls) of England, Scotland and Ireland had legal existence in peacetime only with parliamentary approval. This consent was maintained by (what came to be annual) scrutiny of so-called Mutiny Bills. Statutes at first narrowly concerned with military discipline in peacetime – 'For punishing mutiny and desertion and false musters' – towards the end of the reign of Queen Anne were rudimentary Army Acts, concerned with the size and financing of the land forces: 'For better regulating the forces to be continued in her majesty's service, and of the payment of the said forces and of their quarters'. This evolving phrasing marked the gradual acceptance of a standing army, although some contemporaries were reluctant to acknowledge that fact.

Under this constitutional arrangement, a British Army proper emerged from the Anglo-Scottish Union of 1707. The crown's land forces in North Britain, a regional command financed and controlled from London, replaced the Scottish establishment. A key factor in the relatively peaceful passage

the British Army, pp. 92–111, *passim;* H.C.B. Rogers, *The British Army in the Eighteenth Century* (1977), *passim;* A. Kemp, *Weapons and Equipment of the Marlborough Wars,* (1980), *passim.*

of the Union was that units on the English and Scottish establishments already served operationally as a unified British army. Furthermore, the great majority of Scots parliamentarians serving in the army or with familial connections to it backed the Union. Most Scots among the officer corps wholeheartedly accepted the concept of a British state. The unitary British Army embraced the martial tradition of Scotland, but the merger required the abandonment of discrete national identifiers. This included regimental titles. The Scots Royal Dragoons, for example, became the North British Royal Dragoons, and the Scots Fusiliers became the North British Fusiliers.[3]

The establishment in Ireland, unaffected by the union of those in Great Britain, remained under the devolved command and jurisdiction of the lord lieutenant and parliament there. Since 1692 the Irish establishment had a nominal strength of 12,000 men. Not only in terms of numbers did the Irish establishment appear more durable than that for the British mainland, it also maintained permanent barracks. In addition to being an army of occupation of a largely Roman Catholic land, the Irish establishment was a reserve for that in Britain (allowing the interchange of units), and a pool of regiments for service overseas.[4]

During the War of the Spanish Succession, the British Army gained proficiency and international respect under the Duke of Marlborough's leadership. Unlike the Royal Navy, however, the early 18th century army was not yet regarded as a vital national institution. This was due partly to practical realities, partly to abstract ideals. Because of governmental parsimony and reluctance to institutionalise the army there were few barracks in England and Scotland, so soldiers were routinely billeted among the civilian population. The friction inherent in this arrangement was exacerbated by use of the army as a force of law and order in the absence of an established police force. The army's role, in for example, countering smuggling was widely resented by those benefitting from the practice. The army also sat uncomfortably with certain libertarians on constitutional grounds. Given that the navy was the guardian of the nation and maritime trade, they argued (on the basis of flimsy historical precedent) that the militia, recruited from householders officered by the landed classes, was the traditional, cost-effective and constitutionally robust alternative to a standing army (notwithstanding the reality, that the militia remained largely moribund in England and Wales until the 1750s).[5]

Fears of a standing army on constitutional grounds were twofold. On one hand, it might become the tool of an over-mighty parliament, the looming precedent being the Cromwellian republican army of the 1650s; the powerbroker of national government that acted as the regime's policing force in England and Wales, and army of occupation in Ireland and Scotland. On the other hand, a powerful royal army could become an instrument of absolutist

---

3   Lenman, 'Union of 1707 to the Franchise Reform', p. 319; Childs, 'Marlborough's Wars and the Act of Union', pp. 343–4.

4   Rogers, *British Army*, p. 20; Guy, 'Army of the Georges', p. 100.

5   Barnett, *Britain and Her Army*, pp. 167–70, *passim;* Guy, 'Army of the Georges', p. 97.

monarchy, as was appearing to be the case under James II. The constitutional settlement of 1689 had been designed to prevent both possibilities.[6]

Public antipathy coupled to imaginings of military despotism ensured the army was kept a small force in peacetime, hurriedly expanded in time of war. So as not to draw too much attention to the standing army as a matter of fact, in 1718 the annual army estimates still euphemistically referred to 'his majesty's guards and garrisons'. Constitutional sensitivities were also a convenient pretext for cost-conscious ministers to keep the army at an affordable minimum size. This also appeased parliamentarians wary of increased taxation. During the War of the Spanish Succession, the strength of the British Army had peaked in 1711 with 75,000 subject soldiers (i.e. national subjects of Queen Anne, as opposed to the similar number of foreign auxiliary and allied troops in British pay). By 1715, however, the British establishment allowed just over 8,000 men, with a further 7,800 based overseas (including 1,900 infantry in Flanders). In July 1715, to enhance national security parliament authorised expansion of the British establishment by 3,000 Horse and 4,000 Foot.[7] But retrenchment followed the defeat of the Jacobite rising in 1716. The estimates presented to parliament in November 1717 for the 'Establishment of his majesty's guards, garrisons and land forces in Great Britain' the following year anticipated 16,347 officers and men.[8] But during parliamentary debates in February 1718, an influential bloc of 28 peers argued that:

> 16,347 men is declared necessary […] the kingdom being now (God be praised) in full peace without any just apprehension, either of insurrection at home, or invasion from abroad, so numerous a force is near double to what hath been allowed within this kingdom by authority of parliament in time of public tranquility […] such a standing force, dangerous in itself to a free people in time of peace.[9]

During 1718 the British establishment was reduced by a quarter. Six regiments of Foot were transferred to Ireland (in place of six regiments disbanded there), and four regiments of dragoons disbanded in Britain.[10] The estimates for the 1719 British establishment presented in November 1718 allowed for just 12,435 men of all ranks. This force came into effect on 25 December, notwithstanding the recent declaration of war on Spain.[11] The Earl of Stair, for one, understood it was to give a hostage to fortune for a nation vulnerable to seaborne invasion to have so small an army. 'It is a ridiculous thing', he told fellow minister James Craggs in March 1719, when a Spanish invasion threatened, 'for us always to be in such a precarious position, as to be at the mercy of any prince that will send four or five thousand men to England'.[12]

---

6   Childs, 'Restoration Army', p. 47; Guy, 'Army of the Georges', p. 93.
7   D. Chandler, 'The Great Captain General, 1702–1714', *Oxford History of the British Army*, p. 69; *Journals of the House of Commons*, vol. 18 (1803), pp. 46–7, 235, 237.
8   *Journals of the House of Commons*, vol. 18, p. 643.
9   *Political State of Britain, XV*, pp. 214–15.
10   *Journals of The House of Commons*, vol. 19 (1803), p. 20.
11   *Ibid.*, p. 17.
12   Cited by Michael, *England under George I*, p. 193.

In 1717, after the revelation of the Gyllenborg plot exposed the threat of invasion from Sweden, Daniel Defoe pragmatically set out to reconcile the necessity of a standing army:

> The word Standing Army appears in several shapes; but ought, as it is esteemed a grievance, to be understood only thus: (viz.) a Standing Army maintained in time of peace. It remains to state, what is, or is not a time of peace. And to the present case it is sufficient to say, that a time of a threatened invasion, unconquer'd [sic] disaffection [i.e. Jacobitism], and formidable [political] faction, is not a time of peace; and that therefore in those cases the word Standing Army is out of the question. But when alliances and treaties, pacifications and accommodations, guarantees, and such like things, have dissipated all our just fears from abroad; and rebellion, faction, and disaffection is suppress'd [sic] and disarm'd [sic] at home; then indeed the nation may be said to be in peace, and a Standing Army may be called a grievance. But as even then some forces are necessary to be kept up, and are kept up by all nations, to secure and preserve that state of peace, which alone makes a Standing Army needful at other times: The only question then lies, what is, or is not a necessary medium between the extremes? What number of troops may be acquiesc'd [sic] in, as necessary for the publick [sic] safety, and what shall be esteemed dangerous to the nation's liberty?
>
> The answer to this is short and easy, and was long ago discuss'd [sic], in answer to a tract published against King William's army, at the time of the Peace of Ryswick; (Viz.) That the parliament are and ought to be the judges in the case: That such a force as the parliament shall judge needful, and that force being always subjected to parliamentary authority, as to their continuance, increase, and decrease; such a force, and no other, the nation will always be easy with, and safe in: And such a Standing Army is not inconsistent with the constitution of a free nation.[13]

In 1714 the standing army transferred its loyalty to King George I. When the King's Whig ministry, facing internal disorder and foreign invasion, necessarily deployed the army against protestors, its opponents viewed this as unconstitutional use of armed force to prop up the new regime. After its enactment in July 1715 soldiers became the ultimate enforcers of public order under the Riot Act. This was introduced to counter disturbance and rioting associated with anti-Whig, anti-Hanoverian protest. Genuine Jacobite sentiment often underlay public expression of support for Toryism and the High Church. However, ostensible displays of Jacobitism were also a convenient short-term foil to bring wider economic or social grievances into focus. Nonetheless, the Georgian regime inevitably suspected street demonstrations of Jacobite influence. Protest had, however, diminished when the rising in Scotland began in September. Jacobite expectations that the army would turn against the government proved unfounded. The army (including the Scots regulars, whose loyalty since the Act of Union

---

13 D. Defoe, *What if the Swedes should come? With some thoughts about keeping the Army on foot, whether they come or not* (1717), pp. 36–7.

had never really been doubted) instead fulfilled its prescribed constitutional role, acting in support of the reigning monarch and established government against foreign and internal threat.

Any possibility of a Jacobite rising in southern England in autumn 1715 was prevented by show of force. In September, Bristol was occupied by two regiments of Foot and one of Horse, reinforced in October by a third infantry regiment. Elsewhere in the West Country, Major-General George Wade secured Bath with two regiments, arrested gentry conspirators and seized some cached arms. In the south Midlands, fears that in the wake of Jacobite-inspired street demonstrations in Oxford university scholars were preparing to declare the city for the Pretender resulted in the deployment there of Major-General Pepper's Regiment of Dragoons, and occupation later by Brigadier Roger Handasyde's Regiment of Foot. In 1722, the Whig government similarly had troops paraded through London as a show of strength after the revelation of the Jacobite Atterbury plot. Like the navy, the Georgian army came to express its loyalty by dutiful observance of royal occasions – by firing salutes, parading, lighting celebratory bonfires and drinking the royal family's health. Army units also encouraged local officials where they were billeted to sponsor civic and street celebrations demonstrating loyalty to King George and his government.[14]

The Georgian army existed under parliamentary jurisdiction, while owing its allegiance to the Crown. The sovereign was commander-in-chief, and wielded powers of patronage by approving officers' commissions. King George I had an active and informed interest in the army. He intervened to standardise musketry drill in 1716, and to regulate officers' commissions four years later.[15] Representing the monarch in executive command of the army was the captain-general. Not always occupied, the post had recently been held by the Duke of Marlborough succeeded by the Marquess of Ormond. Marlborough was restored as captain-general in August 1714 and held the position until 1721, the year before his death. However, because of Marlborough's ill health, much of the military response to the 1715–16 rising was managed by the ex-soldier turned politician and secretary of state James Stanhope, 1st Earl Stanhope.[16] Demonstrating how there was then no single individual or department of state solely responsible for military affairs, Stanhope had combined diplomatic duties with coordinating strategy with the commander-in-chief in Scotland, the Duke of Argyll.

In addition to commanders in theatre like Argyll, responsibility for the army and its deployment was shared between several state officials as members of the royal council, or cabinet. The secretaries of state for the Southern and Northern departments were the key ministerial appointments – with Scotland

---

14 H. Smith, 'The Army, Provincial Urban Communities, and Loyalist Culture in England, c.1714–50', *Journal of Early Modern History*, 15 (2011), *passim*; Rae, *History of the Rebellion*, pp. 215–16; Guy, 'Army of the Georges', p. 92; A. Randall, *Riotous Assemblies: Popular Protest in Hanoverian England* (2006), pp. 2, 24, 38, 46-7; Lord, *Stuarts' Secret Army*, pp. 69–70; J. Oates, 'Jacobitism and Popular Disturbances in Northern England, 1714–1719', *Northern History*, 41 (2004), pp. 111–28, *passim*.

15 Barnett, *Britain and Her Army*, p. 177; Guy, 'Army of the Georges', p. 99.

16 Atkinson, *Marlborough*, pp. 482–5, *passim*.

under the charge of the latter. The Southern Department, since March 1718 the responsibility of James Craggs the younger, embraced France and the Mediterranean region, colonial affairs and worldwide naval operations. The Northern Department, since March 1718 the portfolio of the Earl of Stanhope, seconded by his under-secretary Charles Delafaye, was concerned with northerly Europe and general military administration. In their respective spheres of responsibility, both secretariats coordinated the actions of commanders on land and sea with colonial governors and diplomats. This also involved government bodies including the Admiralty and the Board of Trade. Security and military affairs in North Britain also came within the remit of the secretary of state for Scotland. In 1719 this third secretary of state for Great Britain was John Kerr, 1st Duke of Roxburghe. The ministerial office of growing importance to the army was the secretary at war, occupied since December 1718 by George Treby. Originally the personal secretary to the captain-general, during the War of the Spanish Succession the secretary at war was increasingly the army's chief administrative officer. The post was evolving as the vital link between army, government ministers and parliament.[17]

23. Although by then in failing health, in 1719 John Churchill, first Duke of Marlborough, commanded British land forces as both captain-general of the army and master-general of the Board of Ordnance.

By far the largest office of state involved with the early Georgian army was the Board of Ordnance. The Board, alongside the army and navy, formed in effect the third branch of the armed forces, although involving civilian personnel. Its head was the master-general, a high-ranking state official in charge of a huge administrative and logistical organisation. The Duke of Marlborough was master-general in 1719. The Board of Ordnance provided the army with its military supplies, the army and navy with artillery and munitions, and built and maintained military installations. The gunners and engineers attached to the army at home and overseas also fell within its remit. The Board similarly employed the gunners for the guards and garrisons of Great Britain equipped with artillery. In 1718 there were 43 of these, mostly coastal, forts and castles manned by about 250 gunners and their officers. They were salaried from the separate budget of the establishment for land forces. In 1719 the role of the Board of Ordnance in providing the army's artillery was in a state of transition. In May 1716, under Marlborough's combined authority as army captain-general and master-general of the Board, the first two permanent 'Marching [or mobile] companies of gunners

17 J.B. Hattendorf, 'English Governmental Machinery and the Conduct of War, 1702–1713, *War & Society*, 3 (1985), *passim*; Barnett, *Britain and Her Army*, pp. 173–5, *passim*; Chandler, 'Great Captain General', p. 80.

of the Royal Artillery' had been established. This ushered in the ending of the time-honoured practice of forming temporary artillery trains for the duration of particular campaigns. These were permanently replaced in 1727 by the standing Royal Regiment of Artillery.[18]

The stratification of early Georgian society was reflected in the manning of the army. Officers mostly came from the landed aristocracy and gentry, often from minor gentry families regarding soldiering as a respectable career. The army was thus led from the propertied classes, whose vested interests in the accepted order of things made an army coup or militarisation of the state highly unlikely. At a time when patronage and the purchase and sale of offices were features of public life, army commissions were also subject to advocacy and a pecuniary system. The fact that colonels purchased the title to a regiment meant they in effect managed it as a business interest, disbursing the annual parliamentary funding granted for its upkeep. Regiments were therefore usually known by the name of the current colonel.[19] Officers generally achieved promotion by sale and purchase of commissions, an inequable system that nevertheless provided a career path and elementary pension scheme.[20] But promotion could be gained on merit alone. Perhaps one-third of vacancies were filled without purchase, usually as a result of death in post or in reward for bravery. Active service greatly increased these opportunities. Lieutenant Hugh MacKay, for example, for having served gallantly as a volunteer at the battle of Glenshiel was awarded a cash bounty by royal command, and recommended for a commission in a regiment of Foot. Captain James Abercromby, like MacKay an ex-regular officer retained on half-pay who also fought at Glenshiel, had his candidacy for the vacancy of a captain killed there promptly referred to secretary of state James Craggs with Major-General Wightman's endorsement.[21] In 1720 King George intervened to reform the purchase system, setting maximum fees for commissions and regulating to ensure candidates' experience was commensurate to the depth of their pockets. The ceiling for purchasing a colonelcy or captaincy in a line regiment of Foot, for example, was set at £6,000 and £1,000 respectively. No officer above lieutenant could purchase a higher rank without having being commissioned for 10 years or thereabouts, while a colonel could sell only to a fellow colonel or a lieutenant-colonel.[22]

NCOs and private soldiers (known as 'sentinels') were recruited from the opposite end of the social spectrum to their officers. The British Army remained a volunteer force, notwithstanding the use during the War of the Spanish Succession of a limited form of conscription. Recruiting acts had empowered civil officers to nominate for enlistment 'such able-bodied men

---

18 Chandler, *Art of Warfare*, pp. 154–5, 161–2; Barnett, *Britain and Her Army*, p. 134; *Journals of The House of Commons*, vol. 18, pp. 644–8.

19 Numbering regiments by precedence according to founding date became established procedure in 1751: Guy, 'Army of the Georges', p. 99.

20 Childs, 'Restoration Army', p. 63; Barnett, *Britain and Her Army*, p. 137.

21 Guy, 'Army of the Georges', p. 105; Dalton, *George I's Army*, vol. 2, p. 302; TNA, SP 43/61, folio 97: Secretaries of State, State Papers Regencies, George I and George II, papers of secretary of state Charles Delafaye.

22 Dalton, *George I's Army*, vol. 2, p. 109.

as have not any lawful calling or employment, or do not follow or exercise the same'.[23] Soldiering could appear to be an adventurous and socially enhancing alternative to a mundane existence. Redcoats regarded themselves as loyal servants of the state and a cut above the ordinary citizen. The fictional Sergeant Kite's call for volunteer 'gentlemen soldiers', patriotically mindful 'to serve her majesty and pull down the French king', reflected enticements to enlistment at the height of the War of the Spanish Succession that included a cash bounty.[24] But enlistment was often a means of last resort of earning a living rather than a career choice. Unemployment was a powerful motivational force. While the rank and file included misfits of the under-classes the rest of Georgian society was pleased to see the back of, including vagrants and petty criminals, many soldiers had been respectable under-employed labouring or trades men.

Recruits were 'drummed up' by touring regimental recruiting parties, acting in collaboration with the civil powers. In order to prevent enlistment against their will or by the deceit of a real-life Sergeant Kite, recruits had to confirm their consent before the local magistracy. In an example of this proceeding lawfully, justices of the peace sitting at Cheltenham, Gloucestershire, in 1727 ruled a recruiting party culpable for 'false mustering', after a recruit proved he had been tricked into enlisting. His appeal was upheld and he went free because he had not been brought before local JPs to declare consent: 'and till then was deemed not to be a soldier'.[25]

In 1719, the 12,435-man British establishment was the largest part of the army. It could be reinforced from the four regiments of Horse, six of dragoons and 20 regiments of Foot based in Ireland, on an establishment that since 1717 seems to have remained not far off its full strength of 12,000 men.[26] The remainder of the army, 5,431 men on paper, was based overseas. In the western Mediterranean, six regiments of Foot between them garrisoned Minorca and Gibraltar. In the 'Plantations' – the colonies of the North American seaboard and West Indies – were posted two regular regiments and eight independent companies of Foot. The British Army all told therefore probably numbered about 29,500 men.[27] Following current western-European military practice, it was organised into regiments of infantry (the Foot) and cavalry (the Horse and dragoons).

The infantry was the main strength, formed in usually single battalion 'marching' regiments (signifying their mobile role, as opposed to static garrison troops). There were 8,708 Foot soldiers on the British establishment for 1719. 3,813 of them were Foot Guards serving in the London-based royal household 'division' – the First (Duke of Marlborough's), Coldstream (Earl of Cadogan's)

23 'A Proclamation for the better Recruiting of Her Majesty's Land Forces and Marines' (1708), cited in A. Browning (ed.), *English Historical Documents, Volume VI, 1660–1714* (1966), pp. 814–15.

24 Smith, 'Army […] and Loyalist Culture', pp. 143–4, 147–8; G. Farquhar, *The Recruiting Officer. A Comedy. As it was Acted at the Theatre Royal in Drury Lane*' (c.1706), p. 1.

25 D.B. Horn (ed.), *English Historical Documents, Volume X, 1714–1783* (1966), pp. 612–13.

26 *The Journals of The House of Commons of the Kingdom of Ireland*, vol. 4 (1763), pp. 545, 550–1, 553.

27 J. Chamberlayne *Magna Britannia Notitia: Or the Present State of Great-Britain* (1718), p. 136; *Journals of The House of Commons*, vol. 19, p. 17.

and Third (Earl of Dunmore's) Regiments of Guards. The remaining 11 regiments were infantry of the line, one of which at the time of the 1719 rising was serving as marines distributed aboard Admiral Byng's Mediterranean fleet. A line regiment had 10 companies including one of grenadiers, each having an establishment of 44 officers and men: the captain, his lieutenant, an ensign, two sergeants, three corporals, one drummer and 35 sentinels.[28] The majority of Foot soldiers were known as 'hatmen', after the workaday tricorne hat they wore, while their taller mitre caps distinguished the grenadiers.

With the infantry universally equipped with the flintlock musket (known as a firelock or fusil) and bayonet, drill and tactics were mostly concerned with engaging the enemy by concentrating firepower in a firefight at close range – well within 100 yards (91 metres), and preferably less than 50 yards (46 metres). Once a battalion was deployed on the battlefield in line, in close order three ranks deep, the companies were told off into a number of equally sized tactical sub-units called platoons. The size and number of platoons depended on the strength of the battalion, 30 men being considered the effective minimum. Although during the War of the Spanish Succession platoons had been formed irrespective of the company structure, the reduced battalion establishment of 10 companies by 1719 meant that in effect each of the nine companies of hatmen acted as a platoon. With the grenadier company divided into two smaller platoons posted one at each end, a battalion formed an 11-platoon firing line.[29] Each platoon was allocated to one of three 'firings' distributed along the battalion front firing in unison. Once the platoons of the third firing had done so, in theory the platoons of the first firing were reloaded and ready to fire again. The intention was to expose the enemy to a continuous damaging and demoralising rolling spread of musketry fire. This was witnessed in 1715 from the Jacobite side at the battle of Sheriffmuir, as 'a general salvo from the enemy, which began at their left, opposite to us, and run to their right'. Major-General Wightman explained how the infantry's platoon fire effectively contributed to the British army's initial success at Sheriffmuir: 'the Horse on our right, with the constant platoons of Foot, soon put the left of their army to the rout'.[30]

The mounted arm of the British establishment in 1719 numbered 2,071 Horse and 1,656 dragoons.[31] The Horse were cavalry proper, trained for their primary battlefield role of delivering decisive charges against opposing horsemen. The elite cavalry units were those of the royal household: four troops of Life Guards (each with an establishment of 181 officers and gentleman troopers); two troops of Horse Grenadier Guards (both with a strength of 176, all ranks); and the Royal Regiment of Horse Guards (strength 310, all ranks). The fourth troop of Life Guards and second of Horse Grenadier Guards under the pre-Union Scottish establishment had been respectively the

---

28   TNA, WO 24/92; TNA, SP 41/5, Item 112: Secretaries of State, State Papers Military, 1702–1782 'List and Quarters of His Majesty's Forces in Great Britain', May 1719.

29   D. Blackmore, *Destructive and Formidable: British Infantry Firepower, 1642–1765* (2014), pp. 86, 90–2, 97–8.

30   Sinclair, *Memoirs of the Insurrection*, p. 217; Dalton, *George I's Army*, vol. 1, p. 103.

31   TNA, WO 24/92; TNA, SP 41/5, Item 112.

24. British Foot (including grenadiers, in their distinctive mitre caps) in action during the War of the Spanish Succession. Print after a contemporary triptych of the battle of Blenheim painted by Louis Laguerre.

Scots Life Guards and the Scots Grenadier Guards.[32] The senior regiment of cavalry of the line was the King's Own Regiment of Horse (strength 292, all ranks). There were two other regiments of Horse, each having 196 officers and troopers organised into six troops. The dragoons of the Georgian army had shifted some way from their original 17th-century purpose as mounted infantry, and deployed on the battlefield as Horse proper. They were, however, still trained and expected when required to fight on foot, and so were proficient in musketry. Dragoons were suited to patrol, outpost and convoy duty and the skirmishing that might go with it. This made them more useful and adaptable to conditions in Scotland than Horse. Dragoons were also cheaper to maintain than Horse so, there were eight regiments in Britain in 1719. Each numbered 207 officers and men of all ranks, organised into six troops.

In addition to the regulars, there was a rudimentary army reserve. These were discharged soldiers on the books of the Royal Hospital at Chelsea. Not considered unfit enough by active service to receive a full pension, they were retained on an allowance. In 1719 these reservists numbered 4,764 men.[33] The Royal Hospital recruited from this body of out-pensioners on an ad hoc basis to form or maintain so-called 'Invalid' units for home defence. Invalids served and were paid as regular soldiers in lieu of a full pension. The basic requirements, to be independently mobile and handle a musket from a defensive position, probably did not do justice to a body of veterans of mostly

---

32 Childs, 'Marlborough's Wars [...] and Union', p. 344.
33 *Journals of The House of Commons*, vol. 19, p. 16.

middling age still useful as garrison troops – including the 20 Invalids based in Scotland during 1718 at Blackness Castle on the Firth of Forth.[34]

Remaining in Scotland, had it not been in abeyance in 1719 an auxiliary force that would have reinforced the regular army was the Independent Highland Companies. By an Act of 1667 of King Charles II, the Duke of Atholl had raised the first such unit, 'to be a constant guard for securing the peace of the Highlands'. The Independent Highland Companies were paramilitary policing units, raised, as in Atholl's case, by prominent figures regarded as government loyalists. Their role was to police those Highland regions deemed lawless and inaccessible to regular troops. Valued for their local knowledge and skills in scouting and surveillance, the men of the clan-recruited Companies were very much poachers turned gamekeepers. Companies were raised on an ad hoc basis, with a small handful in being at any one time; there were three in 1704, for example. By 1715, however, the usefulness of the Independent Companies had been called into question. Their methods of law enforcement were prejudiced by bribery and inter-clan rivalry. The commanding officers also defrauded the government by claiming pay for more men than enlisted (although this practice also troubled the regular army). During the rising the three Companies then established – one each of Campbells, Grants and Munros – performed useful minor duties, escorting convoys and scouting, for example. Overall, however, their performance was disappointing and loyalty questionable. This, coupled to the fact that their probity was under scrutiny, had in 1717 caused the Independent Highland Companies to be disbanded.[35]

The British Royal Navy

Throughout the period of Jacobitism the Royal Navy was a powerful obstacle, blocking attempts to land Jacobite exiles and military aid for them on the British coastline. During the Hispano-Jacobite invasion scare of 1719, King George I's private secretary acknowledged that 'our Admiralty have manifested an almost incredible diligence'.[36] The full extent of naval operations during the 1719 rising has, however, remained a largely untold story.

The early Georgian navy was the senior armed service, popularly regarded and trusted as the nation's traditional and proper bulwark.[37] The early 18th century was a period of accelerating wealth-creating expansion in British overseas trade. The public and political nation alike accepted the necessity of a strong navy, in order to protect colonial mercantile interests, police the seaways,

---

34 C.L. Nielsen, *The Chelsea Out-Pensioners: Image and Reality in Eighteenth-Century and Early Nineteenth-Century Social Care* (PhD Thesis, 2014), pp. 5, 213; *Journals of The House of Commons*, vol. 18, p. 644.

35 Dalton, *George I's Army*, vol. 1, pp. 236–7; Dalton, *Army Lists and Commission Registers*, vol. 5, p. 213; V. Henshaw, *Scotland and the British Army c.1700–c.1750* (PhD Thesis, 2011), pp. 63–4; J. Prebble, *Mutiny: Highland Regiments in Revolt 1743–1804* (1977), pp. 24–5; P.J. Haythornthwaite, 'The First Highland Regiment', *Military Illustrated Past and Present* (1988), p. 23.

36 Cited by Fritz, *English Ministers and Jacobitism*, p. 55.

37 This summary of the early Georgian navy references mainly: Harding, *Seapower and Naval Warfare*, pp. 184–7; Rodger, *Command of the Ocean*, especially pp. 292–306, *passim*; and Wilson, *Empire of the Deep*, pp. 282–4.

and to maintain sovereignty over home waters. The English in particular were emotionally attached to the navy and prepared to fund it. The navy was central to a virtuous economic circle: maritime trade generated taxable wealth to finance the navy; the growing merchant fleet provided a pool of trained seamen the navy could call upon; and the navy in turn policed the routes of seaborne commerce and protected the homeland.[38] The navy's status benefitted the stability of the service, but tended to form exaggerated expectations in the public and political mind of what it could achieve in wartime.

The Royal Navy in 1713 at the end of the War of the Spanish Succession was the strongest navy, more than twice the size of any other.[39] Its role throughout the war had involved tenacious rather than spectacular service. Most operations had been mounted in support of land forces and amphibious assaults, or in combating enemy privateering and maintaining blockades, rather than engaging enemy battle fleets on the high seas.

The Peace of Utrecht allowed a reduction in the size of the navy, but the powerful peacetime fleet demonstrated British naval supremacy. Squadrons and individual station ships maintained permanent patrols in home waters, in the Mediterranean, in the Caribbean and off the coast of colonial North America. Warships also convoyed merchantmen when and where necessary. The Royal Navy at this time was also a powerful annual presence in the Baltic Sea, representing British interests.

The navy benefitted from parliamentary support, steady income and sound finances, and enjoyed considerable independence in expenditure. It was by far the nation's largest single employer and contractor of trades and services. Indeed, supplying the navy was stimulating emerging industrialisation.[40] Financial stability enabled royal naval yards to continue to grow in size and complexity, maintaining historically high levels of skilled employment in peacetime. Ships and their crews at sea benefitted from the accumulated experience of long-standing administrative naval bodies: The Admiralty (the hub of naval operations); the Navy Board (overseeing ship building and maintenance, materials and naval stores); the Victualling Board (supplying food and drink); and the charitable Sick and Hurt Board.

The design of Royal Navy warships was not, however, outstanding. Shipbuilding policy was unimaginative, although British vessels were seaworthy and workmanlike. Although conservative in building techniques, English yards implemented significant incremental technical improvements – in steering and rigging, for example. Since the 1670s Royal Navy warships had been categorised into six classes, or 'rates', according to the number and weight of their guns. Rating also allowed ships' complements to be calculated from the number of gun crews required.[41] The first four rates were deemed ships of the line, powerful enough to take their place in the line of battle fleet. In June 1718, there were on paper 185 rated Royal Navy warships (or 'men-of-war'). These comprised: seven first rates of 100 guns; 13 second-rates of

---

38 Rodger, *Command of the Ocean*, p. 180; Kennedy, *British Naval Mastery*, pp. 71–3.
39 Harding, *Seapower and Naval Warfare,* p. 184.
40 Kennedy, *British Naval Mastery,* p. 72.
41 Rodger, *Command of the Ocean*, pp. 220–2, 414.

90 guns; 32 third-rates, of 70 or 80 guns; 68 fourth-rates, of 50 or 60 guns; 41 fifth-rates, of 30 or 40 guns; and 24 sixth-rates, of 20 or 24 guns.[42]

Many of the larger warships in particular, as was customary in peacetime, were kept 'in Ordinary' – under maintenance or mothballed in reserve. Nonetheless, the Royal Navy kept far more ships at sea than any other fleet, reflecting Great Britain's status as the premier naval power. Come wartime, peacetime continuity in naval infrastructure and administration would enable effective mobilisation of the ships in Ordinary.

The Highland Clans and their Way in War

While Scotland more actively embraced Jacobitism than elsewhere in the British Isles, the Highlands in particular were enduringly vital to the cause. The reasons for this were geographical and societal. The region was distant from seats of government and difficult to administer, making it more likely for an uprising to take root there undisturbed. The lengthy coastline punctuated with deep-water sea loch anchorages was accessible to seaborne assistance for the Jacobites from abroad. Moreover, Highlanders lived in tribal groupings of clans with warlike traditions and a social hierarchy adapted to military organisation. This enabled Jacobite Highland chiefs (and Jacobite landed magnates of the coastal lowlands of north-east Scotland bordering the Highlands proper) to mobilise armed followings in a way no longer possible in England. There, by the early 18th century, forms of land tenure linked to obligations of military service that lingered in northerly Scotland were abandoned and largely long forgotten. It would be beyond the reach of English landowners to recruit more than a few servants, tenants and estate workers.[43]

Highland clansmen formed the core of Jacobite armies. In the mid-1720s, the Lowland Jacobite George Lockhart reminded the titular James III & VIII, that 'the Highlanders are a body of men of such valuable consideration both to your interest and that of the country'.[44] Most Jacobites fighting at Killikrankie in 1689 were Highlanders, and while greater numbers of Scots Lowlanders joined the Jacobite armies of 1715 and 1745, still up to 45% of the strength came from the Highlands.[45] In 1719, apart from a body of Spanish regulars, the Jacobite army at Glenshiel would consist almost entirely of Highlanders. In 1724, the best estimate the Georgian government had was that across northerly Scotland there were 22,000 men fit to bear arms. Some 10,000 were optimistically considered to be from loyal clans, the remaining 12,000 regarded as likely Jacobite rebels. Mobilisation of this potential manpower was not, however, easily achieved. In autumn 1716 Colin Campbell of Glendaruel reckoned that a successful rising in Scotland would depend on the backing of just six influential chiefs and their probable 4,700 armed followers.[46]

---

42 *Political State of Britain, XV*, pp. 614–17.
43 Lord, *Stuarts' Secret Army*, p. 188.
44 Aufnere, *Lockhart Papers*, vol. 2, p. 187.
45 M. G. H. Pittock, *The Myth of the Jacobite Clans* (1999), p. 46.
46 Allardyce, *Historical Papers*, vol. 1, p. 132; Daniell, *Calendar of the Stuart Papers*, vol. 4, p. 82.

To those who never ventured there, the Highlands of Scotland in the early 18th century seemed a remote, wild and awful place. And those who knew the region tended to propagate that view. Edmund Burt, a Lowland Scot, travelled the Highlands widely during the 1720s and 1730s as a government official and advisor to the commander-in-chief in North Britain, Major-General George Wade. Burt wrote that:

> I have often heard it said by my countrymen, they verily believed, if an inhabitant of the south of England were to be brought blindfold into some narrow, rocky hollow, enclosed with these horrid prospects, and then to have the bandages taken off, he would be ready to die with fear, as thinking is impossible he should ever get out to return to his native country'.[47]

Burt (in letters he probably authored with an eye for future publication, as turned out to be the case) exaggerated for a credulous English readership the awesome prospect of a mountainous Highland glen. Outsiders similarly regarded the inhabitants as alien and outlandish. Another contemporary wrote of the Highland people: 'They differ as much in their dress, manners and language, from the Low-country [of Scotland], as the Indians in Mexico do from the Spaniards'.[48] Major-General Wade on his first tour of duty in Scotland in summer 1724 found Highland culture difficult to comprehend, concluding that 'their notions of virtue and vice are very different from the more civilised part of mankind'.[49]

Highlanders were physically hardy, and habitually carried weapons in social display. Their distinctive clothing and spoken Gaelic marked them as culturally and linguistically different from Lowland Scots and the English. While the two latter peoples commonly regarded Highlanders as barbarous, Highlanders considered themselves superior to other men. Burt reckoned Highland dress, especially the plaid (an over-garment combining cloak, overcoat and blanket in one), distinguished 'the natives as a body of people distinct and separate from the rest of the subjects of Great Britain, and thereby is one cause of their narrow adherence among themselves, to the exclusion of all the rest of the kingdom'.[50] Like other incomers, Burt was fascinated by the characteristic Highland garb, which he described as comprising:

> A bonnet made of thrum without a brim, a short coat, a waistcoat, longer by five or six inches, short stockings, and brogues, or pumps without heels. Few besides gentlemen wear the trowze [sic, trousers], that is, the breeches and stockings all of one piece, and drawn on together; over this habit they wear a plaid, which is usually three yards long and two breadths wide, and the whole garb is made of chequered tartan, or plaiding: this, with the sword and pistol, is called a full dress […]. The common habit of the ordinary Highlanders is far from being acceptable to the eye:

---

47 Jamieson, *Letters from a Gentleman*, vol. 1, p. 288.
48 J. Macky, *A Journey through Scotland. In Familiar Letters from a Gentleman Here, to His Friend Abroad* (1729), p. 126.
49 Allardyce, *Historical Papers*, vol. 1, p. 132.
50 Jamieson, *Letters from a Gentleman*, vol. 2, pp. 87–8

with them a small part of the plaid [...] is set in folds and girt round the waist, to make of it a short petticoat that reaches half way down the thigh, and the rest is brought over the shoulders, and then fastened before, below the neck [...] so that they make pretty nearly the appearance of the poor women in London when they bring their gowns over their heads to shelter them from the rain.[51]

Highlanders inhabited that part of Scotland defined geographically as lying north-west of a line drawn roughly diagonally from Dumbarton, near the head of the Firth of Clyde on the west coast, to an area inland of Aberdeen on the east coast. The west coastal islands, including Mull and the Hebrides, extend this region of 'Highlands and Islands'. At the time of the 1719 rising the Highlands and Islands held an estimated 30 percent of Scotland's likely population of 1,250,000.[52] The Highlands encompassed the heartlands of Jacobite support, found especially in the Grampian Mountains and the coastal lowlands north of the River Tay. The extent of the region was summarised in 1724 by Major-General Wade, writing to enlighten King George I:

The Highlands are the mountainous parts of Scotland, not defined or described by any precise limits or boundaries of counties or shires but are tracts of mountains in extent of land, more than one half of the kingdom of Scotland; and are for the most part on the western ocean, extending from Dumbarton to the north end of the island of Great Britain, near 200 miles in length, and from about 40 to 80 miles in breadth. All the islands on the west and north-west seas are called Highlands as well from their mountainous situation, as from the habits, customs, manners and language of their inhabitants. The Lowlands are all that part of Scotland on the south of [the rivers] Forth and Clyde, and on the east side of the kingdom from the Firth of Edinburgh [i.e. the Firth of Forth] to Caithness near the Orkneys is a tract of low country from four to 20 miles in breadth.[53]

Most inhabitants of the Highlands and Islands belonged to clans. These tribal communities maintained an independent way of life, adapted to the unforgiving environmental conditions.[54] Competition for natural resources in this mountainous region made inter-clan rivalry a fact of life, for immediate practical and deeper historical reasons. Members of each clan shared a belief in a common ancestry. Although these imagined blood ties were rooted more in tradition or mythology than genealogical fact, their acceptance bound the clan to rights and duties as members of an extended family headed by the chief. Clans might be numerically very large, or small in their own right; the smaller being septs, or cadet branches, of larger namesake confederations.

The immediate head of a clan was the hereditary chieftain, usually bound in allegiance to a supreme clan chief. The chieftain held title to the land of his

---

51   *Ibid.*, pp. 84–5.
52   Lenman, 'Union of 1707 to the Franchise Reform', pp. 280–1; Ferguson, *Scotland,* p. 90.
53   Allardyce, *Historical Papers,* vol. 1, p. 131.
54   For discussion of Highland life and Highland Jacobitism, see: Prebble, *Glencoe,* pp. 26–40, *passim*; McLynn, *Jacobites,* pp. 45–60, *passim*; Szechi, *Jacobites,* pp. 15–20, *passim*; Lenman, *Jacobite Risings,* pp. 47–8, 138–50, *passim*; Ferguson, *Scotland,* pp. 90–3.

clan, although by custom and ancient habit rather than in writing. Chieftains and higher chiefs exercised by traditional right and privilege absolute power over their people, who in turn held their leader's honour in high esteem; 'The Highlanders in Scotland are of all men in the world, the soonest wrought upon to follow their leaders or chiefs into the field', a Jacobite officer wrote admirably, 'having a wonderful veneration for their lord and chieftains'.[55]

The ownership and distribution of clan land was the chieftain's preserve. Some he kept as his own, some land traditionally was gifted to families of clan notaries such as the bard or piper. Most land the chieftain sub-let under leases known as 'tacks', usually a long-standing hereditary agreement. The tenant 'tacksmen' and their families constituted the clan gentry, a social grouping including the higher-ranking lairds. As well as landlord-tenant relationships, tacksmen were bound to their chieftain by kinship and tradition. They, in turn, sub-let their tacks to be lived on and farmed by the common folk of the clan, the families of crofters and cottars.

Highland society farmed for its livelihood and survival. Animal husbandry was most important, keeping sheep, goats and especially the native black cattle. Geology and climate restricted arable to valley floors and coastal areas, and to hardy crops such as oats. Fish and shellfish from sea, loch and river were plentiful, supplementing a diet subject to the vagaries of agricultural subsistence.

Edmund Burt described the situation of 'the lower order of the Highlanders' inhabiting a typical farming community. Although his view was coloured by contemporary prejudice, Burt was not unsympathetic to the Highlanders. A typical settlement, comprising low buildings with walls of stone and packed earth with turf-covered roofs, was:

> Composed of a few huts for dwellings, with barns and stables, and both the latter are of a more diminutive size than the former, all irregularly placed, some one way, some another, and, at any distance, look like so many heaps of dirt; these are built in glens and straths, which are the corn-countries, near rivers and rivulets, and also on the sides of lakes, where there is some arable land for the support of the inhabitants.[56]

In summer, Highland life followed traditional patterns of transhumance, when the cattle were grazed on mountainside pastures. As Burt continued:

> In summer the people remove to the hills, and dwell in much worse huts than those they leave below; these are near the spots of grazing, and are called sheilings, scattered from one another as occasion requires. Everyone has his particular space of pasture, for which, if it be not a part of his farm, he pays [...]. When the grazing fails, the Highlanders return to their former habitations, and the cattle to pick up their sustenance among the heath as before.[57]

---

55 Patten, *History of the Rebellion*, p. 130.
56 Jamieson, *Letters from a Gentleman*, vol. 2, p. 27.
57 Jamieson, *Letters from a Gentleman*, vol. 1, pp. 31–2.

25. (left) Reconstruction of the appearance of a clan chief in full Highland dress, based on a *c*.1712 portrait of the Jacobite Kenneth Sutherland, third Lord Duffus. His musket is British pattern. John Macky in the early 1720s described Highlanders gathered for the great cattle fair at Crieff: 'The Highland gentlemen were mighty civil, dressed in their slashed short waist coats and trousing [*sic*] (which is breeches and stockings of one piece of striped stuff) with a plaid for a cloak, and have a blue bonnet. They have a ponyard [i.e. dagger], knife and fork in one sheath hanging at one side of their belt, their pistol at the other, and their snuff-mill before; with a great broad sword by their side. Their attendants […] had also each their broad swords and ponyard, and spake [*sic*] all Irish [i.e. in Gaelic], an unintelligible language to the English'.
(Illustration by Ed Dovey, © Helion & Company Limited)

In late summer drovers collected the fattened beasts to be driven to market beyond the Highlands, including at the great trysts, or livestock fairs, at Crieff and Falkirk, from where many continued southward in the lucrative cattle trade with England.[58] The central importance of cattle to the Highland (and indeed wider Scottish) economy encouraged the traditional inclination to rustle, or 'uplift', animals from neighbouring clans. When the more aggressive clans on occasion also ranged southward into the Lowlands, the protection money they extorted, the so-called Blackmail, could be given in cattle as well as cash.

Rents (in kind more often than coin) filtered from tenants to chieftain, who was also due armed service when required. Tacksmen were duty-bound to raise their sub-tenants in arms when their chieftain or higher chief called upon them to do so. In this way the able menfolk of the clan were mobilised into a warrior band cum militia. The social hierarchy enabling this appeared to contemporary outsiders to mirror conventional military organisation:

> The head of every clan in the Highlands is called the chief, and those of the small families that compose the clan are called chieftains, resembling the colonel and captains of a regiment, and when they are in arms they rank thus: the lieutenant colonel and major are sons or brothers of the chief; the captains are those of next authority among them, and the [tacksmen] cadets of the lesser families compose the subalterns'.[59]

The lowest social orders of the clan formed the majority rank and file.

Traditional martial culture was vital to clan self-identification. In 1727 Major-General Wade acknowledged that since time immemorial, Highlanders had regarded ownership of arms 'as their greatest pride and glory':

> Insomuch, that it was looked on to be a reproach to a Highlander to be seen without his musket, broadsword, pistol and dirk. These by a long custom were esteemed part of their dress and at my first coming to the Highlands were worn by the meanest of the inhabitants even in their churches, fairs and markets, which looked more

---

58 Ferguson, *Scotland*, p. 168; Brown, 'Reformation to Union', p. 207.
59 A. Lang (ed.), *The Highlands of Scotland in 1750. From Manuscript 104 in the King's Library, British Museum* (1898), pp. 86–7.

like places of parade for soldiers, than assemblies for devotion, or other meetings of society.[60]

Although not all were so well armed, a clansman fully equipped bore the panoply of Highland weaponry. This comprised a flintlock musket; a brace of flintlock pistols (of all-steel manufacture, known as dags); a basket-hilted broadsword; and a targe – a leather covered and iron-studded circular shield. Given the centrality of hand-to-hand combat in clan warfare, Jacobite exiles planning to bring arms into the Highlands from the Continent always looked to secure stocks of both broadswords and targes. Gunpowder for firearms was carried in a powder horn and ammunition in a pouch. In addition, Highland men as a universal sidearm wore a dagger, or dirk, with a 12-inch (30.5 cm) blade. This, Burt mentioned, with macabre relish, was a 'dangerous weapon' not to be underestimated: 'They pretend they cannot do well without it, as being useful to them in cutting wood, and upon many other occasion; but it is a concealed mischief [...] ready for secret stabbing; and, in a close encounter, there is no defence against it'.[61]

It was this formidable personal armament the Disarming Act effective from November 1716 was intended to prohibit, making it unlawful for Highlanders 'to have in his or their custody, use or bare, broad sword, or targe, poynard, whingar,[62] or dirk, side pistol or side pistols or gun, or any other warlike weapons, in the fields, or in the way, coming or going to, from, or at any church, market, fair, burials, huntings, meetings or any other occasion whatsoever'.[63]

As Major-General Wade recognised, even the humblest male Highlanders bore these arms by right. Although their training methods are not understood, weapons handling was integral to a male Highlander's upbringing. However, most clansmen cannot have been seasoned warriors, or indeed particularly skilled in war. By the early 18th century, inter-clan 'warfare', such as it was, involved cattle rustling by parties of 20 or 30 men, the occasional attendant minor skirmish, retributive burning of buildings and crops, and occasional murders of informants.[64] Full-scale battle, for the proportionately few clansmen experiencing it, was a rare, generational event. Twenty-six years separated the battles of Killikrankie in 1689 and Sheriffmuir in 1715, and similar time passed between the battles of Glenshiel and Prestonpans – the first major engagement of the 1745–46 rising. Given the rarity of battle and lack of formal military doctrine among the clans, arguments for an evolving sophistication in Highland tactics during this period are unconvincing.[65] Rather, it seems that on the occasional battlefields of the Jacobite risings individual ability in weapons handling and the social *esprit de corps* of the

60 Allardyce, *Historical Papers,* vol. 1, p. 160: Wade to George I, 1727.

61 Daniell, *Calendar of Stuart Papers,* vol. 4, p. 85; Allardyce, *Historical Papers,* vol. 1, p. 133; Quotation from Jamieson, *Letters from a Gentleman,* vol. 2, p. 120.

62 Alternative forms of long knife.

63 Pickering, *Statutes at Large from the Twelfth Year of Queen Anne to the Fifth Year of King* George I, p. 307.

64 Allardyce, *Historical Papers,* vol. 1, pp. 134–6.

65 As proposed in *passim* by J. Michael Hill, in both *Celtic Warfare, 1595–1763* (1986) and 'Killiecrankie and the Evolution of Highland Warfare', *War in History,* 1 (1994), pp. 125–39.

clan, coupled to the Highlanders' fearsome reputation, compensated for both wider combat experience and regulation training.

On those occasions when a clan's menfolk gathered in arms, social status governed both individual standards of equipment and commitment to the fight. General Hawley's oft-quoted standing order of 12 January 1746 to his British regulars in Scotland, that the 'best' and 'true Highlanders' formed the front rank, and the remainder of the Jacobite battleline comprised 'Lowlanders and arrant scum', further cautions against the view that clansmen were all fearsome fighters.[66] However, Hawley – as the defeat of his army at the battle of Falkirk five days later demonstrated – underestimated his enemy, and misunderstood that clansmen took position on the battlefield according to social hierarchy. Social inequality, some contemporaries opined, diminished the apparent warrior culture. In the later 1740s, although the manpower of the steadfastly Jacobite Clan MacKenzie was reckoned to be 3,000, 'by the reason of the great poverty and slavery of the commons' [due, in the writer's opinion, to the crofters' disadvantageous tacks], 'a third of them are but dross'. Similarly, while the menfolk of the MacKenzie-allied territories of Kintail and Loch Alsh – the focus of the 1719 rising – were reputed brave and warlike, no more than 300 were considered fit to bear arms.[67] The variable military effectiveness of clan forces occasionally formed from farmers and husbandmen was magnified when chiefs exercised coercion. In November 1715, for example, the Duke of Atholl reckoned his Jacobite son the Marquess of Tullibardine had threatened the family tenantry with having their corn and cattle seized unless they joined him. One reluctant recruit swept up in Tullibardine's recruitment drive articulated the plight of humble clansmen in similar circumstances, that he was 'unfit for the employment [as a soldier]', being 'a poor cottar man'.[68] Edmund Burt thought that social norms compelled common Highlanders into taking up arms: 'And were it not for their fond attachment to their chiefs, and the advantage those gentlemen take of their slave-like notions of patriarchal power, I verily believe there are few among them that would engage in an enterprise so dangerous as rebellion.'[69]

26. Although showing a piper in the uniform of the Royal Highland Regiment *c.*1740, this engraving provides a depiction of Highland dress largely unchanged from the earlier 1700s. Note the characteristic basket-hilted broadsword. (New York Picture Library Digital Collection)

66 E. Charteris (ed.), *A Short Account of the Affairs of Scotland in the Years 1744, 1745, 1746 By David, Lord Elcho* (1907), p. 460.
67 Lang, *Highlands of Scotland,* p. 40.
68 Atholl, *Chronicles,* vol. 4. pp. 200–1.
69 Jamieson, *Letters from a Gentleman,* vol. 2, p. 203.

The tactics of Highlanders as irregular warriors were uncomplicated. 'Their manner of fighting is adapted for brave but undisciplined men', a senior Jacobite observed during the 1745–46 rising. Highlanders were 'quick, and ardent and impetuous in their attack', he added. 'The sword is the weapon which suits them best. when they are kept passive they lose their ardour'.[70] The Highlanders' traditionally preferred tactic was the charge. It had originated in Medieval Gaelic warfare on land and at sea, in which after an exchange of missile weapons there was a rapid close into hand-to-hand fighting with a resultant pursuit or rout. This suited clansmen as irregular warriors fighting on foot with both missile and melee weapons.[71] A rush to drive off the enemy, or, if they stood, engage in close combat with broadsword and dirk, was adapted to the battlefield from the ambush and cattle raid.

Because of their mountainous homeland, Highlanders were inclined to charge downhill; 'they endeavour to possess themselves of the higher ground, as knowing they give their fire more effectually by their situation one above another, being without discipline [i.e. formal training]; and also that they afterwards descend on the enemy with greater force'.[72] The preceding missile fire was intended to discourage and soften up the enemy line. In the inter-clan warfare of the Middle Ages this involved exchanges of javelins, sling-shot and especially arrows, but during the 17th century archery gave way to musketry. Highlanders customarily gave only one scattered volley, delivered at close range for maximum effect, before charging the enemy line. The historical transition in weaponry adapted to the charge was mentioned by a visitor to the Highlands around the year 1700:

> The ancient way of fighting was by set battles, and for arms some had broad two-handed swords, and headpieces, and others bows and arrows. When all their arrows were spent, they attacked oneanother with sword in hand. Since the invention of guns, they are very early accustomed to use them, and carry their pieces with them wherever they go. They likewise learn to handle the broadsword and targe. The chief of each tribe advances with his followers within shot of the enemy, having laid aside their upper garments; and after one general discharge, they attack them with sword in hand, having their targe on their left hand (as they did at Killikrankie) which soon brings the matter to an issue'.[73]

The successful Highland charge against the left wing of the British army at the battle of Sheriffmuir in 1715 was conducted in a similar way:

> The two thousand Highlandmen, who were then drawn up in very good order, run towards the enemy in a disorderly manner, always firing some dropping shots which drew upon them a general salvo from the enemy [...]. No sooner that begun,

---

70 J. Johnstone, *Memoirs of the Rebellion in 1745 and 1746 by the Chevalier De Johnstone*, (ed.) Anon. (1821, second edition), p. 115.

71 M. MacGregor, 'Warfare in Gaelic Scotland in the later Middle Ages', *Military History of Scotland*, pp. 223–4.

72 Jamieson, *Letters from a Gentleman*, vol. 2, p. 120.

73 M. Martin, *A Description of the Western Islands of Scotland* (1703), p. 210.

the Highlanders threw themselves flat on their bellies; and when it slackened, they started to their feet. Most threw away their fuzies [i.e. fusils, or muskets], and drawing their swords, pierced them everywhere with an incredible vigour and rapidity, four minutes' time from receiving their order to attack.[74]

When delivered effectively at the right moment, the Highland charge was regarded and feared as an 'attack so terrible that the best troops in Europe would with difficulty sustain the first shock of it'.[75] Nonetheless, clansmen lacked the predictability of regular troops. To allow them more freedom in a melee, Highlanders before charging often discarded their bulky plaids and their muskets once fired; apparently matter-of-factly accepting they could collect clothing and firearms if victorious, or would have no need of them in defeat.[76] James Keith recollected how having been unable to recover their plaids from the battlefield at Sheriffmuir, many Highlanders suffering in the cold weather were sent home to be clothed. They were also meant 'to bring back those who had fled straight from the battle to the mountains'.[77] This unconventional approach to warfare tended to undermine the usefulness of Highlanders in a prolonged campaign. As the Earl of Mar sourly put it: 'Amongst many good qualities, the Highlanders have one unlucky custom, not easy to be reformed, which is, that generally after an action they return home'.[78]

Because they were untrained and unaccustomed to do so, Highlanders on the battlefield would not long engage in a firefight. However, many were capable marksmen. Indeed, they would fight the battle of Glenshiel with musketry. In November 1715, the clansmen at Preston fought defensively firing from buildings and behind street barricades. A fellow officer agreed, 'that none are more capable [i.e. than Highlanders] to make a more vigorous defence of a breach, for they fire as well as any, from under cover, against attackers'.[79] Highlanders also engaged in longer-range sniping. 'To shoot at a mark', Burt told, 'they lay themselves all along behind some stone or hillock, on which they rest their pieces, and are a long while taking their aim; by which means they can destroy any one unseen'. In example, Burt described how in the early 1720s a concealed party of clansmen ambushed and shot down a government patrol: 'Though they were themselves out of all danger, or might have descended and disarmed so small a party, yet they chose rather, with their fire-arms, as it were wantonly to pick them off, almost one by one, till they had destroyed them all, except two, who took to their heels'.[80]

Motivations of Highland Jacobitism
While the remoteness of the Highlands and the unique, warlike social organisation of its inhabitants were both valuable to the Jacobite cause, why was

---

74   Sinclair, *Memoirs of the Insurrection,* p. 217.
75   Johnstone, *Memoirs of the Rebellion,* p. 114.
76   *Ibid.*
77   Keith, *Fragment of a Memoir,* pp. 21–2.
78   Patten, *History of the Rebellion,* p. 212.
79   Sinclair, *Memoirs of the Insurrection,* p. 130.
80   Jamieson, *Letters from a Gentleman,* vol. 2, pp. 77–8, 120.

Jacobitism so strong there? In counter-point, it must be stressed that far from all clans were Jacobite, and those deemed to be so could not always be relied upon to rise for the Stuarts. The Campbells, the most powerful clan, were staunchly Whig and loyal to the Georgian regime, as were the Munros and MacKays, among others. Opposition to the expansionist dominance of Clan Campbell undoubtedly placed some clans, especially their historically inveterate enemies the MacDonalds, into the Jacobite camp. However, by the early 18th century some clans enjoyed quite cordial relations with the Campbells.[81]

The Stuarts were a Scottish royal house, and their adherence to the divine and hereditary rights of kings doubtless chimed with chiefs and chieftains who drew their own authority from traditional inherited rights and powers. Historians remain undecided how far the actions of the future James II when, as Duke of York, he served in effect as his brother King Charles II's viceroy in Scotland in 1679–82, including heading the Commission for Pacifying the Highlands, endeared him to the Highland chiefs, although on the whole he seems to have had their support. James's suppression of dissenters favoured Episcopalians and Roman Catholics and fell on Presbyterians and Whigs, including the Campbell Duke of Argyll, forced into exile. But as king, in 1688 James sent troops into the western Highlands of Lochaber and seemed doubtful of the wider region's loyalty.[82] Nonetheless, a king of Scots descent in the person of James III & VIII had greater emotional pull on Highland allegiance than Hanoverian King George. Critical contemporaries, however, argued that the introspectiveness of the Jacobite western clans always had inclined them to disregard royal authority:

> The MacDonalds pretend that their attachment to the Stuart family proceeds from a principle of honour and duty but it is observable of several highland clans, particularly the MacDonalds, that they have been mostly loyal to some king or other who was not in possession, but seldom to any king on the throne, and when they could not find a pretender they were never at a loss for a pretence of some kind or other for rapine and plunder'.[83]

In this way Jacobitism could be a convenient outlet for the traditional opportunist predatory instincts of impoverished Highlanders.[84] In the early 1720s, the Scots writer and peripatetic British spy John Macky agreed, Highlanders had: 'Taken a mighty fit of loyalty upon them since the Revolution [i.e. of 1688], and have taken up arms on any invasion for the invaders, which shows that their resentments were not so much against the family of the Stuarts, as against the established government of Scotland, which in all reigns they have endeavoured to disturb'.[85]

81 McLynn, *Jacobites*, pp. 66–71; Prebble, *Glencoe*, p. 68; Lenman, *Jacobite Risings*, pp. 47–8.
82 McLynn, *Jacobites*, p. 71; Lenman, *Jacobite Risings*, p. 48; Ferguson, *Scotland*, p. 16; Brown, 'Reformation to Union', p. 257; Prebble, *Glencoe*, pp. 62–3.
83 Lang, *Highlands of Scotland*, pp. 53–4.
84 Ferguson, *Scotland*, p. 18.
85 Macky, *Journey through Scotland*, p. 129.

Religion also fueled Highland Jacobitism. Episcopalianism was strong across the Highlands, as in other Jacobite-inclined parts of Scotland, and the regard the Stuarts held for High Church practice encouraged recruitment. Roman Catholicism as a small minority faith in early 18th-century Scotland hung on in the north-east Lowlands and parts of the western Highlands and Islands. Catholic clans, including the Chisholms of Strathglass, the MacDonalds of Glengarry and Moidart, and the McLeouds of Barra, and notable individual Catholics such as the Earl of Seaforth, were inevitably Jacobite for religious reasons.[86]

Jacobite ideology was attractive to Highland gentry and the elite. Ordinary Gaels, however, were more likely to understand Jacobitism as safeguarding traditional ways of life against perceived threats from social and economic change in early 18th century Scotland accelerated by the Act of Union. Certainly, educated Lowland Jacobites like George Lockhart believed a 'hearty aversion to the Union' would encourage Jacobitism. In April 1719, he would appeal to the Earl Marischal with the Jacobite expeditionary force just landed in the western Highlands to proclaim a manifesto, declaring that King James III & VIII would dissolve the Union, restore to the Scots their parliament and 'ancient rights and independent state', remove the dead-hand of English commercial dominance, and end 'the violation of Scots liberties and civil rights'.[87] Quite how far this libertarian outlook would have engaged with traditionally patriarchal Highland society was another matter, but the threat of English military occupation under a foreign king could be more easily envisaged. As a Jacobite exile pointed out after the 1715–16 rising, 'They [i.e. the common folk of the Jacobite-inclined clans] have a deep resentment against the Duke of Brunswick [King George I][88] and his government, for they see their chiefs, whom they adore, ruined and forced to banishment and themselves disarmed, which they look on as a badge of slavery'.[89] Anglophobia, then, also fuelled clan Jacobitism, and Highlanders came to be regarded by Lowland Jacobites as embodying Scottish nationalism; Lockhart reckoned they were 'the only remains of the true old Scots blood and spirit'.[90]

---

86 Pittock, *Myth of the Jacobite Clans*, pp. 50–1, 62; Ferguson, *Scotland*, pp. 129–30; Allardyce, *Historical Papers*, vol. 1, p. 145.
87 Aufnere, *Lockhart Papers*, vol. 2, p. 20.
88 Hanover was also known as the Duchy and Electorate of Brunswick-Lüneburg.
89 Daniell, *Calendar of Stuart Papers*, vol. 4, p. 86.
90 Aufnere, *Lockhart Papers*, vol. 2, p. 161.

5

The Threatened Spanish Invasion of England

'Press the fitting out of the ships, raise as many troops as you can.'

In mid-April 1719, the English press ran the first reports of Jacobite forces landed in Scotland. The London newspaper *The Weekly Packet*, for example, reported in its edition for 18–25 April:

> There are authentic letters from Scotland, which give an account: that the late Lord Seaforth and others were landed in the northern Highlands, with some men, the numbers of which are very uncertain: But it is probable they are the same which sailed under convoy of two men of war from Port Passage, and were to have made a diversion in Scotland.

The British government also had ample advance warning of the Spanish invasion threat. Interception of Cardinal Alberoni's correspondence had by December 1718 revealed the extent of Hispano-Jacobite relations. In the New Year, spies working for the Earl of Stanhope, notably one John Pringle, a Scots merchant in Spain, provided more detailed information. The French also supplemented British intelligence. In January, France's foreign minister Cardinal Guillaume Dubois, an intractable opponent of Cardinal Alberoni's schemes for the aggrandisement of Spain, provided James Craggs, secretary of state of the Southern Department, with reports of Alberoni and Ormond's invasion plan and the Pretender's intent to leave Rome for Spain. French governmental intelligence from Spain was also shared with the Earl of Stair, who in turn informed London. At first it was assumed the Cádiz armada was bound for Ireland. Accordingly, on 19 January at Dublin the Lords Justices and Council of Ireland, the executive there of the British government, issued a proclamation offering £10,000 in reward for the apprehension of the Duke of Ormond; 'attainted of high treason [...] actually landed, or will soon attempt to land in this kingdom'. On 21 February, however, Stair wrote to Craggs it seemed likely the Spanish would land in north-west England. Their objectives were assumed to be the port of Liverpool and the city of Chester, opening the way for a Hispano-Jacobite advance into the Welsh borderlands and valley of the River Severn.[1]

Towards the end of February, Dubois gave Craggs conclusive intelligence of Spain's intent. A force led by Ormond would land in south-west England, and with the support of West Country Jacobites seize Bristol as a precursor to marching on London.[2] Given this threat, Dubois expressed the Regent's offer to loan Britain French troops as reinforcements, and French sailors to bring the complements of Royal Navy ships up to wartime strength. On 4 March from Paris the Earl of Stair wrote with urgency to Craggs, to 'press the fitting out of the ships, raise as many troops as you can and send to the Dutch to have their troops ready. The Spaniards could not sail before the 7th or the 8th of this month. I hope our squadron will be ready in time'. Stair concluded with the pointed caveat, that 'I think the Duke of Orléans is heartily in earnest to help us, but it is good not to want French assistance'. In the event, none of the 10 squadrons of cavalry and 18 battalions of infantry offered by the Regent went to England. The British government also declined the services of most of the 1,500 sailors offered, although during March 600 French seamen were accommodated at the navy base at Portsmouth. However, none of them were called upon to crew a Royal Navy warship, and were soon all paid off and repatriated.[3] As Craggs was pleased to explain, 'Our navy prides themselves on doing their own service without any obligation of foreign helps'.[4]

Anti-invasion Preparations

Rumours and speculation about an invasion now provoked some alarm among the English public.[5] In the face of the Spanish threat, parliament rallied to support the Georgian regime. On 10 March King George attended the House of Lords. Before the assembled peers and members of the House of Commons who had been instructed to gather there, the Lord Chancellor delivered the king's address communicating what the government knew of the situation; 'having received [...] repeated advices, that an invasion will suddenly be attempted from Spain against my dominions, in favour of the Pretender to my crown'. The Lords expressed their united willingness to stand by the king, 'with the utmost zeal, in the support and defence of his sacred person and government, in opposition to all his enemies'. For their part, MPs solemnly pledged consent to any additional expenditure necessary for home defence.[6]

Naval preparations were the first and foremost priority. In London on 7 March, the Admiralty had issued orders for Admiral Sir John Norris to lead a squadron to cover the Western Approaches. By cruising off the

1   Fritz, 'Anti-Jacobite Intelligence System', pp. 271, 278; Fritz, *English Ministers and Jacobitism*, pp. 52, 54; Dickson, *Jacobite Attempt*, xxxviii–ix, pp. 224, 227, 234. Quotation from Anon., *The Historical Register, Containing An Impartial Relation of all Transactions, Foreign and Domestic* (1719), pp. 45–6.
2   Fritz, *English Ministers and Jacobitism*, p. 54.
3   Dickson, *Jacobite Attempt*, p. 232.
4   Cited in *Ibid.*, p. xxxix.
5   Fritz, *English Ministers and Jacobitism*, pp. 57–8.
6   *Journals of the House of Commons* vol.19, p. 127; *Journals of the House of Lords* vol. 21 (undated), Nov. 1718 to Mar. 1721, p. 96.

27. James Berkeley, 3rd Earl of Berkeley. Portrait by John Faber Jr. after Sir Godfrey Kneller, Bt. Mezzotint, 1731. In spring 1719, Berkeley for a while commanded the British fleet covering the Western Approaches seeking to intercept the Spanish armada. (© National Portrait Gallery, London)

Scilly Isles and Land's End, Norris was expected to intercept and defeat the Spanish fleet. Norris was a highly experienced long-serving officer. He had been promoted to full admiral in 1709 as admiral of the blue, and in 1715 commanded the Royal Navy's first summer squadron sent to the Baltic Sea. In March 1718 he became a lord of the Admiralty. 18 men-of-war at anchor along the south coast of England were put at Norris's disposal. However, not all were readily seaworthy and so it was with seven ships of the line that Norris sailed on 11 March from Spithead (the roadstead used by the Royal Navy as an anchorage outside Portsmouth harbour). Norris's squadron was reinforced next day by the arrival of two warships that left Plymouth on the 8th.[7] 'I do not doubt', Craggs confidently wrote to Stair from Whitehall on 9 March, that Norris would 'be able to give a very good account of a dozen Spanish ships, should they meet with them. He has orders and is resolved notwithstanding any inequality in numbers to attack them'.[8] To reinforce Norris and extend the patrolled area to the seas off southern Ireland, on 23 March the Admiralty instructed Admiral James Berkeley, 3rd Earl of Berkeley, to put a second squadron to sea. Berkeley had been the first lord of the Admiralty since May 1717. Recent appointments in March 1719, on the 13th as admiral and commander-in-chief of the fleet, and on the 21st as vice-admiral of Great Britain, had made Berkeley Britain's most senior naval officer. On 29 March he set sail westward from the anchorage at St. Helen's off the Isle of Wight with seven men-of-war: His Majesty's Ships *Dorsetshire* and *Hampton Court*, third-rates of 80 and 70 guns respectively; the 60-gun *Medway* and 50-gun *Weymouth*, both fourth rates; *Rye*, a 30-gun fifth-rate; and the 20-gun sixth-rates *Hind* and *Dursley-Galley*.[9]

While Royal Navy warships put to sea, measures were taken to redeploy and to expand the land forces. Once it was known the Spanish intended to land in the English West Country, where there were known and suspected pockets of Jacobitism (the thousands of Cornish tin miners, in particular, had traditionally favoured the Stuarts), four battalions of Foot, including three of guards, and 15 troops of Horse and four regiments of dragoons were ordered to march or make ready to march there.[10] In early April, the London newspaper the *Post Boy* reported the ongoing deployment of troops from

---

7   *Political State of Great Britain*, XVII, p. 317.
8   Dickson, *Jacobite Attempt*, p. 235.
9   TNA, ADM 2/49, folios 593–5, 609: Admiralty Out-Letters, Lords' Letters, Orders and Instruction, 19 July 1716–8 May 1719; *The London Gazette*, 28–31 March 1719.
10   *Political State of Great Britain*, Volume XVII, p. 325.

the capital: 'the same morning [11 April] the three other companies of the Foot Guards set out for the west, and are soon to be followed by eight more companies of the First Regiment [of Foot].'[11] The government considered re-forming the six regiments of Foot and six of dragoons disbanded during 1718. However, instead four infantry regiments on the Irish establishment were shipped to western England as reinforcements. Numbering in all about 1,780 officers and men, these were Major-General Joseph Sabine's Royal Regiment of Welsh Fuziliers, Edward Lord Hinchingbroke's Regiment, and the regiments of Colonels William Egerton and Thomas Chudleigh. Sailing out of Cork, the troops disembarked in Somerset, at Minehead, and at Bristol during the third week of March and were listed on the British establishment on the 21st.[12] In all, probably 5,000-6,000 troops were deployed in south-western England centred on Bristol. Other anti-invasion preparations in the West Country involved senior officers identifying potential landing places; the close monitoring of inland and coastal trade for concealed arms and munitions; and establishing intelligence links with trusted informants in Bristol and certain key towns. The British and Irish establishments were placed on alert, and officers on leave or otherwise absent ordered to re-join their units.[13]

William Cadogan, Earl Cadogan, was put on standby to command the forces gathering in south-west England in the event of the Spanish landing. For much of the War of the Spanish Succession Cadogan had been quartermaster-general (a role equivalent to the chief of staff in a modern army) to the Duke of Marlborough and very much his trusted right-hand man. As already mentioned here, during the latter part of the 1715–16 Jacobite rising Cadogan had replaced the Duke of Argyll in command in Scotland.

In order to release marching regiments from duty in coastal defence and guarding key locations, Invalid companies of pensioner soldiers were raised. On 11 March orders were given to establish 20 new companies of invalids, each with 50 privates and eight officers and NCOs (later reduced to 56 of all ranks), 'formed out of the pensioners belonging to the Royal Hospital near Chelsea'. The officers were selected from candidates on the army's half-pay list. Ten companies would form a regiment commanded by Colonel Edmund Fielding, the remainder serving as independent companies under individual captains' command.[14] On 4 April an additional 15 independent companies were established, increasing the overall Invalid reinforcement to nearly 2,000 officers and men.

While the recruitment and equipping of 35 new invalid companies did not go smoothly – the captains of both companies posted to Chester, for example, complained that most of the muskets issued to their men were unserviceable – the national deployment went ahead during April. The posting of four companies to the east-coast port of Hull, for example, allowed

---

11 Issue for the week 9–11 April 1719.
12 TNA, WO 24/95: 'Establishment of the four regiments of foot removed from Ireland to Great Britain, commencing 21 March 1719'; *The London Gazette,* 28–31 March 1719.
13 Fritz, *English Ministers and Jacobitism,* pp. 55–7.
14 TNA, WO 24/96, 'Establishment for a regiment and ten independent companies of invalids, commencing 11 March 1719'.

28. Invalid companies raised in 1719 were similarly uniformed and equipped to the invalid from the 1740s pictured here. (New York Picture Library Digital Collection)

five companies of General Wightman's Regiment of Foot there to rejoin the remainder of the unit concentrated by May nearer the Scottish border at Newcastle-upon-Tyne, while Colonel Fielding's entire regiment reinforced the key naval base at Portsmouth. By May, invalid companies held positions around the coast of England, including the Scilly Isles, Pendennis Castle in Cornwall, Newport on the Isle of Wight, Guernsey and Jersey in the Channel Islands, in Essex at Tilbury Fort, and Tynemouth Fort in the north-east. Two companies were posted at the historically strategically important Anglo-Scottish border town and castle of Carlisle, joined by three troops of Major-General Evans's Regiment of Dragoons.[15]

Notwithstanding the Invalid reinforcement (albeit a force useful only for garrison duty) and the regiments from Ireland, the small regular army in Britain would be hard pressed if the invasion came. While units had to be concentrated in the expected invasion area, the army had also to maintain its presence across the kingdom in support of the civil powers in case of Jacobite-inspired civil unrest or more threatening armed insurgency. The British government therefore looked to allied powers to contribute auxiliary forces under treaty obligation.

The Dutch Reinforcement

France was militarily committed to Great Britain (and to the United Provinces), both by the Treaty of Quadruple Alliance of summer 1718 and the Treaty of Defensive Alliance of January 1717. As has been seen, however, the British could not yet stomach accepting military aid from their colonial rival and old and recent enemy. The Earl of Stair distrusted the French, as he confided in private correspondence to Secretary Craggs on 20 March 1719: 'To tell you the truth I have no manner of taste to be assisted by French troops in England, the bias of all this nation towards the Pretender is inconceivable. More reassuringly, Stair added that 'the Regent's good disposition [...] will have a very good effect and help to keep the Jacobites in awe'.[16] Disregarding French aid, Britain turned instead to Imperial Austria and to the United Provinces, her former partners in the second Grand Alliance during the War of the Spanish Succession.

Great Britain was allied to Imperial Austria by the Quadruple Alliance and by the terms of mutual military support of the Treaty of Defensive Alliance concluded on 25 May 1716. This so-called Treaty of Westminster was a reciprocal arrangement, whereby the Emperor Charles VI agreed to send up to 8,000 infantry and 4,000 cavalry to Britain's assistance, and King George I pledged to commit in support of the Empire a similar number of British troops, or else (and far more likely) naval forces of equivalent strength.[17] At the beginning of March 1719, the British government approached Baron

---

15 TNA, SP 41/5/103; TNA, WO 4/22, folios 93, 112: Secretary-at-War, Out-letters; TNA, SP 41/5/112.

16 Dickson, *Jacobite Attempt*, xxxix.

17 *Collection of all the Treaties*, vol. 1, pp. 277–9.

Penterridter, the Imperial ambassador in London, to invoke the terms of the treaty of Westminster. Penterridter accordingly sent instructions to Brussels to the Marquis de Prie, governor of the Austrian Netherlands, to place Imperial troops on standby for deployment to Britain in the event of a Spanish invasion. De Prie in turn liaised with the Imperial governor of Brussels, Lieutenant-General Count Vehlen. By the evening of 12 March, Vehlen had six battalions of Foot from the Brussels garrison ready to march. By the 15th the infantry had reached Bruge on their way to the coast at Ostend, where they would be shipped to England under Vehlen's command. Two battalions arrived and were billeted at Ostend. In order that sufficient transports could be requisitioned at Ostend, on 25 March instructions were sent from Brussels to the governor there to embargo the departure of all shipping. However, in the event no merchantmen were needed, and the four battalions away from the coast marched no further than Bruge and Ghent; the British government decided not to deploy Imperial troops.[18]

Instead, Britain called only on the Dutch to commit forces. The States General (the federal government of the United Provinces) had not so far ratified the military conventions of the Treaty of Quadruple Alliance. However, the Netherlands was allied to Great Britain (and also to France) by the Treaty of Alliance of January 1717. Furthermore, the Treaty of Succession and Barrier of October 1709 more tightly committed the Dutch to the British. Under its terms, the United Provinces had committed to uphold the Protestant Hanoverian succession to the throne of Great Britain. Britain for its part, once the war over the Spanish Succession was ended, in the post-war diplomatic settlement was to guarantee Dutch occupation of a string of frontier strongholds known as the barrier fortresses. Situated in what was then the Spanish Low Countries, these strongholds would protect the borders of the United Provinces against any future French invasion. The further Anglo-Dutch Treaty of Guarantee agreed in February 1713 had bound the existing Treaty of Succession and Barrier to the Peace of Utrecht. However, by the associated Treaty of Rastatt, that in 1714 officially ended the state of war between France and Imperial Austria, the Spanish Low Countries were ceded to the Empire as the Austrian Netherlands. This necessitated the negotiation of an additional barrier treaty to commit the Empire to the existing Anglo-Dutch frontier agreement. The resultant tripartite Treaty of Barrier and Restitution was signed at Antwerp on 15 November 1715 by plenipotentiaries of the States General, Great Britain and Imperial Austria. The territorial military and financial measures underpinning this treaty had been confirmed in a further convention agreed by representatives of all three powers at The Hague as recently as 22 December 1718.[19]

Within three months the British government invoked the terms of the Barrier Treaty, calling on the United Provinces to provide auxiliary troops to safeguard the Protestant succession against the threat from Catholic Spain. There was, moreover, recent precedent for such a deployment. In

---

18 *Ibid.*, p. 235; *The Whitehall Evening Post*, 21–24 March 1719; *The London Gazette*, 28–31 March 1719.

19 *Collection of all the Treaties*, vol. 1, pp. 250–75, 330–45; *The Historical Register*, p. 41.

29. The appearance of Dutch Foot during the War of the Spanish Succession, little altered by 1719. (New York Picture Library Digital Collection)

November and December 1715 6,000 native Dutch and mercenary Swiss troops in Dutch pay had been sent to Scotland to reinforce British Army operations against the Jacobites.[20] In early March 1719, the Earl of Stanhope as secretary of state for the Northern Department wrote to the States General requesting four battalions of infantry.[21] Colonel (later Lieutenant-General) John Huske was sent to the Netherlands to act as military liaison officer, and arrived at The Hague with Stanhope's instructions towards the end of March. On 3 April agreement was reached for five Dutch battalions to be sent to England.

While Huske arranged provisioning and transportation for the troops, one Mr. Pesters, the representative in Brussels of the States General, gave marching orders and planned the route to the embarkation port at Willemstad (a harbour south of Rotterdam) for the selected regiments, three of which were drawn from the Dutch garrisons of the barrier fortress towns of Tournai and Ypres. The Admiralty in the meantime chartered English merchantmen to serve as troop transports. Given the importance of their voyage, and because it was the custom of Royal Navy ships to take sailors from merchantmen at sea to make up their own complements, the Admiralty instructed that crews of the designated transports were exempt from naval impressment. By 4 April, 12 ships were made ready out of the 13 in all employed as transports, of which three were Dutch vessels sailing out of Rotterdam.

Approximately 2,500 Dutch Foot were shipped as auxiliaries to England and later to Scotland, forming five battalions from four regiments. Brigadier Sturler's regiment of Swiss in the Dutch service provided two battalions, each comprising five companies with a nominal strength of 100 men. Two battalions of this regiment had served in the Dutch expeditionary force in Scotland during the 1715–16 rising.[22] The other three battalions were native Dutch provincial regiments with 44-man companies: Major-general Baron

20 J. Oates, 'Dutch Forces in Eighteenth-Century Britain: A British Perspective', *Journal of the Society of Army Historical Research,* 85 (2007), pp. 23–4.

21 Dickson, *Jacobite Attempt,* p. 235. The reconstruction of the Dutch reinforcement given here is derived mainly from: TNA, AO 1/2310/26: Records of the Auditors of the Imprest, Commissioners of Audit, Exchequer and Audit Department, National Audit Office and related bodies, a roll of later date, accounting for Huske's expenditure in organising the deployment; TNA, WO 24/100, another account of expenditure on the Dutch forces; TNA, SP 41/5/112, giving dispositions of the regiments when in Scotland; TNA, SP 41/5/141–2, a directive concerned with the transport and victualling of the Dutch and Swiss troops for returning to the Netherlands; and news from the Low Countries and England reported in the following English newspapers: *The Daily Currant,* 25 March 1719; *The London Gazette,* 28–31 March 1719; *The Weekly Journal or British Gazetteer,* 18 April 1719; *The Weekly Packet,* 18–25 April 1719.

22 Rae, *History of the Rebellion,* p. 372.

Van Huffel's regiment of 10 companies; Colonel Van Amerongen's Regiment of 12 companies; and Colonel Sixmar's Regiment, also of 12 companies. The battalions were reinforced before departure by drafts from other units, although a plan to send 300 recruits to strengthen Huffel's, Amerongen's and Sixmar's regiments when in Scotland was not put into effect.

The Dutch were regarded as reliable troops. During the War of the Spanish Succession the infantry of the United Provinces had gained a reputation for their disciplined steadiness and stoicism under fire. The Jacobite James Keith acknowledged the 'regularity of the Dutch' in comparison to the Highland clansmen; 'who are of a disposition as hot and quick as the Dutch are slow and phlegmatic'.[23]

Command of the Dutch reinforcement was given to Major-General Baron van Keppel. He was brother of the late Arnold Joost van Keppel, Earl of Albemarle, an army officer and courtier favoured by King William III who became one of the Duke of Marlborough's trusted subordinates in Flanders during the War of the Spanish Succession. Keppel's second in command was Brigadier-General Walderen. Keppel embarked at Willemstad on 9 April aboard the fast-sailing English packet boat *Prince*, ahead of the first lift of five transports carrying Sturler's regiment to the River Thames. He landed at Harwich on the 14th.[24] However, the following convoy was delayed for several days by contrary winds on the Channel coast at Hellevoetsluis. It was probably on 17 April therefore that the Swiss troops disembarked at Tilbury in Essex on the lower reaches of the Thames. Major-General Keppel's personal baggage arrived with them. Transported from Essex on six wagons escorted by a detachment of Swiss grenadiers, Keppel's impedimenta arrived in London at his apartments near St. James's Palace on 20 April.[25]

The Spanish Armada

By the time they arrived in England, however, the Dutch troops had no immediate role. The Spanish invasion armada had not materialised. No ships had been sighted, let alone intercepted by the combined fleet of Admirals Norris and Berkeley. 'I have been this fortnight looking out for the enemy', penned Berkeley on 10 April in a situation report to the Earl of Stair, written aboard his flagship HMS *Dorsetshire* an estimated 35 miles (56 km) southward of Lizard Point in Cornwall:

> When I first came I went off Cape Clear in Ireland, thinking that might be a place they were to rendezvous at, but saw nor heard nothing of them. Since I'm come back, we have resolved to keep on our own shore as much as we can, that intelligence may come quicker to us, and that our cruisers may be sure where to find us, if they should get sight of the enemy. This we think better than running the risk of letting them slip by us in the sea […] and in the station we are in between the Lizard and Scilly, if our cruisers should bring us an account of them, we should be able to go into either channel, and not be long after them. […]. I believe that part of their

---

23 Keith, *Fragment of a Memoir*, p. 10.
24 *The Evening Post*, 14–16 April 1719.
25 *The Post Boy*, 21–23 April 1719.

being sailed is certainly true, but if with so little provisions as they say, they must certainly be perished in the sea. Indeed I am apt to believe their expedition is over, and that we shall have a very dismal account of them whenever we hear of them, for they can have met with nothing but contrary winds.[26]

Berkeley a day or two previously had sent two ships to reconnoiter the port of Corunna. Not far round the coast eastward from there was the harbour village of Sada. The Duke of Ormond and his attendants had arrived here on 13 February to await contact with the Spanish fleet. Mindful of the foul weather then affecting Spain's west coast, in dispatches to Cardinal Alberoni Ormond expressed his hope that the armada had delayed its departure from Cádiz, and also his concern how, if conditions at sea remained difficult, to contact Rear-Admiral Don Balthasar de Guevarra once he neared Corunna. 'We cannot possibly think of sailing', fretted Ormond on 19 February, 'until we have seen each other, for he will not know where I propose to go'.[27] When news arrived that Guevarra had in fact sailed on 23 February, Ormond shifted to Corunna on 6 March. Arrangements were made to station boats off Cape Finisterre to look out for the fleet. Five days later, however, without further news of Guevarra, Ormond wrote worriedly to Alberoni that further delay could make 'our enterprise very difficult and almost impossible'. Ormond feared, rightly, that the British knew the Cádiz armada was heading for England, not Ireland, and the vital element of surprise was lost: 'for otherwise I should not have been so rash as to propose to attack England with 5,000 men when they were informed of our intentions'. Given the changed strategic situation, Ormond proposed to Alberoni that the armada should instead make for Scotland to join forces with Marischal's expedition, known by Ormond to have sailed. 'We shall have plenty of men', in the Highlands Ormond opined, to 'defend ourselves and hold out. It is well to have a footing [...] accidents might happen to our advantage'. Scotland therefore would once again be the springboard for the Stuart restoration, providing a third opportunity for the would-be King James III and VIII to play a leading role in reclaiming the crown of the three kingdoms. 'Should your eminence agree to what I propose', Ormond wrote to Alberoni on 11 March, 'the king my master ought to come to go on board the fleet'; he knew by then that James Francis Edward Stuart was in Spain.[28]

Upon receiving in January Ormond's correspondence intimating what was planned, James had decided to shift to Spain. He no longer felt secure in Italy and of course hoped to lead the invasion in person. However, because taking the overland route through northern Italy and into France would most likely result in James's arrest and detention, a voyage to Spain was deemed a less hazardous undertaking, notwithstanding the continuing presence in Italian waters of Admiral Byng's British fleet. In order to keep James's departure from Rome secret for as long as possible a deception was arranged. While he clandestinely

26 J.M. Graham (ed.), *Annals and Correspondence of the First and Second Earls of Stair*, 2 vols. (1875), vol. 1, pp. 116–17.
27 Dickson, *Jacobite Attempt*, p. 74.
28 *Ibid.*, pp. 92–3.

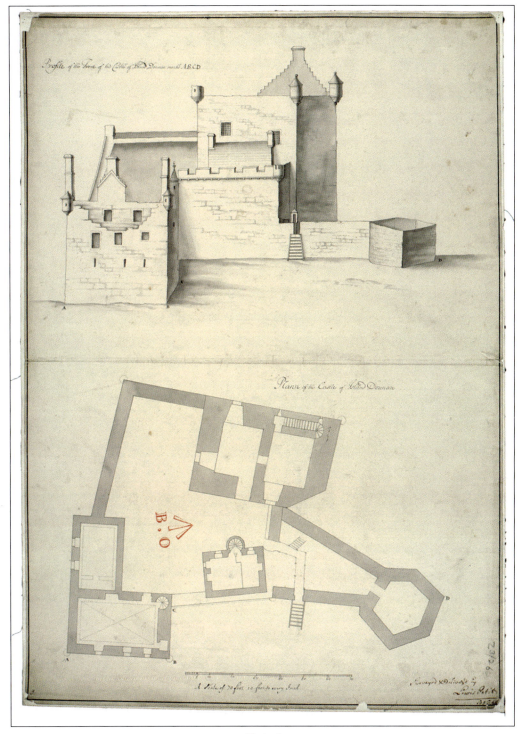

Plate A
'Plann of the Castle of Island Dounan [*sic*];
Profile of the Front of the Castle of Island Dounan markt [*sic*] ABCD'
(Reproduced by permission of the National Library of Scotland)
See Colour Plate Commentaries for further information

i

Plate B
'Attack on Eilean Donan Castle'
(Painting by Ed Walker. Copyright © and reproduction by permission of the artist)
See Colour Plate Commentaries for further information.

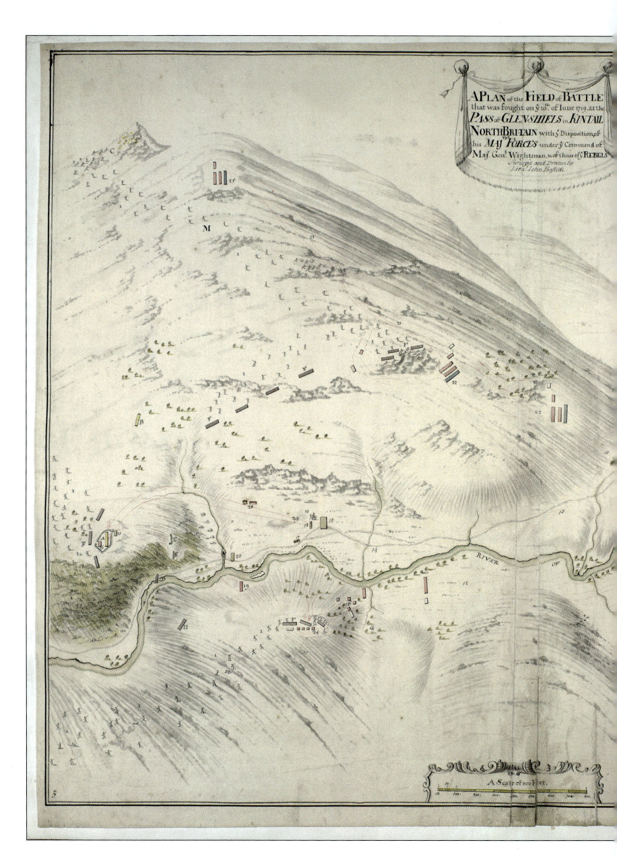

A PLAN of the FIELD of BATTLE that was fought on ỹ 10th of Iune 1719 at the PASS of GLENSHIELS in KINTAIL NORTH BRITAIN with ỹ Disposition of his Maj. FORCES under ỹ Command of Maj. Gen. Wightman, w.th those of ỹ REBELS Surveyd and Drawn by Lieut. John Bastide.

A Scale of 500 Feet.

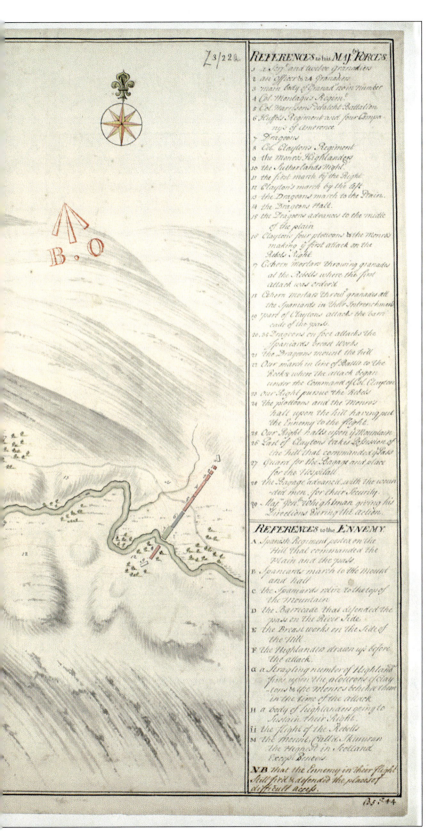

Plate D
'Plan of the Field of Battle that was fought on ye 10th of June 1719, at the Pass of Glenshiels [*sic*]'
(Reproduced by permission of the National Library of Scotland)
See Colour Plate Commentaries for further information

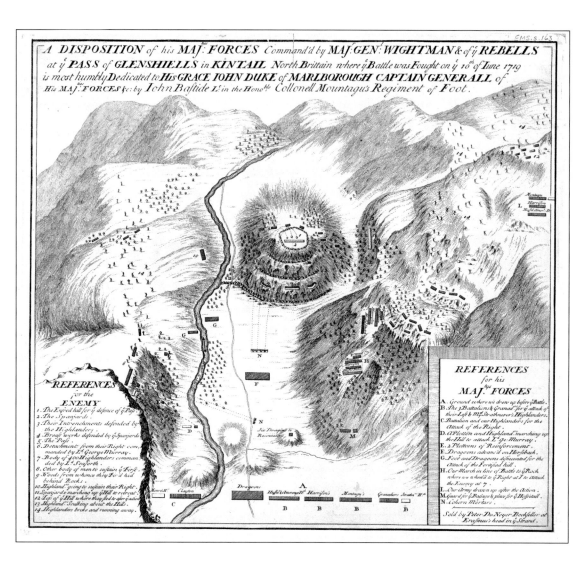

Plate E

'A Disposition of His Majesty's Forces commanded by Major-General Wightman & of the Rebels at the Pass of Glenshiells [*sic*] in Kintail North Britain where the battle was fought on the 10th of June 1719'

(Reproduced by permission of the National Library of Scotland)

See Colour Plate Commentaries for further information

left the city early on 27 January, later that day the Dukes of Mar and Perth in another party believed also to include James more conspicuously departed northward. Heading for Genoa, soon after entering Imperial Austrian territory the group were duly arrested and detained at Milan. The Imperial authorities soon found out, however, that the individual taken to be the Pretender was in fact a member of James's household. James in the meantime had travelled to a fishing village south of Rome. There he took passage in a merchantman sailing under the Genoese flag chartered at Alberoni's behest by Admiral George Camocke, a Jacobite former officer of King James II's fleet now serving in the Spanish navy. After a difficult voyage, during which he suffered seasickness and a fever, James landed at Rosas in Catalunia on 26 February. He entered Madrid on 15 March with due ceremony, reportedly 'in one of the king's new coaches, followed by his majesty's lifeguard and officers of his household, and by some grandees, who rode some leagues out of town to meet him'. King Phillip greeted and accorded James full honours, and for his accommodation and that of his small entourage provided a palace guarded by troops of the royal household corps.[29]

While Alberoni had backed Ormond's change in strategy, James Francis Edward now stubbornly opposed it. He instead instructed Ormond to hold to the plan of landing in England. Ormond dutifully replied on 24 March, that he would not 'mention Scotland any more'. Alberoni had had to advise Ormond to obey James's wishes, but he countermanded this in a dispatch from Madrid on 25 March. James had now changed his mind, and was in agreement that Scotland was a desirable objective. 'I will do what I can to land in Scotland', replied Ormond, 'which will only be the last resort'.[30]

However, abnormal conditions at sea would prevent either Ormond or his king from leaving Spain. On 30 March, five weather-beaten Spanish transports arrived at Corunna, one of which was badly damaged. From reports received over the next few days, of other storm-lashed ships seeking shelter elsewhere on the west coast of the Iberian Peninsula, it became clear that the Cádiz armada had scattered in exceptionally bad weather.

Numbering about 5,000 men, the invasion force had by the second week in February embarked at Cádiz aboard Rear-Admiral Guevarra's ships. However, adverse winds and then fog delayed departure. According to intelligence from Paris in mid-March, Ormond's would-be army comprised 13 battalions of Foot, mostly from the Irish Brigades of the Spanish Army, and one regiment of dragoons.[31] The armada reportedly included at least 22 transports of various sizes, although accounts of the return of the ships to port indicate more vessels were involved. A later British account mentioned 40 or so transports, and this seems a much more likely figure.[32] The naval escort consisted of just five men-of-war, also carrying troops and heavily laden with supplies. Guevarra's squadron comprised his flagship the 64-gun *Commadore*, two 50-gun men-of-war, and two others of 20 guns (equivalent to British sixth-rates). This modest

---

29 Dickson, *Jacobite Attempt*, xxxiii, xxxvi–ii; *The Weekly Journal or Saturday's Post*, 18 April 1719.

30 Dickson, *Jacobite Attempt*, p. 107.

31 *Political State of Great Britain, XVII*, p. 317

32 *The Historical Register*, p. 163.

30. A company drummer of Spanish Foot, early 18th century. A drummer's ornate uniform was distinguished from the plain off-white coats worn by most Spanish infantry. Regiments were identified by distinctive coloured coat linings ('facings'), displayed prominently on the deep turned back cuffs. The detached battalion of Colonel Don Pedro de Castro's Regiment of Foot that fought at Glenshiel was described by an eyewitness as having 'one livery, viz white lin'd [*sic*] with yellow'.

force reflected the weakened state of the Spanish Royal Navy after the War of Succession. From 1713 the Spanish monarchy had invested heavily in naval facilities and growing the fleet, but the losses in 1718 at Cape Passaro had setback the warship-building programme. It has been estimated that in 1715 the Spanish navy had just 23 ships of the line and smaller cruisers, compared to 182 equivalent ships in the British fleet. By 1720 Spain had only 26 such warships.[33]

The armada finally left Cádiz on 23 February. For the first leg of the voyage it sailed west south-westward together with a navy sloop and a merchantman heading for the West Indies.[34] Having stood sufficiently into the eastern Atlantic to avoid contact with British warships cruising off Portugal, the fleet parted company with the Caribbean-bound vessels and altered course northward for Cape Finisterre. But an estimated 170 miles (274 km) south-west of the Cape, in the early morning of 18 March the armada was struck by an unusually violent storm persisting for two days. The prevailing weather patterns south of the British Isles at this time in March were not particularly unfavourable, and so putting the fleet to sea was not an unacceptable risk. However, it seems that the Spanish were unluckily caught up in a major weather event that for a while affected much of Western Europe. Recent historical-meteorological research has convincingly argued this was a massive cut-off low, a low-pressure system detached from the usual prevailing Atlantic weather systems. The cut-off low was for the time of year unusually centred on the western Mediterranean Sea. This meant that de Guevarra's ships in the eastern Atlantic were unknowingly sailing at the westerly edge of the low, the region most likely to be affected by the cold frontal zone generating the stormiest conditions.[35]

The armada dispersed in riding out the storm for 48 hours. While no ships seem to have foundered, many were damaged. They took on water in the heavy seas, and in desperately attempting to maintain buoyancy crews cast guns and supplies overboard. The *Commadore* was dismasted, and to keep her afloat upper deck guns were pitched into the ocean. The number of casualties seems to have remained undisclosed, but the troops especially must have suffered badly in the crowded conditions below deck. Certainly, many of the dragoon horses died. When the storm eventually abated, lacking provisions and critically short of water individual ships sought shelter in Spain's northerly and westerly ports; arriving at Bilbao, at Corunna,

---

33 Rodger, *Command of the Ocean*, p. 25.

34 The main source here is the eyewitness account of an English merchant sailing master, one Richard Spartman of Southampton, published in *The London Gazette* of 21–25 April 1719. Spartman told he had been impressed in Cádiz and served on a Spanish transport.

35 P.J. Klinger, 'Weather and the Jacobite Rebellion of 1719', *Environment and History*, 23 (2017), pp. 197–216, *passim*.

southward of there at Muros, at Vigo and at Cádiz, while several ships made it to Lisbon in Portugal. A report from Lisbon towards the end of March mentioned how on the 25th:

> One of the transports which sailed with the Spanish fleet from Cádiz came into this port, as did the next day another with French colours, which the master says was forced into the service at Cádiz; and on the [28th] arrived two more. The two first are about 200 tons each, and the other two of about 140 tons each. All the four have not above 300 soldiers and 54 horses on board, one of them having thrown overboard all the horses that were embarked in her, and all of them threw overboard their guns, casks of water and provisions; yet they received no damage in their masts or rigging, except one of them whose main mast is split.[36]

James Francis Edward Stuart eventually arrived at Corunna on 6 April, joining the stranded and dejected Duke of Ormond. At first, James's Spanish allies encouraged him to believe that despite this huge setback the invasion was not abandoned. King Phillip wrote reassuringly that the fleet had been ordered to refit, although Alberoni cautioned that repairs and reorganisation would take several months. On 15 April the Cardinal wrote confirming that while Spain remained committed to the operation, a second armada would not be ready before August. Ormond hoped that two ships allocated go to Scotland with supplies and orders for Marischal's expedition would still sail, but in early May Alberoni instructed the crews to stand down.

However, as will be seen, another of the Cardinal and Ormond's plans seems to have been put into effect. This involved the ex-Spanish ambassador to the States General covertly arranging shipment of military supplies from the United Provinces to Scotland. Jacobites held the province of Holland to be a good source of arms – broadswords, for example, could be bought there in quantity at reasonable prices – and it was understood that British warships were less inclined to stop and search Dutch merchantmen than those of any other nation.[37] Indeed, in April one such arms-runner from the Netherlands had been located and seized by British government excise officers on the south-east coast of Scotland, in Largo Bay near Kilkaldy in Fife.[38]

Spanish shipyards did begin to make seaworthy the storm-damaged fleet. In early May it was reported in England that at Cádiz:

> Men work here night and day in refitting the two men of war and 16 transports which make a part of the fleet that sailed hence the 6th of March last [i.e. 23 February Old Style], and were driven back by storms; but they are so shattered, that they will not be ready for to put to sea again these six weeks.[39]

---

36   Sailing Master Spartman's account, *The London Gazette*, 21–25 April 1719.
37   Dickson, *Jacobite Attempt*, pp. 84, 109–25, passim; Daniell, *Calendar of Stuart Papers,* vol. 4, p. 86.
38   J. Reddington (ed.), *Calendar of Treasury Papers, 1714–1719* (1883), p. 449.
39   *The Weekly Journal or Saturday's Post,* 30 May 1719.

By then, however, Spain's strategic priorities had shifted dramatically. Not only did ongoing operations in the central Mediterranean have to be sustained, but Spain itself had been invaded. In April, the French had opened a new front in the War of the Quadruple Alliance, when the Duke of Berwick led an army through the westerly passes of the Pyrenees and on the 21st crossed the river Bidassoa into the Basque country of northern Spain. Intending and succeeding to avoid battle with the smaller Spanish army mustered against him, Berwick instead mounted a campaign of sieges. In June, the French captured the coastal fortress of Fuenterrabia, and the port and citadel of San Sebastian in August. Later that month Berwick switched the main theatre of operations to north-east Spain, launching a similarly deliberately paced autumn offensive into Catalunia.[40]

Spanish military support for the Jacobites necessarily evaporated in consequence of the French invasion. But back in early March, Marischal's expedition was believed to be underway. If it reached Scotland, then, as Ormond had speculated, 'accidents' might still occur to Jacobite advantage.

---

40   Michael, *Quadruple Alliance*, pp. 99–104, *passim*.

6

The Jacobite Expedition

'To force a rising at all hazards, on so small a foundation'.

With the departure of Marischal's force from San Sebastian on 25 February 1719 and the sailing of Tullibardine's party from Honfleur 11 days later, the Jacobite expedition had got underway. However, neither element knew for sure the other was successfully heading for Scotland.

Soon after they sailed, contrary winds forced Marischal's frigates to shelter for a few days in the fishing port of Bermeo, westward of San Sebastian. Resuming the voyage, the flotilla headed due west into the Atlantic for some distance to the north-west of Cape Finisterre. At this point sealed orders were announced, revealing to the junior Spanish officers and the rank and file that Scotland was their destination. They had been led to believe they were bound for the Mediterranean. The unease among the Spanish soldiery must have increased when the Earl Marischal, who, it seems, had so far kept to his cabin, appeared on deck to announce through an interpreter that he was in overall command. The other Scots on board apparently maintained their anonymity until the ships neared Scotland.

The frigates kept a northerly course, far enough into the easterly Atlantic to minimise the risk of encountering British warships covering the Western Approaches. On 17 March, a customs officer sighted them sailing in company off County Mayo on Ireland's west coast. On the 20th the warships entered the mouth of Broadhaven Bay, allowing the officer watching their progress from the coastal headlands to confirm: 'they are two French or Spanish men-of-war; they are just as big as English six-rates; they carry above 30 guns apiece. I do believe they are some enemy'.[1] Next day he despatched a report to the lord lieutenant of Ireland in distant Dublin, but this would arrive too late to trigger a military response. The frigates voyaged undisturbed to the Isle of Lewis, the rendezvous agreed between Ormond, Marischal and the Keiths. They made landfall off the south-east of the island on 26 March.

---

1   Graham, *Annals and Correspondence*, vol. 1, pp. 118–19.

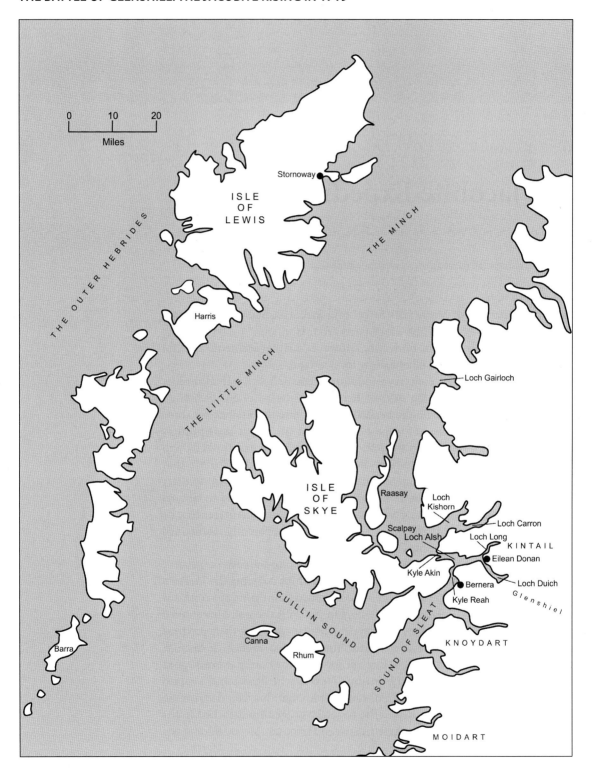

Map 3. The Western Isles and coastal mainland of Scotland, where the Jacobite expeditionary force arrived in March–April 1719.

In the meantime, the master of the bark carrying Tullibardine's party intended to reach Lewis by navigating the straits of Dover into the North Sea, and to round Scotland via the Pentland Firth south of Orkney. However, the small merchantman for some days was unable to make headway against the prevailing easterly winds. On 13 March she was turned about to set a westerly course for the Hebrides, either by St. George's Channel and the Irish Sea, or by rounding the Atlantic coast of Ireland. Late in the evening of 15 March, some way westward of Land's End, the bark was 'in the middle of a fleet', as James Keith recollected:

> Seven of which had out-lights and the others none; these we conjectured to be men-of-war, and the rest transports; and finding the number of the former to agree with what the Duke of Ormond had, I made no doubt but it was his fleet. However, the wind being favourable, we passed through them without speaking to them, in which we were very lucky; for it proved a squadron of English men-of-war transporting a body of troops from Ireland to England, where they had at last got the news of the invasion intended against them.[2]

The Jacobites had fortunately avoided the naval escorts of the convoy transporting from Ireland to the English West Country the regiments of foot of Colonels Egerton, Sabine, Hinchinbroke and Chudleigh.

The Landings in Scotland

'From thence', Keith recalled, the bark 'stood for Cape Clear [Ireland's southernmost point] and the west coast of Ireland, and after favourable but blowing weather', made landfall off the west coast of Lewis on 24 March.[3] Returned to his domain, the Earl of Seaforth sent to the east coast for news. But the returning messengers only confirmed what the local islanders had already told; that no Spanish ships had been seen and nothing was known of more distant events. This disheartened the Jacobites, hopeful of news of Ormond's successful landing in western England. Now they could do little more than to wait on events, so Tullibardine busied himself writing letters to inform sympathisers in the Islands and on the mainland of their arrival. However, probably on the 28th they received reports that two foreign warships had been sighted off the east of Lewis. By his own account, James Keith was first to set out to cross the island to make contact with the hoped-for Spanish warships and so with the Earl Marischal, but arriving on the stretch of coast where they had been seen found the ships had left. However, a local laird confirmed to Keith that they were indeed Spanish vessels, and had sailed up coast to Stornoway. There, as a visitor in the early 1700s described, was 'a harbour well known by seamen' – a sheltered bay providing a deep-water anchorage for larger vessels. The village of Stornoway was the largest settlement on Lewis, and so in effect the island capital. The place was then home to about sixty families, had a church and a school, and several inns serving visiting mariners.[4]

---

2   Keith, *Fragment of a Memoir*, p. 45.
3   *Ibid.*
4   Martin, *Description of the Western Islands*, pp. 4, 30.

Arriving at Stornoway during the evening of 29 March, Keith found both frigates at anchor in the harbour with the troops still aboard. Gratefully reunited with his brother, James described his success in France rallying the exiles; 'but at the same time told him what I suspected of the disposition of some of the company, who seemed to be dissatisfied to the work because the Duke of Mar had not been so much employed in it as they wished'. Furthermore, he voiced his suspicion that Tullibardine held certain commissions from Lieutenant-General Dillon. The Earl Marischal, however, appeared unperturbed that he might have to relinquish command. Declaring that 'he had never pretended to more than a share in the enterprise', he would respect a commission senior to his own, as a major-general in both the English and Spanish service. He then gave James a commission as a colonel in the Spanish service, authorising him to recruit in Scotland a regiment of two battalions in the name of the King of Spain.[5]

During 30 March Tullibardine, the Earl of Seaforth, Campbell of Glendaruel and the rest of the party arrived at Stornoway. That evening they met in the first of what became a series of factious councils of war. The council of war was an accepted way to direct military and naval operations, as it was then customary for commanders-in-chief to measure the opinion of leading subordinates. This was especially so in situations where, for reasons of distance from the seat of high command, or changed local circumstances, commanders on the spot had to reconsider their original orders; just the kind of situation faced by the Jacobites at Stornoway.

So far, the expedition had met with remarkably good luck. Both elements, notwithstanding the uncoordinated departures from warring nations, had missed the storms that ruined the armada, avoided patrolling warships of the British navy, and arrived at the far-distant rendezvous without loss. Their party included individuals of influence and military experience who could expect to rally support to the cause of King James III and VIII. The Spanish firearms and munitions (together with whatever armaments had been brought from France) could equip a useful Highland army. It was also the first time since French troops had arrived in Ireland in 1690 that a body of regular soldiers from an allied European power had landed in the British Isles in supporting of the Jacobites. By a show of force demonstrating foreign backing for a rising, the Spanish soldiers, as the Duke of Ormond anticipated, would prove their worth in Scotland. However, the military capability of the expedition fell far short of what Scots Jacobites would hope for, given that shortage of military supplies and lack of foreign troops contributed to the failure of the 1715–16 rising. Indeed, in mid June, shortly after the battle at Glenshiel, the Marquess of Tullibardine in concluding a dispatch intended for the Earl of Mar, made the point that: 'seeing we came with hardly any thing that was really necessary for such an undertaking [...] it is not to be imagined how much people are dispirited at the manner of our coming'.[6]

---

5 Keith, *Fragment of a Memoir*, p. 46.
6 Dickson, *Jacobite Attempt*, p. 273.

Disagreements about strategy and leadership arose that would undermine the expedition. As a diversionary force timing was the overriding concern; when and how to act effectively in support of the anticipated Spanish landing more than 500 miles (800 km) away in south-western England – but of the success, failure or delay of which the Jacobites at Stornoway had no news. For that reason, over coming weeks the councils of war, informed by rumour and uncertain intelligence, were indecisive. Some argued that taking immediate action was essential, in the expectation that Ormond had already landed. Others advocated caution (that the activists saw as dangerous procrastination). They preferred to await certain news of Ormond before encouraging a Highland rising, which if the landing in England failed would have no support.

George Lockhart had sat as an MP in the Parliament of Scotland and then at Westminster until implicated in the 1715–16 rising. In 1719 Lockhart was living in Edinburgh as a Jacobite activist and agent. He expressed the strategic dilemma facing militant Lowland Jacobites and the expedition in the far north-west of Scotland alike:

> As there were many accidents to which the Spanish fleet might be exposed in so long a voyage, we did by no means think it advisable to move in Scotland till we were sure the Duke of Ormond was landed; for if any appearance should be made for the king in Scotland, and the grand design fail in the execution, we should meet with no quarters [i.e. any leniency] from the government, and the king at the same time reap no benefit.[7]

Lockhart articulated concerns about the expedition's discordant leadership: 'One thing is sure, that he [Marischal] and Tullibardine were soon at variance about the command; and it seemed very odd that such matters were not adjusted before their embarkation'.[8] Of similar age, rivals in social status and for military rank, and with contrasting personalities, the 27-year-old Earl Marischal, testy and headstrong, and the 30-year-old Marquess of Tullibardine, affable and phlegmatic, by 1719 had little liking for each other, especially on Marischal's part. This animosity, coupled to the fact they represented factions within the Jacobite movement, meant that the expedition lacked unified leadership.

Marischal, as already mentioned, after the 1715–16 rising was an outspoken critic of the Earl of Mar. Slighted, Mar in turn nursed his grudges against Marischal. ''Tis [sic] hard to imagine what that boy the Earl Marischal would be at', Mar wrote from Rome in late December 1718 to Campbell of Glendaruel, 'but I see all the kindnesses and condolences to him from the king and Mar are thrown away. […] Mar has forgot all the bad requitals he has had from him, it being for the king's interest to do so, but the aggressor never forgives'.[9] Mar would have been further annoyed to know that Marischal was already acting under the Duke of Ormond's orders.

---

7 Aufnere, *Lockhart Papers*, vol. 2, p. 18.
8 *Ibid.*, p. 19.
9 Daniell, *Calendar of Stuart Papers*, vol. 7, p. 673.

31. (left) Reconstruction of the appearance of an impoverished cottar man in Mackenzie territory compelled to join the 1719 rising. His tattered clothing is based on archaeological evidence from an early-18th century male burial on the Isle of Lewis, found lacking the usual plaid. He has been issued with a Spanish musket. (Illustration by Ed Dovey, © Helion & Company Limited)

Ormond as his patron had favoured Marischal with command of the present expedition over the Marquess of Tullibardine; whether or not he knew of Tullibardine's commission in 1717 as commander-in-chief in waiting of Jacobite forces in Scotland. That June, when the Jacobites had hoped for Swedish military support, James Francis Edward Stuart himself had written instructing Colonel James Hay, a close advisor, that instead of going to Scotland Marischal should serve under Ormond in England: 'The Earl Marischal would never agree with Tullibardine', opined James, 'and I had also in my view the preventing of the Earl Marischal's venting his spleen against Mar in his own country'. In reply Hay agreed, 'It was not proper for the Earl Marischal to go along with Tullibardine for several reasons I need not mention, and his being left behind would have made the world believe he was neglected out of revenge'.[10] On Lewis in 1719 Marischal's followers appear to have been in the minority. They included his brother James, and his associate Brigadier Colin Campbell of Ormidale. Campbell shared Marischal's fighting spirit, and so was distrusted by the cautious Tullibardine. On 29 April, when the expedition was on the mainland, in a dispatch intended for James Francis Edward Stuart Tullibardine remarked, how 'I am sorry that Brigadier Campbell seems to run headlong into the most violent proceedings, which I am afraid will appear too much at this occasion'.[11]

Tullibardine, given Mar's patronage, headed the party from France. Among them Campbell of Glendaruel, another of Mar's associates, had particular influence over Tullibardine. Glendaruel came from Argyll in south-westerly Scotland, and his Jacobitism probably stemmed from a strong sense of Scottish nationalism. In February 1715, Mar, in covert correspondence with certain Jacobites, had mentioned 'I cannot but mention the travels and pains Glendaruel has been at in serving his country in general and particularly the Highlands'. At Mar's gathering at Braemar in August 1715 Glendaruel had represented the elderly and lukewarm Jacobite John, Earl of Breadalbane. During the rising Glendaruel was a political rather than military figure, but had remained in Scotland until evacuated to France in July 1716.[12] He had since recognised Tullibardine's potential as a figurehead for a future rising. Writing to James Francis Edward Stuart in June 1717, Glendaruel characterised Tullibardine as 'an honest man and your friend', with the caveat that he would have to be 'managed effectively'. Thus, it seems that less than two years later in Scotland Glendaruel, probably acting under instruction from Lord Dillon, encouraged Tullibardine to take command of the expedition. That this was the nature of the relationship is supported by

---

10   Cited in Cuthell, *Scottish Friend of Frederick the Great*, vol. 1, p. 80.

11   Dickson, *Jacobite Attempt*, p. 269.

12   Daniell, *Calendar of Stuart Papers*, vols. 1 & 2 combined, p. 350; Sinclair-Stevenson, *Inglorious Rebellion*, pp. 84, 86–7.

James Keith's remark, explaining the reason why Glendaruel before leaving France insisted on seeking instructions from General Dillon was so that Tullibardine's 1717 commission could be asserted; 'This Glendaruel thought absolutely necessary for his own private ends, being surer to govern the easy temper of the Marquess than those who otherwise would naturally have command of the army'.[13]

The Jacobite council of war held on the evening of 30 March 1719 aboard one of the Spanish frigates in Stornoway harbour was opened by the Earl Marischal. According to his brother's recollection of the meeting, having first asked whether anyone present held a commission senior to his own as major-general (when Tullibardine kept quiet), Marischal declared his command of the expedition under the Duke of Ormond's orders: 'which gave power to him or any superior officer to make war upon the Usurper [i.e. King George I] when and where they thought most convenient'.[14] With Campbell of Ormidale's backing, Marischal proposed taking the course of action agreed with Cardinal Alberoni, based on the assumption that Ormond had landed. The expedition should quickly disembark on the mainland, and the Spanish troops with local clansmen rapidly march upon and storm Inverness – reckoned to be then only weakly garrisoned. Inverness would be the rallying point for a general rising across the Highlands.

However, the majority saw this as reckless. They reckoned that without certain news of Ormond it would be difficult to rally Highland support so soon after the failures of 1715–16. Furthermore, they asserted that to rise prematurely, or 'if the designs on England should happen to miscarry [...] would prove a mighty disadvantage to his majesty's interest as well as bring destruction on the country'. More positively, it was reasoned 'that a general rising might be as quick and easier upon the certainty of a landing in England'.[15] Tullibardine and Campbell of Glendaruel proposed remaining on Lewis until such news arrived. However, the majority opposed this, out of concern that if British warships blockaded the island the expedition would be marooned. The council broke up having agreed to sail for the mainland in three days' time. In the meantime, the Spanish troops would be allowed ashore to refresh, having spent 42 days aboard the frigates.

Next morning, however, Tullibardine (presumably having overnight been persuaded by Glendaruel to do so) called the council to reassemble. After delivering a rather inarticulate address (later dismissed by George Keith, as 'a sort of speech, which nobody but himself understood'), Tullibardine revealed his commission as King James's lieutenant-general in Scotland. Marischal thus had no choice other than to accept his rival's seniority and relinquish the command-in-chief. While he seems to have done so without open disagreement, Marischal insisted on retaining his command of the frigates granted by Cardinal Alberoni, and also control over one-fifth of the Spanish cash. He remained, in effect, second in command to Tullibardine, although there would be little cooperation between them.

---

13 Daniell, *Calendar of Stuart Papers*, vol. 4, p. 82; Keith, *Fragment of a Memoir*, p. 44.
14 Quotation from Oliphant, 'Distinct Abridgment', *Jacobite Lairds of Gask*, p. 453.
15 *Ibid.*, p. 454.

With Tullibardine in charge the debate about strategy resumed. Tullibardine and Glendaruel advocated inactivity, and the Earl of Seaforth was of the same mind. Much depended on raising the MacKenzies and aligned clans, but Seaforth was mindful that another failed rising would most impact his estates and followers. Concerned how few Spanish troops there were, Seaforth was said to have been dismayed by 'what slender encouragement there was for rising disarmed people'. Marischal had also rather lamely admitted in council that in negotiating with Cardinal Alberoni he had followed Ormond's instruction not to press for more than 300 soldiers, as guards for the arms and ammunition. Ormond had feared that insisting on making greater demands on Spanish military resources ran the risk of annoying the Cardinal, who may then have withdrawn support for the expedition to Scotland altogether.[16] However, counter arguments among the council prevailed: that news of Ormond would take longer to reach isolated Lewis; that the onset of adverse weather would delay the expedition reaching the mainland; and that the arrival of British warships would certainly prevent it from doing so. Seaforth therefore reluctantly agreed to shift to mainland Scotland, to Kintail in Ross-Shire.

Kintail was MacKenzie territory and the land of Clan MacRae. In 1750 the MacRaes were still regarded by the British government as 'by far the most fierce, warlike and strongest men under Seaforth'. In the vicinity of Loch Alsh Kintail was also home to the Mathesons – reckoned to be 'next to the Kintail men in statute and valour'. In 1715 both septs had fought alongside the MacKenzies at Sheriffmuir.[17]

Orders were given to make ready to sail from Stornoway, and local pilots hired and brought aboard. These experienced native seafarers would guide the Spanish crews in the unfamiliar Hebridean waters. On 4 April the flotilla set out for the mainland. However, adverse weather forced the frigates to seek shelter in Loch Gairloch, well to the north of Kintail.[18] Going ashore, the Jacobites heard from the locals about a rumour the Spanish had landed in England.[19] This encouraged Tullibardine, writing aboard the frigate *Fidela* at anchor in Loch Gairloch on 6 April, to pen dispatches to supporters, including followers on his family estates around Blair Atholl in Perthshire, warning them to prepare for a rising. Notwithstanding the encouraging bellicose introductory tone, that the Jacobites had arrived 'aboard the Spanish ships that are come here with some troops, arms and ammunition and money, which is sent for enabling the king's good subjects to appear immediately in his majesty's and their country's service', Tullibardine's instructions were typically circumspect and ambiguous:

---

16 Keith, *Fragment of a Memoir*, p. 47; Oliphant, 'Distinct Abridgment', *Jacobite Lairds of Gask*, p. 454.
17 Lang, *Highlands of Scotland*, pp. 31–2.
18 Contemporary sources appear silent in regard to whether the French bark had already sailed for home or now did so.
19 Oliphant, *Jacobite Lairds of Gask*, p. 454.

> To be ready to rise against any part of his majesty's army come to these parts, or as
> that shall otherwise be required by me, who leaves it to your prudence, being on the
> spot, to rise sooner in   case you cannot else keep yourselves from being taken
> up, or other ways as you shall find it most conducing to the service.[20]

Glendaruel was put ashore and went inland to circulate the dispatches. These included hopeful letters to supporters from the Duke of Ormond, entrusted to Marischal when leaving Spain. That intended for Donald MacDonald of Benbecula, cousin of Clanranald, for example, ran:

> My Lord Marischal comes to you with arms and ammunition and I am waiting for
> a fair wind to embark with a body of Spanish troops. I know the zeal that you and
> your family have shown for the king's interest, and I hope you will help my Lord
> Marischal in making a diversion to employ some of the enemy's forces, when I am
> in England. The king will be in this embarkation or will follow as soon as possible.[21]

Later on 6 April Tullibardine ordered the frigates to sail for Kintail. This was contrary to the advice of the local pilots, who reckoned the weather unfavourable. Storm-force conditions developed overnight as predicted, so on the morning of the 7th they made for Stornoway. James Keith took a jaundiced view of Tullibardine's leadership when recollecting the episode:

> Our chief, being impatient, ordered the signal to be given to way anchor, 'tho [*sic*]
> our pilots declared that the wind was still contrary to the port we intended, which
> was not above ten leagues from thence. We soon found that they were in the right,
> for we were not a league out of the bay when we could neither continue the course
> we intended nor gain the harbour out of which we had come; and it blowing very
> fresh we were forced once more to bear away for the Isle of Lewis.[22]

Continued bad weather detained them at Stornoway until the 11th, when setting out the ships again made it only as far as Loch Gairloch. No headway could be made next day, when they were driven towards Lewis. However, a favourable shift in the winds on 13 April finally allowed the expedition that evening to make landfall off Kintail, when both frigates anchored at the eastern end of Loch Alsh.

Kintail has been said to be have gained its name from the Gaelic Chean-dha-hall, 'the head of two salt water bays'.[23] The district is indeed partly bounded by two sea lochs, Loch Long to the north and Loch Duich to the east. Situated at the confluence of both lochs with Loch Alsh is the rocky tidal islet of Eilean Donan. Here offshore stands Castle Donan, an originally 13th century stone-built stronghold of the MacKenzies and MacRaes. While by 1719 the medieval fortress was largely derelict and roofless, its walls remained sound and defensible. A prominent landmark, Castle Donan would

---

20 Atholl, *Chronicles*, vol. 2, pp. 277–8.
21 Dickson, *Jacobite Attempt*, pp. 70–1.
22 Keith, *Fragment of a Memoir*, p. 48.
23 J. Sinclair (ed.), *The Statistical Account of Scotland*, 21 vols. (1791–1799), vol. 6, p. 242.

serve the Jacobites as a rallying point and later as a depot. Eilean Donan and the adjacent shoreline, then, 'was thought the fittest place for debarkation'.[24]

Establishing the Beachhead

Next day, Campbell of Glendaruel arrived at Eilean Donan accompanied by a notable Jacobite (unnamed in the sources), said to be 'hearty and very ready for the service the minute there came any certainty of the landing, and told that was the advice came from the king's friends both in Scotland and England'.[25] In preparation the expedition deployed beyond the landing place, camping further afield and establishing separate magazines. This allowed provisions to be gathered and accommodation found among the scattered coastal communities, and positioned the force to move inland with the expected reinforcements of clansmen.

Government sources reckoned the main Jacobite camp lay about two miles (3.2 km) from Eilean Donan; so too near to be have been in the area of the present settlement at Dornie, within half a mile north of the castle. The Jacobites therefore probably camped at Bundalloch, two miles north-east of Castle Donan on the southerly shore of Loch Long.[26] Here the River Glennan provided fresh water (the lochs were or course of sea water). They would also occupy Glen Elchaig, leading from the head of Loch Long five miles (8 km) or so from Eilean Donan. Here agricultural land in the valley of the River Elchaig made a suitable camping ground. The government official Edmund Burt defined a Highland glen as 'a little spot of corn country, by the sides of some small river or rivulet, […] bounded by hills'.[27] About six miles

32. The castle at Eilean Donan on the shore of Loch Alsh. The Jacobite expeditionary force landed here in April 1719. Note the islet's tidal situation. (Reproduced courtesy of eileandonancastle.com)

---

24 Quotation from Oliphant, 'Distinct Abridgment', *Jacobite Lairds of Gask*, p. 455.

25 *Ibid.*

26 A settlement at Bundalloch is shown on the area map from William Roy's Military Survey of Scotland of 1747–1755, known as the 'Great Map'. See the National Library of Scotland's online digitised collection of 18th century military maps.

27 Jamieson, *Letters from a Gentleman*, vol. 1, p. 290.

(9.6 km) south of Eilean Donan, at the head of Loch Duich the Jacobites also occupied an area then known as the Crow of Kintail. This was Strath Croe (near present Morvich), where the valley of the River Croe as it broadens towards Loch Duich provided another well-watered camping area. 'A strath is a flat space of arable land', continued Burt on Highland topography, 'lying along the side or sides of some capital river, between the water and the hills; and keeps its name till the river comes to be confined to a narrow space, by stony moors, rocks, or windings among the mountains'.[28]

While the Jacobites kept the arms and some munitions at the Bundalloch camp, 'the great quantity of ammunition was lodged in a country house near the Crow of Kintail'.[29] This was a substantial stone-built building, a significant farmstead, or a gentleman's house, situated five miles (8 km) or so south-east of Eilean Donan near the shore of Loch Duich (in the vicinity of the present dispersed settlement at Inverinate).[30] Both magazines were intended as temporary distribution points, from where once the rising was underway the expected reinforcements of clansmen would be equipped. Shifting the supplies to both sites took considerable time and effort, and it was not until 'the 28th [April] before the arms and everything else could be got ashore, for want of boats and other conveniences'.[31]

On 8 May an informant (or Jacobite deserter) reported to the garrison at Inverness, how the expeditionary force had dispersed in detachments of about 50 men: 'lodged in houses, and huts built by themselves within two miles of the place where they landed'. A week later, a government loyalist described how the Jacobites 'kept close sentries at a distance of five or six miles [from Eilean Donan], the reason for which I conjecture to be that their number might not be known'.[32] These were outposts at Glen Elchaig and near Strath Crow. Another report mentioned 'they have an out-guard about 12 miles distant from their quarters'.[33] This accords with the approximately 13 miles (21 km) along present roads from Eilean Donan to Glenshiel itself. A picquet posted there could observe the drove-way leading through the pass. This track was both a way of easterly communication for the expedition and a potential route of advance for enemy forces approaching from Fort William and from Inverness.

Dispersal to outposts and by detachments was a stratagem concealing the size of the Jacobite force. A correspondent writing from Inverness in mid-May advised the recipient, a government loyalist: 'What I wrote of the numbers of those people I had from such as none would distrust, and I do assure you that whatever numbers are given less is industriously done to conceal their strength'.[34] Simon MacKenzie from Inverness spent three days at the Jacobite camp. When he was later 'taken up, searched, [and] examined'

---

28 *Ibid.*

29 Oliphant, 'Distinct Abridgment', *Jacobite Lairds of Gask*, p. 458.

30 According to Dickson, in *Jacobite Attempt*, xlvii, quoting local tradition, the building stood near the small fresh water lake Loch nan Corr at the head of Strath Croe.

31 Oliphant, 'Distinct Abridgment', *Jacobite Lairds of Gask*, p. 455.

32 *The London Gazette*, 16–19 May 1719; Atholl, *Chronicles*, vol. 2, p. 282.

33 *The Weekly Packet*, 16–23 May 1719.

34 D. Warrand (ed.), *More Culloden Papers* (1925), p. 196.

by the Inverness garrison (whether as a spy or deserter remains uncertain), MacKenzie explained that 'the enemy […] gave themselves out to be 1,500 but he never saw them together, nor exercise their arms'.[35]

This raises the question of the size of the Jacobite expedition. As already explained here, it included about 320 Spanish military personnel. Servants and followers had also accompanied the leading Jacobites. A number of supernumerary officers – professional mercenary soldiers of Scots or Irish extraction and Jacobite persuasion – had also joined the expedition. Government intelligence reports are again useful in drawing a conclusion about likely numbers. Simon MacKenzie testified that as well as the notable Scots Jacobites, there were 'several other British gentlemen, whom he did not know'. According to another version of his story in the London press, there were 'about 60 Scotch and Irish gentlemen and supernumerary officers, and that their whole number does not exceed 400'.[36] 'The best intelligence I have been capable of collecting since my arrival here', reported Lieutenant-Colonel John Reading, second in command of Colonel Jasper Clayton's Regiment of Foot, on 1 May from Inverness, where he had recently arrived to take charge, was that the enemy numbered 'about 300 men and 55 officers […] at this present encamped […] waiting to be joined by such of the clans as will have received arms'.[37] Reading's estimation supported dispatches sent from Inverness to London around 17 April, reporting the force landed in Kintail

33. Eilean Donan Castle, in May 1719 garrisoned by Spanish troops, then part demolished by the Royal Navy. It was rebuilt in its present form, in a flamboyant late Medieval style, by Lieutenant-Colonel John MacRae-Gilstrap from 1912 to 1932. In 1719 there was no bridge connecting the islet to the mainland.

35 *The Weekly Journal or British Gazetteer,* 30 May 1719.
36 *The Weekly Packet,* 16–23 May 1719.
37 Atholl, *Chronicles,* vol. 2, p. 281.

numbered about 400.[38] Thus it seems that the expeditionary force numbered few more than 400 men – of all ranks and of several nationalities.

For a while they had the support of shore parties from the Spanish frigates, and were joined by transient parties of Highlanders. A Royal Navy dispatch in later May reported 150 of Lord Seaforth's men were then with the Spanish troops, and until early June there were probably not many more clansmen than that with the expedition at any one time.[39] However, away from the beachhead groups of armed Highlanders would oppose landing parties from Royal Navy warships deployed to the region.

To return from these later dispositions to the situation of the expedition as it disembarked. Later on 17 April Seaforth and Marischal, who had both gone inland immediately after the landing, returned to the beachhead accompanied by several MacKenzie gentlemen. Seaforth may well have travelled as far as his family seat at Brahan Castle near Dingwall. It was reported in Edinburgh on 21 April 'that on the 16th instant, the said Seaforth was at Brahan, and that he had written circular letters to all his friends in that country to be ready with their best horses &c. [etc.] to join him, under pain of hanging without mercy'.[40] Given the distance from Dingwall to Kintail, it seems more likely Seaforth was in the area of Brahan on 15 April rather than the 16th. While Seaforth's reported intent to hang tenants unwilling to obey his call to arms may have been propagandist exaggeration (although Highland chiefs did, on occasion, threaten violence in summoning their people), the report suggests that although he remained reluctant to commit fully to a rising, Seaforth was preparing for that eventuality.

His return also encouraged a resurgence in brigandage. 'In the meantime', ran a report from Edinburgh dated 21 April, 'Seaforth's men began already to carry off cattle in the places where they came'. Bands of armed MacKenzies and their allies roved freely in their home territories and encroached on the neighbouring lands of pro-government Whig clans, including the Frasers to the west of Inverness, under their chief Simon Fraser, Lord Lovat. A report from Inverness dated 8 May mentioned that 'the late Earl of Seaforth has, with some armed men, possessed himself of the height of Lord Lovat's country'.[41]

Meeting with Seaforth, Tullibardine and others on 17 April, Marischal shaped the discussion into an impromptu council of war. He repeated the case for taking action – before Ormond's situation was known and before a general rising of the clans – using MacKenzie manpower alone. In a premeditated thinly veiled vote of no confidence in Tullibardine's leadership, Marischal and Campbell of Ormidale, who had fallen sick and so was unable to attend in person, had put in writing their opinion that:

> As he [Marischal] had Ormond's instructions, his majesty's forces ought to be assembled, it being for the king's service that they should be immediately employed

---

38 *The London Gazette*, 25–28 April 1719.

39 Captain Holland's dispatch written aboard HMS *Assistance* anchored in Loch Carron on 25 April, published in extract in London on 11 June in *The Daily Currant*.

40 Reported in London in *The Post Boy*, 25–28 April 1719.

41 Reported in *The Weekly Packet*, 16–23 May 1719.

in securing some post where not only the Highlanders, but the gentlemen of the low country might more securely join, or whatever other expedition is judged most for the service, *and that they were not to wait any news of the Duke of Ormond's landing* [author's emphasis], considering the distance.[42]

Tullibardine's faction, including Seaforth, who reportedly 'declared his mind was still the same as he had told in the Lewis, thinking it folly and distraction to stir without a landing in England', counter-argued; to the effect, that Ormond had not intended 'people should endeavour to force a rising at all hazards, on so small a foundation, especially since there was no directions how to behave on all events in case of any accident or disappointment as to the main design'.[43]

The meeting broke up in stalemate. However, with the arrival of the clan chiefs John Cameron of Lochiel, Ranald Macdonald of Clanranald, John Dubh Mackinnon, and Roderick Chisholm of Strathglass, a formal council of war was held on 20 April. Recovered from his illness, Brigadier Campbell of Ormidale argued for seizing Inverness. There were good reasons for doing so. Campbell of Glendaruel in his strategic recommendations made in autumn 1716, held the view that Inverness 'must be reduced and entirely secured before you march south, which will encourage all that country that are in the king's interest to join you, and wholly discourage the king's enemies'.[44] A surprise attack on Inverness under Marischal's leadership as Ormidale proposed probably had a good chance of success. It was then only thinly garrisoned, by four companies of Clayton's regiment, about 175 men, who were hastily putting the place into a state of defence. Furthermore, Ormidale argued, if Ormond's invasion was unsuccessful, because Inverness was a seaport the expedition could be evacuated to Spain. However, the council baulked at that course of action; as James Keith expressed it, 'the same demon who had inspired them with the design of staying in the Lewis hindered them from accepting this proposition'.[45]

Arguments for caution prevailed: that it would be difficult to raise clansmen of the attainted chiefs without declaring a general rising; that Inverness would not prove easy to take; that Clayton's regiment, reinforced by local militiamen, would be there in full strength by the time the Jacobites arrived; and that in street fighting the clansmen would struggle to overcome the garrison's defences and firepower. Argument and counter-argument continued into the evening until the council dispersed. This inertia was attributed by James Keith to have been a product of the guarded tone of Tullibardine's earlier circular dispatches; sent 'to most of their friends, acquainting them that it was the king's intentions that nobody should take arms till the Spanish troops were landed in England'.[46] That was pragmatic reason enough to disincline the chiefs from taking action until such news was certain.

---

42 Oliphant, 'Distinct Abridgment', *Jacobite Lairds of Gask*, pp. 455–6.
43 *Ibid.*, p. 456.
44 Daniell, *Calendar of Stuart Papers*, vol. 4, p. 82.
45 Keith, *Fragment of a Memoir*, p. 49.
46 *Ibid.*

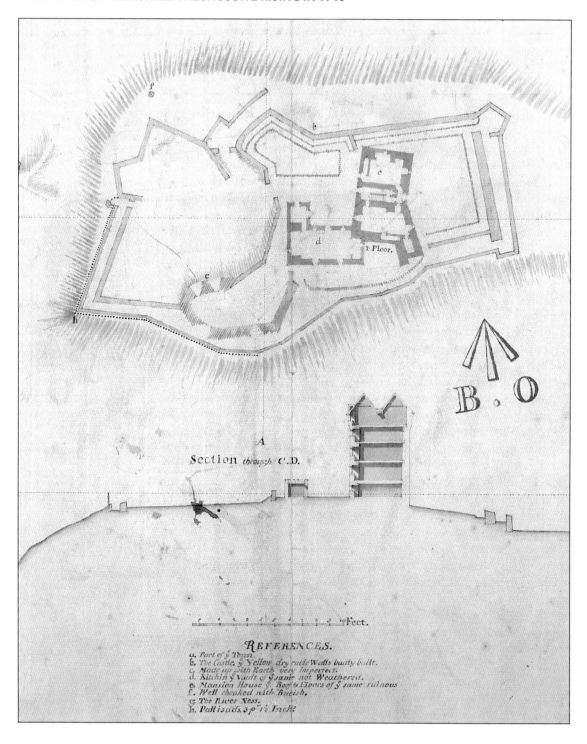

34. Detail of the Board of Ordnance survey plan of the castle at Inverness, completed later in 1719. The lower half of the plan depicts a section through the outer walled and earthwork defences and the tower house converted to a five-storey barrack block. (Reproduced by permission of the National Library of Scotland)

The Expedition is Marooned

The council, except for a disgruntled Earl Marischal, reconvened next day. 'All who had followings [i.e. the chiefs]' agreed that taking immediate action would be 'destructive to the service, and were entirely against a rising before it could be general'. There was, however, agreement that the Kintail beachhead should be held. When Clanranald and Lochiel departed with their followers they therefore took their allocation of arms and ammunition. It was also accepted that the Spanish warships were endangered. As James Keith recollected, 'they being no longer in safety where they were, for [the expedition] being already discovered, it was natural to believe that the government of England would immediately send ships to block them up, or to interrupt them in their passage home'.[47]

Keith related how his brother told Tullibardine of his decision to order the frigates to leave. Marischal had come to believe that Tullibardine had lost his nerve; that instead of waiting for news of Ormond, he would order the evacuation of the expedition. Marischal may have been right. 'We are in great pain how to behave without instructions in case there be not quickly a landing in England', Tullibardine wrote dejectedly at Castle Donan on 29 April, in a dispatch intended for James Francis Edward Stuart: 'Your grace will soon perceive our precarious condition'.[48] However, the final decision over the frigates seems to have been made by the senior Spanish officers, by the ships' captains and moreover by Lieutenant-Colonel Bolaño in command of the infantry. Just as the Highland chiefs were disappointed by how few Spanish troops there were, Bolaño had been led to believe they would join forces with as many as 10,000 well-armed clansmen: 'but finding very few, he kept the frigates there 10 days [it was in fact a fortnight] resolving to go off again, 'tho [sic] at last he was prevailed with to stay, and to let them sail'.[49] On 28 April Tullibardine was notified that the Spanish crews were prepared to leave. With Marischal's dispatches aboard, next day the frigates headed partway down Loch Alsh and anchored off the southern shore near the Sgeir na Caillich skerry to await suitable tidal and weather conditions. With Tullibardine's dispatches and a note giving his tacit consent for their withdrawal taken aboard, on 30 April both frigates headed for the open sea and for Spain.

Meanwhile, on the 28th Seaforth wrote warning Tullibardine of a rumour that an attack was being planned from Inverness against their positions about Loch Alsh. Tullibardine replied asking Seaforth to raise men, and wrote instructing Clanranald and Lochiel to do the same. On 1 May the Jacobites received news that Ormond had landed in England. However, their relief was short-lived. Three days later, one Mr Wallace, representing informed Jacobite opinion in Edinburgh, came to Kintail and told that 'the Spanish fleet was dispersed, and drove back by storms, advising by all means they should immediately re-embark the 300 men, and everybody get off as quickly as possible'. This demoralising news was reflected in a letter from another

---

47   Keith, *Fragment of a Memoir*, p. 50.
48   Dickson, *Jacobite Attempt,* p. 269.
49   Summary of the Spanish lieutenant's account, published in *The London Gazette,* 30 May–2 June 1719.

(unnamed) influential Jacobite – 'a person of consequence' – warning that 'it would [under]mine the king's friends and affairs if they pretended to make a stir as things stood'. Tullibardine responded by sending after Clanranald and Lochiel to meet at Castle Donan, so 'that joint measures might be taken how to behave most for the service under such a precarious situation'. Both chiefs were to leave orders for their clansmen to join them quickly when called upon.

Now the expedition was faced with defending its position in Kintail, it was decided to place much of the ammunition and gunpowder into Castle Donan. Upon closer inspection the buildings had been found suitable for use as a magazine; 'the old walls and vaults would be sufficient to keep it from any flying party by land, or attack by sea'. Supplies were hurriedly shifted to the castle and a Spanish company posted there in garrison under the command of Captain Peter Stapleton, an Irishman in the Spanish service.[50]

The munitions and guard were in place by 9 May, and that evening Clanranald and Lochiel returned. However, any discussions that may have then begun in a further council of war were clouded by disconcerting news that British warships had anchored in Loch Alsh.

---

50 Quotations from Oliphant, 'Distinct Abridgment', *Jacobite Lairds of Gask*, pp. 457–8.

7

The Royal Navy Intervenes

'Three English men-of-war came to anchor at Caliach's Stone'.

A Squadron to the Highlands

Since arriving in Lewis the Jacobites apprehensively had expected the intervention of the British Royal Navy, and the Spanish frigates left in anticipation of that threat. The return of Lochiel and Clanranald to the Jacobite camp on 9 May was overshadowed by the appearance of British warships in Loch Alsh. As later described, 'the same evening three English men-of-war came to anchor at Caliach's Stone'. This was the same deep-water anchorage off the Sgeir na Caillich skerry, five miles westward of Eilean Donan, from where the Spanish had sailed just nine days before.[1]

The arrival of His Majesty's Ships *Worcester*, *Enterprise* and *Flamborough* was due to Admiralty orders issued in London on 22 April. The latest intelligence received from Edinburgh was that the Earl of Seaforth with several hundred 'foreigners' had landed on the Isle of Lewis on 5 April, and that, as a result of further landings two days later, the Jacobites in arms were reckoned to number 2,000 men. Acting on that information, the Admiralty sent instructions to Sir John Norris, at sea with the fleet covering the Western Approaches, to detach five warships 'to cruise between the Western Isles of Scotland'. This squadron was to seek out and destroy enemy vessels, hamper operations by Jacobite land forces, and generally act to suppress rebellious activity in the region. Orders were also despatched to a sixth warship, HMS *Success*. Then moored at Portsmouth, the sixth-rate was to make her course independently to join the squadron in the Hebrides.[2]

On 22 April, the Admiralty issued further orders, for HMS *Bideford*, another sixth-rate, to sail from the Downs for Inverness.[3] Once arrived off Inverness *Bideford* was to first support the isolated garrison there, then cruise to prevent aid for the Jacobites being landed in north-east Scotland.

---

1   Oliphant, 'Distinct Abridgment', *Jacobite Lairds of Gask*, p. 458.
2   TNA, ADM 2/49, folios 633–6.
3   The Downs was the Royal Navy's traditional anchorage in the English Channel, off Deal on the coast of Kent.

To augment *Bideford*, on the 23rd the Admiralty gave instructions for HMS *Gosport*, a 40-gun fifth-rate, then also anchored in the Downs, to make ready to sail northward. Her orders were to patrol the North Sea before joining *Bideford* searching for arms runners.[4]

The five warships of the squadron bound for the Western Isles already with the combined fleet of Admirals Berkeley and Norris were as follows: the three 50-gun two-decker fourth-rates *Assistance, Worcester* and *Dartmouth*, commanded respectively by Captains Holland, Charles Boyle and Nicholas Eaton; the 40-gun two-decker fifth-rate *Enterprise*, under Captain Mungo Herdman; and the 20-gun sixth-rate *Lively* – which in the event was replaced by Captain John Hildesley's *Flamborough*, a similarly-armed sixth-rate. On 7 March the Admiralty had sent Hildesley orders for *Flamborough* to sail with Norris's squadron from Spithead, while orders instructing *Worcester* to put to sea from Plymouth were issued on 3 April. Both commander and crew were new to the recently refitted *Worcester*. Captain Boyle's orders required him to transfer his officers and men to her from their previous ship, the now unseaworthy fourth rate *Centurion*, which was to be decommissioned and put into reserve. In timely fashion, *Worcester* under her new complement joined Norris on 17 April. *Dartmouth*, then anchored in the Downs, was sent Admiralty orders on 2 April to join Admiral Berkeley 'at his cruising station' and had done so 12 days later. *Enterprise* and *Assistance* were also anchored in the Downs when orders to sail were despatched from London on 14 April. They reached Norris's squadron sailing off Lizard Point in south Cornwall on 22 and 27 April respectively.

Apart from major fortresses, a ship of the line was by far the most expensive, technologically complex and potent weapons system of the early 18th century. The squadron's three fourth-rates were powerfully armed. The firepower of one of these 50-gun warships alone was comparable to the artillery train of a contemporary field army. At the battle of Blenheim in 1704, for example, Marlborough's 52,000-strong Allied army had 60 cannon, while at Almanza in 1707 30 field guns had been deployed in support of Galway's Allied army of 15,000 men.[5]

Assistance, Worcester and *Dartmouth*, launched (in *Worcester*'s case as a rebuild) respectively in 1713, 1714 and 1716, had a regulation complement of 280 officers and crew. As the main battery, these warships carried on the gun deck 22 cannon firing as standard ammunition solid cast-iron ball, or round shot, 18 pounds in weight. The secondary 22-gun battery on the upper deck fired nine-pound shot. In addition, four 6-pdr guns were mounted on the quarterdeck, and two more on the forecastle as forward firing 'bow chasers'. Launched in 1709 and having a complement of 190, HMS *Enterprise* as a fifth-rate was a cruiser rather than a line of battle ship. As such, she was more suited to long-range patrolling and the attack and defence of merchant shipping. Her main armament was the twenty 12-pdrs on the gun deck, with a secondary battery of twenty 6-pdrs carried on the upper deck. Launched in

---

4   TNA, ADM 2/49, folios 636–7.
5   Chandler, *Art of Warfare*, p. 150.

35. Naïve contemporary depiction of a mid-18th century British 20-gun sixth-rate warship in North American waters. HMS *Flamborough* would have been of similar design and appearance. (New York Picture Library Digital Collection)

1712, *Flamborough* as a sixth-rate was a smaller type of cruiser, with a 115-man company. Her broadside of twenty 6-pdr guns was carried on the upper deck.[6]

These five warships, with *Success* arriving later, formed a squadron well balanced for its anticipated tasks: for the 'chase', or pursuit, and engagement of enemy warships at sea, and for inshore operations, involving the bombardment of coastal positions and landing armed parties ashore. The Jacobite James Keith, likely an eyewitness to the arrival of *Worcester*, *Enterprise* and *Flamborough* in Loch Alsh, reckoned that the Spanish frigates had been lucky to sail before they came: 'And indeed just in time, for not a week after their departure arrived three English men-of-war, most superior to ours in force and equipage'.[7]

The squadron parted with the fleet under Admiral Norris's command on 28 April (with no sighting of the Spanish, Admiral Lord Berkeley had left Norris in charge and returned to England. He had landed at Dover on the 15th).[8] The captains of *Worcester*, *Dartmouth* and *Assistance* also sailed

6 D. Lyon, *The Sailing Navy List: All the Ships of the Royal Navy, Built, Purchased and Captured, 1688–1860* (1993), pp. 35–7; J. J. Colledge, *Ships of the Royal Navy: The Complete Record of All Fighting Ships of the Royal Navy* (2010, rev. edn.), p. 618.

7 Keith, *Fragment of a Memoir*, p. 50.

8 The reconstruction of the squadron's operations in this and the following chapter is based on the following Admiralty records: NMM, Admiralty Records, Lieutenants' Logs: ADM/L/A/201,

under Norris's additional orders. Once operations in Scottish waters were satisfactorily concluded they were to proceed to Denmark. In Copenhagen harbour they would rendezvous with Norris's squadron bound for the Baltic station that summer, to take part in a politico-military show of force that had become an annual exercise for the Royal Navy.[9]

Following Admiralty orders, the squadron divided to converge on the Hebrides by separate sea-lanes, eastward and westward of Ireland. *Dartmouth*, *Enterprise* and *Flamborough* together charted a northerly course through St. George's Channel and the Irish Sea, while *Worcester* and *Assistance* maintained company sailing off Ireland's Atlantic seaboard. This division of forces might allow interception of any Spanish ships that had slipped past Norris's cruisers. Accordingly, on 29 April *Worcester* and *Assistance* were sailing north-westward off Cape Clear in southern Ireland, while during the 30th *Dartmouth*, *Enterprise* and *Flamborough* passed Bardsey Island off the north-west coast of Wales.

Making good headway the squadron had made landfall off the Western Isles by 5 May, when off South Harris *Enterprise* closed with and boarded a trading brig bound from Stornoway for Dublin.[10] Her crew provided Captain Herdman with 'intelligence that Lord Seaforth had been at Stornoway but went away with two Spanish ships of war to the main part of Scotland'.[11] Meanwhile, *Assistance*, *Flamborough* and *Dartmouth* had reached Stornoway. Like the Spanish frigates before them, the Royal Navy hired local pilots under whose guidance the warships would more safely operate inshore. The first lieutenants of *Dartmouth* and *Assistance* went ashore, and to some local worthies delivered and proclaimed letters instructing the islanders to act loyally in support of King George I against the rebels.

By late evening on 7 May the squadron had regrouped at a pre-arranged rendezvous eastward of the Isle of Barra. Captain Boyle of *Worcester* as senior captain now assumed command of the squadron as commodore. This was the customary rank for an officer in command of a detached squadron, placing him above a captain but below a rear admiral. Aboard *Assistance* Boyle convened a council of war of his fellow officers. Based on their accrued intelligence, indicating that the Jacobites were on the mainland in Kintail, and that any ships remaining in support would be sheltering in the sea lochs along that coast, the council agreed a course of action involving a pincer movement

---

HMS *Assistance*, 1709–1720; ADM/L/D/14, HMS *Dartmouth*, 1717–1721; HMS *Enterprise*, 1709–1724; ADM/L/E/112A, HMS *Enterprise*, 1718–1720; ADM/L/F/104, HMS Flamborough, 1709–1740; ADM/L/F/105, HMS *Fox* and HMS *Flamborough*, 1716–1721; ADM/L/W/169, HMS *Worcester*, 1716–1741; ADM/L/W/170, H.M.S. *Worcester*, 1719–1720; TNA, Admiralty Records, Captains' Logs: ADM 51/229, including HMS *Dartmouth*, 1719–1720; ADM 51/312, including HMS *Enterprise*, 1719–1720; ADM 51/357, including HMS *Flamborough*, 1716–1720; ADM 51/938, including HMS *Success*, 1717–1723; ADM 51/1057, including HMS *Worcester*, 1719–1720; TNA, Admiralty Records, Sailing Masters' Logs: ADM 52/126, HMS *Assistance*, 1719–1720; ADM 52/144, HMS *Dartmouth*, 1719–1720; ADM 52/158, HMS *Enterprise*, 1719–1720; ADM 52/317, HMS *Worcester*, 1719–1720.

9   On 14 April the Admiralty sent instructions to Norris to prepare the squadron he was to lead into the Baltic Sea that summer: TNA, SP43/61, Items 33, 34.

10   A brig (brigantine) was a twin masted sailing vessel, in this case a small merchantman.

11   NMM, ADM 51/312, no folio.

pivoting on the Isle of Skye; that Boyle 'should proceed with the *Worcester*, *Enterprise* and *Flamborough* south about Skye, while the *Assistance* and *Dartmouth* went north about'.[12] The squadron separated next day. *Worcester*, *Enterprise* and *Flamborough* entered the southerly Cuillin Sound, charting a course northward of the islands of Canna and Rhum, while *Assistance* and *Dartmouth* headed north-easterly, navigating the channel between the Outer Hebrides and the west coast of Skye known as the Little Minch.

Assistance and *Dartmouth* headed for Loch Gairloch, as the Spanish frigates had five weeks previously. At anchor there on Saturday 9 May both warships launched boats carrying armed parties of seamen to gather intelligence. Second-Lieutenant Ralph Archbould commanded one of *Assistance*'s boats on a sailing patrol that stayed out overnight. With the return of Archbould's boat to the ship, next morning First-Lieutenant Fellows led a party ashore. Fellows made contact with the locals, and was able to question 'a chief man of a village and another, but they gave us a very imperfect account of the enemy'.[13] But *Dartmouth*'s first-lieutenant had more success gaining intelligence. On the afternoon of the 10th he 'went a cruising in our longboat with 20 armed men'. Landing on the Island of Raasay he was told the Spanish frigates were to the south in Loch Carron, and that the enemy in Kintail were reckoned to number 3,000 men. Acting on this information both warships set sail from Loch Gairloch southward, but like the Spanish frigates taking the same course in early April were forced by bad weather to stand in to Stornoway. The officers of the squadron recorded in their logs at this time the very 'uncertain' state of the weather, with frequent strong gales bringing rain and sleet.

Improving weather conditions over the next day or so allowed *Assistance* and *Dartmouth* to make landfall off Kintail in Loch Kishorn, where they rode at anchor on the 14th. Early next morning cruising patrols put to sea in the ships' boats. *Assistance*'s longboat in the joint charge of two midshipmen encountered some of Lord Seaforth's clansmen. Landing 'to observe the enemy' on the shore of an unnamed loch (this may have been Loch Reraig, a lesser inlet to the south of Loch Kishorn), the shore party was surprised to be 'saluted [fired upon] two or three times by the enemy's musketry'.[14] A short skirmish ensued, during which as the seamen hastily retreated to the longboat one of the midshipmen was captured by pursuing Highlanders (although he seems soon after to have made his escape, and was picked up and returned to ship some days later).

Second-Lieutenant Archbould in *Assistance*'s pinnace in company with one of *Dartmouth*'s boats had meanwhile ventured further southward. Passing through the narrows at Kyle Akin into Loch Alsh they made contact with the rest of the squadron. Archbould returned to *Assistance* on the morning of the 16th. He noted in his log the encouraging news: 'they had been received by *Worcester*, and [with] the *Enterprise* and *Flamborough* had last Sunday battered

---

12   Boyle's dispatch to the Admiralty dated 12 May, published in the newspaper *The Post Man and The Historical Account*, edition for 28–30 May 1719.

13   NMM, ADM/L/A/201, no folio

14   *Ibid.*

36. View from the shore near Bernera of the Kyle Rhea narrows separating the Isle of Skye (background hills) from the Scottish mainland. On 9 May 1719 HM Ships *Worcester*, *Enterprise* and *Flamborough* navigated this channel heading northward for Loch Alsh.

a castle possessed by Spaniards, and after spending about 200 shot in battery they landed their men and took it with little or no resistance'.[15] Castle Donan had been taken, and with it the Jacobites' main magazine.

The Fall of Castle Donan

Commodore Boyle later reported how after the squadron had divided on 8 May, he had gained 'further information'; that a 'regiment of Spaniards lay encamped opposite to the castle of Donan, and had garrisoned that place with a captain, lieutenant and 48 men'. Boyle probably received this intelligence on the evening of 9 May, after *Worcester*, *Enterprise* and *Flamborough*, having sailed through the Sound of Sleat separating south-easterly Skye from the mainland, towed and guided by their boats had carefully navigated the Kyle Rhea narrows and around seven in the evening come to anchor in Loch Alsh off Sgeir na Caillich. Soon afterwards *Worcester*'s second-lieutenant, George Weston, put a boat ashore and brought back two men for questioning. Whether they were locals or Jacobite deserters remains unclear, but they told Boyle about the enemy dispositions.

Next morning, Sunday 10 May, the warships were underway at the eastern end of Loch Alsh in choppy waters unsettled by frequent squalls of rain. Soundings were taken to gauge the uncertain depth of the sea loch and to avoid the shallows off Eilean Tioram that narrowed the approach to Eilean Donan. At about eight o'clock, with *Worcester* anchored some way off the islet, Commodore Boyle sent Lieutenant Weston in a boat under a flag of truce to demand the castle's surrender. However, a single shot or else a scattered volley (eyewitness accounts differ) of musketry from Captain Stapleton's garrison caused Weston's party hurriedly to row back to *Worcester* – without, as Captain Hildesley of *Flamborough* put it, the enemy 'admitting to any speech'.[16] Weston had, however, had time to notice that Castle Donan appeared to be defended by artillery. In a clever attempt to make a deceptive show of force, the garrison had had tree trunks shaped to resemble the muzzles of four cannon positioned protruding from embrasures in the walls facing the loch. This apparent enemy battery was a serious concern for the

---

15 *Ibid.*
16 TNA, ADM 51/357, no folio.

warships attacking the castle. Whereas guns positioned on land could be exactly aimed, the elevation of those aboard a ship rose and fell with the swell of the sea with considerably reduced accuracy.

Worcester signalled *Enterprise* and *Flamborough* to manoeuvre closer in, and by about nine o'clock anchored within close range of Castle Donan all three opened fire. The warships together bombarded the castle for about an hour and a half, until strengthening gales caused *Flamborough* to drop out of line to adjust her position. *Worcester* and *Enterprise* maintained regular broadsides till about eleven-thirty, and after noon sporadic fire by three or four guns on each ship every five minutes or so. Without artillery in fact, Captain Stapleton and his men could not retaliate; the sailing master of *Worcester* noted that 'we saw the Spanish soldiers running to and fro in the said castle. They have not fired any great or small shot at us'.[17] The warships ceased firing at about one o'clock in the afternoon.

Before noon, *Worcester* and *Enterprise* had launched boats to pick up a Spanish deserter seen waving from the shore. The soldier gave Commodore Boyle the impression that his comrades occupying the castle lacked the will to fight and might easily capitulate. Furthermore, the Spaniard disclosed the position of the magazine sited near the Crow of Kintail. Boyle sent orders for Captain Hildesley to take action against it. Accordingly, at about one o'clock *Flamborough* headed south-easterly up Loch Duich (the 'Black Lake' as it was known to the seamen). By mid afternoon *Flamborough* was anchored off shore of the building housing the magazine. Her crew quickly cleared the deck for action and opened fire. Unable to reply to *Flamborough*'s broadsides and unwilling to oppose a landing party, the 30-man Spanish detachment guarding the magazine made ready to withdraw. However, to prevent the munitions falling into enemy hands, before abandoning the position they set fuses to the gunpowder store. The resultant explosion demolishing the storehouse was, according to Hildesley, 'such a blast as threw great stones to a good distance and laid all the village flat'.[18] As well as damaging outbuildings, the blast wrecked several barrels of musket shot, flinging lead bullets a considerable distance, destroyed all the gunpowder (as many as 80 barrels,

37. 18-pdr and 12-pdr cast iron round shot, fired during the Royal Navy bombardment of Eilean Donan Castle on 10 May 1719. Found during the early 20th-century rebuilding of the castle. (Reproduced courtesy of eileandonancastle. com)

---

17 TNA, ADM 52/317, no folio.
18 Hildesley reported the action in person to Lord Carpenter in Edinburgh later in May, when *Flamborough* was anchored at Leith: Atholl, *Chronicles*, vol. 2, p. 285.

38. Late 19th century photograph showing the ruinous state of Eilean Donan Castle before MacRae-Gilstrap's 1912–32 rebuilding. (Reproduced courtesy of eileandonancastle.com)

or so the sailors were later told), and started a fire that consumed all the flour and oatmeal the Jacobites had gathered there as provisions.[19]

Meanwhile, although the walls of Castle Donan had so far largely withstood the Royal Navy's bombardment, Captain Stapleton by now distrusted his beleaguered garrison, particularly his defeatist lieutenant who wanted to surrender. Stapleton therefore sent a Highlander to deliver to LieutenantColonel Bolaño the message that he could no longer depend on his company to hold out. The messenger found the Jacobite camp in disarray. Two men of Clan Fraser, who claimed to have joined the Jacobites in order to spy for Lord Lovat, but in fact may have been deserters, were eyewitnesses to this. When questioned at Inverness on 14 May, they described having been arrested for spying and held under threat of execution, until the Jacobites were put in 'great confusion' by the action of the British warships. 'Finding the enemy all in consternation upon what had happened', both men had seized the opportunity to make their escape.[20]

The Jacobites decided to send Bolaño to Eilean Donan with reinforcements. If he found the castle untenable, then the magazine was to be detonated – in the desperate hope that debris hurled by the blast would damage the men-of-war. The Jacobites were mindful that the ships' guns commanded the shoreline, and that without boats reinforcements could not reach the castle until low tide. That would be at around 10 o'clock that evening, but by then the castle would have fallen.[21]

---

19 Dickson, in *Jacobite Attempt* xlvii, mentioned that bullets fused together by the force of the explosion had been found in the locality.
20 *The Weekly Journal or British Gazetteer*, 'reporting letters from Inverness', 30 May 1719.
21 Oliphant, 'Distinct Abridgment', *Jacobite Lairds of Gask*, p. 458.

About three o'clock in the afternoon *Worcester* and *Enterprise* recommenced the bombardment. *Worcester*'s crew had executed a standard drill to improve the accuracy of her gunnery. They attached a 'spring' to the main anchor, a means of handling a stationary man-of-war to bring guns to bear on the enemy. A looping hawser was run via the capstan to the aft of the ship, and using a ship's boat attached to the main anchor cable. Turning the capstan allowed the ship to pivot, or spring, by the bow – enabling either broadside to be angled to the required line of fire.

At eight o'clock in the evening both warships fired a final couple of broadsides, under cover of which Commodore Boyle's orders to storm the castle were put into effect. A landing party, numbering 40 or so sailors in several boats, rowed for the islet under the command of second-lieutenants Weston of *Worcester* and Wheatley of *Enterprise*. Scrambling ashore, the sailors were at first checked at the outer entrance to the castle. This was an un-gated gap in the curtain wall about seven feet above ground entered via a wooden stairway, which the defenders had removed. The attackers had to skirt the walls to seek another way in; as Weston put it, 'we were obliged to climb up the walls on the contrary side, when we took it'.[22] In a fleeting skirmish, in which no one was killed or seriously wounded, as the seamen overran the castle the Spanish soldiers returned only a scattered fire in token resistance before surrendering. Boyle seconded Captain Herdman to take command of Castle Donan. Coming ashore he accepted Captain Stapleton's unconditional capitulation of the garrison. Stapleton along with his lieutenant, a sergeant, 39 rank and file and a lone Highlander became prisoners of war.

The captives went aboard *Worcester*, and the morning of 11 May found her crew and that of *Enterprise* busy ferrying the captured munitions to the men-of-war. All told 343 barrels of gunpowder and 52 barrels of musket ball were accounted for, along with provisions. Meanwhile, shore parties went to work prising stones from the walls to form niches for gunpowder mines to render Castle Donan indefensible. Commodore Boyle, seeing no purpose in occupying the place (and the squadron had no marines to form a garrison), and mindful that three ships of the squadron, including his own, were under orders to join the Baltic fleet, had decided to deny the castle to the enemy: 'Thinking it proper (as the [Jacobite] camp lay within two miles) to blow the place up'. In the late afternoon, 16 barrels of gunpowder were returned to the castle because the amount of explosive required had been underestimated. At about nine o'clock in the evening the mines were detonated, bringing down the westerly buildings. Demolishing Castle Donan would, however, require more effort. Early next morning another 11 barrels of gunpowder were landed from *Worcester*, and at nine o'clock mines exploded under the outer walls. Inspection revealed one of the charges had failed to ignite, and this too was finally blown about four that Tuesday afternoon. The result of these blasts was to leave Castle Donan, as Captain Herdman noted with satisfaction in his log that day, 'laid all in ruins'. It would remain so for 200 years.

---

22 NMM, ADM/L/W/169, no folio.

39. Early photograph of Eilean Donan taken from the north-east. The originally 13th century castle was left ruinous and abandoned after Royal Navy demolition in May 1719. (Reproduced courtesy of eileandonancastle.com)

The same afternoon landing parties burnt along the shore of Loch Duich several barns and that had been used by the enemy. A number of boats were also destroyed, an action the squadron repeated elsewhere over the next couple of weeks in order to hamper the Jacobites moving men or supplies inshore, and to prevent their retreat to Skye or further Hebridean islands. While the Jacobites lacked means to attack the warships, the Royal Navy did not have things entirely its own way. On Wednesday 13 May a sailor was severely wounded when Highlanders fired upon a shore party from *Worcester* collecting drinking water. That day, however, lookouts aloft the ships' rigging watched the Jacobite main force withdraw inland; as *Worcester*'s sailing master noted in his log, 'This morning we saw the rebel army march to the eastward through a large valley.'

Deterioration in the weather over the next few days prevented further operations, while the warships rode out gales in Loch Alsh. Conditions had improved by the afternoon of May 21, when Second-Lieutenant Weston of *Worcester* accompanied by the ship's gunner landed on the Skye shore of the Klyle Akin narrows at the inlet of Kyleakin. Here on a headland stood Castle Maol. The Jacobites had not occupied this long-abandoned medieval stronghold of Clan MacKinnon, and it was not in a defensible state. Nonetheless, Commodore Boyle had it demolished as a precautionary measure and further show of force. Castle Maol was blown up somewhat ceremoniously on the morning of 22 May, within view of the crews of *Worcester* and *Enterprise*. As Weston recorded in his log:

I and out gunner went to the Castle of Kyle […] to view it and make lodgements in the walls to blow it up. At one this morning ten barrels of powder [were] ashore, and by seven this morning had our mines ready to spring when our ship passed through the channel of Skye loch. By eight of the clock blew up the castle, the *Enterprise* [following] behind.[23]

40. The fragmentary remains of Castle Maol, the MacKinnon's 15th-century stronghold at Kyleakin, Isle of Skye. Royal Navy demolition in May 1719 left only the north and south walls of the originally three-storey rectangular tower standing to any height.

Worcester sailed on through the Kyle Akin narrows into the Inner Minch. She headed for Stornoway, where it was said Jacobite military supplies had been recently landed. *Enterprise* remained on station at the mouth of Loch Alsh, at an anchorage known to her crew as 'Kalliock Road' – in the vicinity of the present harbour at Kyle of Lochalsh – tasked with preventing the enemy withdrawing to Skye. This redeployment brought the first period of the Royal Navy's intervention against the Jacobite expedition to a successful close. The squadron had seized or destroyed the bulk of the enemy's munitions and reserve food supplies; taken and rendered indefensible their base; disrupted their communications; and, moreover, had forced their retreat inland.

HMS *Flamborough* had meanwhile re-joined *Worcester* and *Enterprise* at anchor off Eilean Donan on 11 May. Commodore Boyle tasked Captain Hildesley with transporting the Spanish prisoners and carrying dispatches reporting the squadron's operations to Edinburgh. Accordingly, on the 13th the prisoners were transferred to *Flamborough,* apart from Captain Stapleton and the Spanish deserter who remained aboard *Worcester*. On the 16th *Flamborough* sailed through the Kyle Rhea narrows, setting a southerly course about Skye heading to circumnavigate the north of Scotland. The fierce gales on the 19th caused the upper section of *Flamborough*'s mainmast to split, when one topman (a crewman skilled in working aloft) fell and was

---

23 NMM, ADM/L/W/169, no folio.

lost overboard and another badly injured falling to the deck. The winds moderated on the 20th, allowing the damaged top yards and rigging to be taken down and the ship's carpenters to cut the splintered mast down to a manageable stump. The voyage thereafter was uneventful. On 24 May *Flamborough* anchored in Leith Roads within sight of Edinburgh Castle, and next day dropped further up the Firth of Forth to the anchorage at Queensferry north-west of the Scottish capital.

The Spanish prisoners of war were landed at daybreak on the 28th, put under the guard of a detachment of Dutch infantry from Colonel Sixmar's Regiment. After a lengthy march through the outskirts and city they were confined in Edinburgh Castle. Parading the Spaniards on this circuitous route was done so conspicuously to dishearten Jacobite sympathisers. The reported reason was that: 'there are divers persons in this town, enemies to his majesty's government, who have endeavoured to persuade others that there were no prisoners taken at Donan Castle'.[24] Meanwhile, from Queensferry between noon and one in the afternoon was heard the report of *Flamborough's* guns, fired in celebratory salvos to mark the birthday of King George I.

The Spanish lieutenant who had seen no purpose in fighting for Castle Donan was brought before the recently ennobled Lieutenant-General Lord Carpenter at his headquarters in Edinburgh Castle. When questioned, the subaltern reportedly spoke 'freely without any reserve', summarising what he saw as the hopeless situation of the Jacobite expedition: 'He judges they can have but little ammunition left, and that those which remain will endeavour to get into the isles in order to make their escape'.[25]

---

24 News from Edinburgh reported in *The London Gazette*, 2–6 June 1719.
25 News from Edinburgh reported in *The London Gazette*, 30 May–2 June 1719.

8

Countermeasures and Containment

'This is likely to be the only scene of action'.

The Jacobites Shift Position

The Spanish lieutenant pessimistically predicted the outcome of the naval action in Loch Alsh and Loch Duich during the second week in May would be the collapse of the Jacobite expedition and flight of its leaders. However, that was not the case. As a Highland laird mentioned in writing to the Duke of Atholl on 21 May:

> Your grace was wrongly informed by them who told that them [*sic*] noblemen dispersed in their party, contrary they keep together, but removed their quarters for convenience, the firing growing scarce, to stronger ground, and a little remoter from the sea coast, a place called Glenelchage [*sic*] in Kintail. How long they may continue in that position I know not, but the place is admirably strong and hardly to be attacked.[1]

The correspondent was well informed. On 13 May Tullibardine had led the Jacobites in an orderly withdrawal inland. The 'large valley' that lookouts in the tops of the British warships anchored in Loch Alsh had seen the Jacobites in a body enter was the mouth of Loch Long. They followed the shoreline eastward to encamp in Glen Elchaig, about five miles (8 km) from Eilean Donan. Using small boats, the Jacobites lifted the munitions and firearms from their old camp to Glen Elchaig. Seaforth ordered the distribution of Spanish muskets with ammunition to arm his followers, while 'Clanranald and Lochiel went home to be ready against the first favourable accounts from abroad to make an effectual rising'.[2]

---

1   Atholl, *Chronicles*, vol. 2, p. 284.
2   Oliphant, 'Distinct Abridgment', *Jacobite Lairds of Gask*, p. 459.

On 16 May, the Earl Marischal with the brigadiers Campbell of Ormidale and Mackintosh of Borlum came to Glen Elchaig. They had been away attempting to engage support, and now suggested a show of force to encourage a general rising – a plan which appears to have had Seaforth's backing. They proposed that Tullibardine would lead the Spanish contingent to the westerly end of Loch Ness and seize the part-built army barracks at Kiliwhimen. This isolated outpost was probably then occupied by just a sergeant and 12 men detached from Colonel Clayton's Regiment of Foot. Clanranald and Lochiel with their contingents would rendezvous at Kiliwhimen, together with Seaforth bringing the 100 or so clansmen he reckoned could be withdrawn from protecting the coastline of MacKenzie territory against Royal Navy incursions.

Tullibardine's unenthusiastic response was said to have been 'that to stir out of the country so near the enemy without a body of men would expose their weakness and show the world that none would join them'. He pressed Seaforth to instead commit at least 400 men in support of Clanranald and Lochiel, on the grounds that it would then be more likely 'these gentlemen would undertake something effectually, and then they might stand their ground till others joined'.[3] Seaforth agreed to a wider call-to-arms of his followers, but could not guarantee how many would respond.

Before taking action, however, the Jacobites were distracted by a convincing rumour that government forces, including many Whig clansmen, were on the march and would reach Glen Elchaig within two days. This caused the rendezvous of forces at Kiliwhimen to be abandoned; and so the opportunity for a minor military victory and significant propaganda coup by overrunning the garrison was lost.

This failure strengthened the view that the Jacobite expedition posed little threat. As the government loyalist Alexander Campbell of Fonab, a Perthshire laird, who in the early 1700s had captained one of the Independent Companies of Highlanders, writing in early May put it: 'I do not hear that the landing in the north has occasioned the least disturbance in the west Highlands; 'tis [sic] easy judging that them that landed in the north cannot be numerous by their not attacking Inverness upon their first landing'.[4]

The imagined enemy advance upon Glen Elchaig provoked another crisis of confidence among the leading Jacobites. Seaforth pressed Tullibardine to abandon the expedition entirely. Tullibardine responded that before doing so they should at least be certain of the number of the enemy, and distribute the remaining arms and ammunition. Furthermore, Tullibardine argued, if there was no other choice than to disperse, then, rather than disband, they should withdraw to remoter places and await instruction from the titular King James III and VIII. Seaforth notified Marischal, who next day with Campbell of Ormidale demanded Tullibardine's permission to maintain a guerilla campaign. Tullibardine discouragingly responded to the effect, that if the enemy 'were so near as was given out […] it would soon but too plainly

---

3   *Ibid.*
4   Atholl, *Chronicles*, vol. 2, p. 280.

appear impracticable that any of them could keep together under such difficulties as they were unavoidably obliged to wrestle with'.[5]

No doubt to the disconcertion of the Jacobite leaders, the rumour of the enemy advance on Glen Elchaig proved to be nothing more than that. Tullibardine recovered his composure and on 23 May the expeditionary force broke camp and shifted position southward to Strath Croe, at the head of Loch Duich. Because few or no packhorses could be obtained in the locality, however, the munitions and firearms the Spanish soldiers and Highlanders could not carry with them were taken by boat. On the night of 21/22 May, in a well-executed operation, one of the few successes of the Jacobite campaign, laden with military supplies small boats hugging the shoreline passed from Loch Long unnoticed by the Royal Navy ships in Loch Alsh into Loch Duich to land safely near Strath Croe.[6]

41. The valley at Strath Croe Jacobite forces used as a camping ground in May and June 1719. The area was then known as the 'Croe of Kintail'.

Further Naval Activity

The Earl of Seaforth was said to have reasoned why it had so far proved difficult to raise numbers of his people was because 'he could bring out no men while the men-of-war were about his coast'.[7] Since arriving in the region during the second week in May, Commodore Charles Boyle's squadron had executed a series of punitive actions against coastal communities in MacKenzie territory. As late as 1750, in the wake of the recent suppression of what proved to be the final Jacobite rising, the British government still regarded the MacKenzies as 'a clan so remarkably poisoned with disaffection'.[8] In May 1719, the sailors of Boyle's squadron had also viewed the MacKenzies and allied clans as dangerous rebels to be overawed. Captain Nicholas Eaton of HMS *Dartmouth* recorded

5   Oliphant, 'Distinct Abridgment', *Jacobite Lairds of Gask*, p. 460.
6   *Ibid.*, pp. 459–60.
7   *Ibid.*, pp. 458–9.
8   Lang, *Highlands of Scotland*, p. 27.

42. Naïve contemporary depiction of a mid-18th century British 40-gun fifth-rate warship in North American waters. HMS *Enterprise* would have been of similar design and appearance. (New York Picture Library Digital Collection)

in his log with professional dispassion how on 31 May his crewmen landed on the Island of Raasay, 'to plunder and burn the town, they being people that was in the late rebellion [i.e. in 1715–16], which was accordingly executed'.[9] Given that the locals fled to remote higher ground on their approach, the seamen may not have deliberately killed or seriously injured any unarmed persons on this and similar occasions. However, by killing livestock, burning or otherwise damaging buildings, and, in particular, by wrecking the small sailing craft the inhabitants of this part of the Highlands and Islands depended on for their livelihood and communication, the Royal Navy inflicted considerable hardship on the affected communities.

While *Worcester*, *Enterprise* and *Flamborough* were engaged in the operations about Loch Alsh, further north Captains Eaton of *Dartmouth* and Holland of *Assistance* had their ships at anchor at the confluence of Loch Kishorn and Loch Carron. From here both ships sent boats 'manned and armed', as it was termed, on a series of inshore reconnaissance missions-cum raids.

On 17 and 18 May, landing parties from *Dartmouth* burnt several homesteads and shot livestock for fresh meat for the crew. On the 17th, *Assistance*'s boats probing the upper reaches of Loch Carron were fired upon by locals and forced to withdraw. Later that day another shore party from *Assistance* torched the house of the MacKenzie laird of nearby Applecross, beforehand having seized his correspondence. This included incriminatory letters dated April from the Earl of Seaforth, apparently 'calling for his

---

9   TNA, ADM 51/229, no folio.

people to risen in rebellion'.[10] On 19 May First-Lieutenant Fellows took *Assistance*'s and *Dartmouth*'s barges further into Loch Carron. The sailors twice exchanged fire with a force of about 40 Highlanders, who shooting from the cover of the rocky shore stopped them landing. On 23 May, sniping clansmen prevented a party from *Dartmouth* getting ashore in Loch Carron. Responding to this opposition, on the morning of 27 May Captains Eaton and Holland launched a combined retaliatory raid; 'against a town in Loch Carron', as First-Lieutenant Fellows put it, 'which had always fired on our boats as they passed that way'.[11] Fellows, in command of *Assistance*'s barge, together with both of *Dartmouth*'s lieutenants, in charge of her barge and longboat, with about 70 armed sailors landed on the northerly shore of Loch Carron near a settlement at Stromemore. While most inhabitants, according to Fellows, 'fled at our coming to the mountains', some Highlanders stood their ground and exchanged fire with the landing parties. At least one clansman was shot and killed before his comrades retreated to higher ground. The sailors then spent about two hours looting houses and killing livestock. Before re-embarking in their boats they set the settlement ablaze.

On probably 29 May *Dartmouth* and *Assistance* sailed westward into the Inner Minch. The following day both warships rejoined *Worcester*, now in company with HMS *Success* near the Island of Raasay. Captain George Clinton's 20-gun *Success* had made landfall at Stornoway on 23 May, the same day *Worcester* returned there. On the 25th, boats from both ships patrolling the approaches to Stornoway intercepted and brought into harbour to be searched three Norwegian merchantmen bound for Glasgow. On the evening of 26 May Lieutenant Weston of *Worcester*, as he noted in his log, took a party ashore 'to burn, destroy and send off all the boats' in and around Stornoway harbour, an operation 'perfected by two in the morning'. According to *Worcester*'s sailing master, Weston's men 'gathered and burnt all the boats to be found great and small, to the number of 30 or 40'.[12] Later that morning *Worcester* put to sea in company with *Success*, and on 30 May both joined *Dartmouth* and *Assistance* off the Crowlin Islands, eastward of the Island of Raasay.

43. Naïve mid-18th century depiction of Royal Navy ship's boats in North American waters. The various barges and longboats of the warships were essential for inshore operations, such as those conducted in Hebridean waters from April–June 1719. (New York Picture Library Digital Collection)

---

10 NMM, ADM/L/A/201, no folio.

11 *Ibid.*

12 NMM, ADM/L/W/169, no folio; TNA, ADM 52/317, no folio.

44. Northerly headlands of the Island of Raasay, photographed from the Isle of Skye. The Royal Navy raided Raasay on 31 May 1719.

Next morning, a Sunday, the squadron launched a raid upon the MacLeods of Raasay. On a signal from *Worcester*, at about 9:00 a.m. boats from all four warships, manned by 150 or more armed sailors, rowed for the island under the overall command of First-Lieutenant Fellows of *Assistance*. Landing on Raasay within the hour, the shore parties divided into two bodies that each then headed to one of two main settlements on the island. The sailors do not appear to have encountered any resistance worthy of note, and with the inhabitants fled they set about driving off or killing livestock, burning houses and outbuildings, and burning or breaking any boats they came across. Aubrey Walker, the sailing master of *Assistance*, recorded in his log that as many as 100 buildings on Raasay were burnt. Walker had not joined in the raid, and so while this was probably an exaggerated figure, bandied about by fellow crewmen who had, it suggests the extent of the material damage inflicted on the crofters and fisher-folk of Raasay. Afterwards the shore parties made a leisurely return to their ships, now joined by *Enterprise*.

During the final week of May *Enterprise* had remained at anchor near the mouth of Loch Alsh. The last operation there by Captain Herdman's company had been to put a 24-man patrol ashore in Kintail on the 29th. They returned to ship early on the 31st, having wrecked seven boats found. *Enterprise* had then set sail through the Kyle Akin narrows, and having spotted their sails joined the squadron off Raasay.

On 1 June the squadron separated for the final time. It can be assumed Boyle and his fellow captains reasoned they had done sufficient to damage and constrain the rebels in Kintail, and to discourage coastal communities from supporting them. Time was pressing for *Worcester*, *Dartmouth* and *Assistance* to make the rendezvous at Copenhagen of the Baltic fleet. Therefore, while *Worcester* headed back to Stornoway, *Success* sailed eastward into Loch Alsh taking over *Enterprise*'s station acting as guard ship to monitor any further enemy activity in Kintail. *Enterprise*, *Dartmouth* and *Assistance* for a while remained in the broad sheltered sound separating the Island of Scalpay from south-easterly Skye. On 2 June a party from *Assistance* raided Scalpay, burning or otherwise wrecking eight boats and taking a larger bark in tow. Part of that day and the next was spent distributing between *Dartmouth* and *Assistance* barrels of gunpowder from *Enterprise* (this was mostly Spanish powder taken at Castle Donan). Along with the bulk of *Enterprise*'s shot, this replenished the magazines of both ships in readiness for the Baltic. On 4 June *Assistance* set sail for Denmark, beforehand setting alight and cutting loose

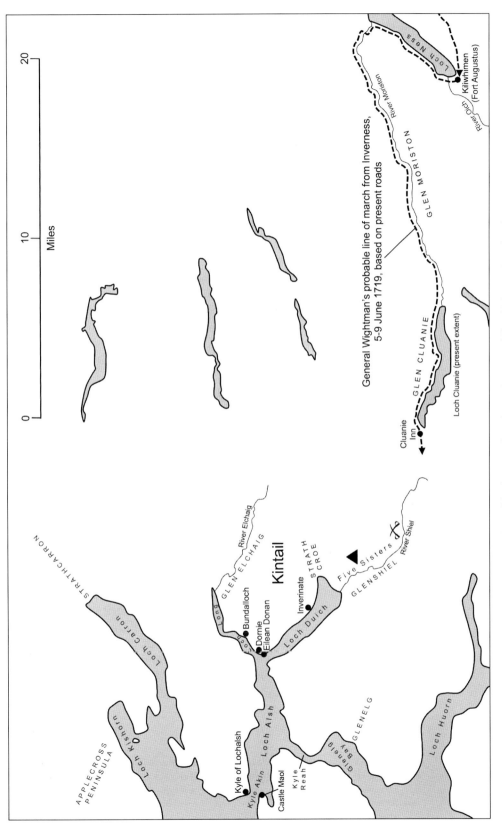

Map 4. Kintail and wider Highland region where the 1719 rising and Glenshiel campaign played out.

General Wightman's probable line of march from Inverness, 5–9 June 1719, based on present roads

the bark taken on the 2nd. By 22 June *Assistance* was riding in Copenhagen Roads in company with other warships of Admiral Norris's fleet. On 4 June *Dartmouth* also sailed for Denmark. After anchoring off Stornoway later on the 5th in company with *Worcester*, on the 7th she headed for Copenhagen arriving there on the 23rd.

On 3 June, *Worcester* on a final patrol out of Stornoway spotted, pursued and boarded a merchantman and escorted her into Stornoway harbour. She was the brig *The Thomas and John* from Campbeltown in south-west Scotland, on an ostensibly routine trading voyage from Rotterdam to the Isle of Man. A search by *Worcester*'s crewmen, however, revealed concealed among her cargo 80 smaller barrels of gunpowder and 500 sword blades. It seems therefore that *The Thomas and John* was one of the vessels the Duke of Ormond and Cardinal Alberoni had engaged to run military supplies from the Netherlands to Scotland. Her sailing master and two merchants on board were detained when *Worcester* sailed from Stornoway on 9 June with the brig in tow as a prize. On the 11th, *Worcester* rendezvoused with *Enterprise* off Skye. The Irishman Captain Peter Stapleton, who had commanded at Castle Donan, together with the two suspected arms merchants and the master of *The Thomas and John* were transferred to *Enterprise*, which also took the brig in tow. The warships then parted, *Enterprise* cruising eventually to Plymouth, while *Worcester* headed for Denmark. She dropped anchor in Copenhagen Roads on 24 June.

The Military Response in Scotland

So far the Jacobite expedition was unopposed by regular British troops. In later April, armed clashes probably occurred on the easterly reaches of the Earl of Seaforth's lands, between his followers and pro-government Whig clansmen. In retaliation to incursions by Seaforth's people into their territory, the Frasers seized Seaforth's seat at Brahan. By May, the castle was occupied by 100 or so of Lord Lovat's men.[13] Elsewhere in Scotland, during the first week in April the authorities of Glasgow and its hinterland, where the majority population, being staunchly Presbyterian and fiercely anti-Catholic backed the Georgian government, had organised volunteers reportedly ready to take up arms 'ever since they heard of an intended invasion by the Spanish, in favour of the Pretender'.[14] In later April, Stirling's civic authorities asked the castle's governor to provide ammunition for the militia and town guard from the garrison magazine while they sought to purchase their own supplies.[15]

The regional magnate with governmental authority to enlist militia against the Jacobites was John Gordon, 15th Earl of Sutherland and chief of the clan of that name. As King George's lord lieutenant, Sutherland held military powers over the vast area of northern Scotland, encompassing the shires of Moray, Nairn, Ross, Cromarty, Sutherland, Caithness, the Isle of Orkney, and Inverness and Banff too.[16]

---

13   *The Weekly Packet*, 16–23 May 1719; *The Weekly Journal or British Gazetteer*, 30 May 1719.

14   *The Weekly Journal or British Gazetteer*, 18 April 1719.

15   R. Renwick (ed.), *Extracts from the records of the Royal Burgh of Stirling, AD 1667–1752* (1889), p. 160.

16   The assumption here is that Sutherland gained the lord lieutenancy of both Inverness and Banff when the previous incumbent Brigadier Alexander Grant, chief of Clan Grant, was dismissed

Sutherland had a track record of loyalty to the Georgian regime. At the outbreak of the rising in 1715 he acted to prevent the Earl of Seaforth joining forces with the Earl of Mar. However, in early October Sutherland's combined force, comprising his clansmen, Mackays, Rosses and Munros, fled at the so-called 'Rout of Allness' before Seaforth's own clan army that had then occupied Inverness. This did not, however, discourage Sutherland from accepting a commission in mid-November as lieutenant-general of Horse and Foot. Thus he remained in charge of loyalist Whig clan forces for the remainder of the desultory war of manoeuvre in northern Scotland, although throughout found it difficult to keep an army together.[17] By 1719, however, Sutherland was often living in London. His military responsibilities to oppose the Jacobites were therefore assumed by his son and deputy lord-lieutenant, William Gordon, Lord Strathnaver. He had some military experience, in 1706 having raised a marching regiment of Foot for the duration of the War of the Spanish Succession.[18]

The view among Whig clans in Strathnaver's region of responsibility was that the 1716 Act for securing the peace had caused their unilateral disarmament. As Simon Fraser, Lord Lovat, reiterated at length in 1724 to King George I:

[The Act] was, without doubt, in theory, a measure very useful and desirable; but experience has showed that it has produced this bad consequence, that those who had appeared in arms, and fought for the government, finding it their duty to obey the law, did accordingly deliver up their arms, but those lawless Highlanders, who had been well provided with arms for the service of the Pretender, knowing but too well the insuperable difficulty for the government, to put that act into execution, instead of really complying with the law, they retained all their arms that were useful, and delivered up only such as were spoiled, and unfit for service; so that, while his majesty's enemies remained as well provided and prepared for all sorts of mischief as they were before the rebellion [i.e. of 1715–16] his faithful subjects, who were well affected, and ventured their lives in his service, by doing their duty, and submitting to the law, rendered themselves naked and defenceless, and at the mercy of their own and the government's avowed enemies.[19]

While the defencelessness of the 'well affected' clans may have been more apparent than real, Lord Strathnaver's priority in April 1719 was to secure to equip loyalist militia the 1,200 stand of arms kept on the government's behalf at his family's seat at Dunrobin Castle. The weapons in the magazine at Dunrobin were property of the Board of Ordnance, and on 21 April the Board meeting in London issued instructions to transfer 700 muskets to the greater security of Edinburgh Castle. The remaining 500 were to be put in the charge

from his offices by King George I for political reasons in July 1717: G. Charles, *History of the Transactions in Scotland, in the Years 1715–16 and 1745-46*, 2 vols. (1816–17), vol. 1, pp. 253; D. W. Hayton, 'Grant, Alexander (aft. 1673–1719), of Castle Grant, Elgin', in *The History of Parliament*, available www.historyof parliamentonline.org/volume/1690-1715, accessed 18 Apr. 2017.

17 H. Paton, 'Sutherland, John, sixteenth earl of Sutherland (*bap.* 1661, *d.* 1733)', rev. J. Spain, in *ODNB* (2004), online edn., accessed 2 Nov. 2016.

18 Childs, 'Marlborough's Wars', p. 327.

19 Jamieson, *Letters from a Gentleman*, vol. 2, pp. 263–4.

of Captain George Munro of Culcairn.[20] His familial estate at Culcairn was not far from Dunrobin, and George was the younger son of Sir Robert Munro, 6th baronet of Foulis, the chief and head of Clan Munro. During the 1715–16 rising because of their father's infirmity George and elder brother Robert, who had a colonel's commission to do so, jointly led the Munros in support of the government, notably to regain and hold Inverness. The brothers later acted to enforce disarmament in the locality, and in 1725 George was given command of one of the re-formed Highland Companies. In 1739 he would become a regular captain in the British Army, when the Companies were amalgamated as the Earl of Crawford's (43rd Highland) Regiment.

Strathnaver set out to assert his powers as his father the lord lieutenant's deputy. However, his authority to raise a militia armed from Dunrobin was disputed. The constitutional standing of the occasional soldiers of the militia (traditionally known in Scotland as fencibles, or 'defensible men') as an auxiliary force of the state was debatable in Scotland at this time, among influential Scots concerned about its political and legal status. The last Act of the independent Scottish parliament regulating militia dated from 1669, and it was unclear whether this had effect after the 1707 Act of Union. The Union itself had not addressed the standing of the militia in Scotland. Therefore, in 1708 a parliamentary Bill was introduced to address the 'Settling the Militia of the part of Great Britain called Scotland'. However, because the Bill controversially set out to replicate in Scotland the Anglo-Welsh system of county-based militias headed by lords lieutenant appointed under the patronage of the London government, it was vetoed by Queen Anne as constitutionally too sensitive. The Bill also fell victim to the aborted French invasion in March, which worried Westminster politicians habitually wary of institutionalising the arming and training of potentially rebellious Scots.[21] A similar Bill (backed by both the Earl of Mar and the Duke of Argyll) was introduced in 1714, during the last parliament of Anne's reign. However, this too failed to become statute because Jacobite-inclined Scots Tory MPs delayed its passage until parliament was prorogued. The leader of this faction, George Lockhart, MP for Edinburghshire,[22] couched his opposition to the bill on libertarian grounds: 'As for the Lords lieutenant […] I would never consent that such a power over those I represented [as an MP] should be lodged with any fellow subject'. While many Scots distrusted the imposition of placeman lords lieutenant holding military authority on the English model, Tories were particularly opposed to the Bill. They worried that Whig officers would come to control the fencibles in the way that Whigs dominated the officer corps of the regular army.[23]

In August 1715, just before the rising began, King George I had instructed his 20 lords lieutenant across Scotland to raise militia to maintain public order. In October, the Duke of Argyll looked to them and their deputies to 'march forthwith with their fencible men, with their best arms and whatever

20   TNA, WO47/32, f. 85.
21   Henshaw, *Scotland and the British Army*, pp. 207, 210-211; Childs, 'Marlborough's Wars', p. 339.
22   A constituency equivalent to the present local government area of Midlothian.
23   Aufnere, *Lockhart Papers*, vol. 1, pp. 452–8, *passim*, quotation from p. 254.

ammunition they have'. Nonetheless, there was confusion over authority among loyalists wishing to raise forces. As a result, the recruitment of rural or urban fencibles and volunteer units had been undertaken in an ad hoc fashion, hampered by local officials reluctant to accept that the lieutenancy had sole responsibility for the militia.[24]

The military powers of the lord-lieutenancy in effect supplanted the time-honoured authority vested in chiefs to raise armed followings. It was for this reason that in April 1719 Lord Strathnaver encountered opposition among the Whig elite of the north-east, when calling upon them to send tenants and servants to work as pioneers fortifying Inverness. Certain gentlemen questioned Strathnaver's authority to command them or to raise a militia of any sort. However, the cooperation of detractors like Colonel William Grant of Ballindalloch[25] was secured under a compromise arrangement brokered by Duncan Forbes of Culloden. Forbes was an influential and respected land-owning lawyer from near Inverness, a staunch opponent of Jacobitism. It was agreed that self-appointed gentleman officers and their men would serve as volunteers only under the orders of regular army officers; therefore under Colonel Jasper Clayton when he came with the remainder of his regiment to take command at Inverness in mid-May, and later under Major-General Wightman when he arrived there.[26]

Strathnaver had also to contend with the prevailing wariness among early-18th century Highland society to avoid armed conflict within itself. Inter-clan ancestral rivalries remained, but rather than being contested under arms these antagonisms were usually tempered by pragmatic social ties of business, kinship and guarded neighbourliness. The more bellicose clans still took cattle, and transgressed into the Lowlands to levy Blackmail and rustle livestock. However, strong social deterrents discouraged repetition of the damaging inter-clan blood feuds of previous centuries. For these reasons the sporadically energetic war in northern Scotland in 1715–16 engaged in by transient Jacobite and Whig clan-based armies had involved a lot of manoeuvring and jockeying for position, but little actual fighting, and looting and petty destruction of property, but very few casualties in actual combat.[27] Indeed, the tendency after 1716 of the Highland elite to embrace gentlemanly reconciliation rather than repudiation of old adversaries prompted General George Wade in 1724 to mention to King George I, that 'I cannot omit observing to your majesty, this national tenderness your subjects of North Britain have one for the other is great encouragement to the rebels and attainted persons to return home from their banishment'.[28]

Notwithstanding the constraints on Lord Strathnaver's recruitment drive, by later May 1719 there were about 500 armed pro-government Highland

---

24 Charles, *Transactions in Scotland,* vol. 1, pp. 252–3; Henshaw, *Scotland and the British Army,* pp. 211–12, 215; Quotation from Rae, *History of the Rebellion,* p. 233.

25 Grant's honorary rank reflected his time spent in command of an Independent Highland Company during the early 1700s – and he would command one of the new companies raised in 1725.

26 Warrand, *More Culloden Papers,* pp. 197–9.

27 Szechi, *Great Jacobite Rebellion,* pp. 181–4, *passim.*

28 Allardyce, *Historical Papers,* vol. 1, p. 139.

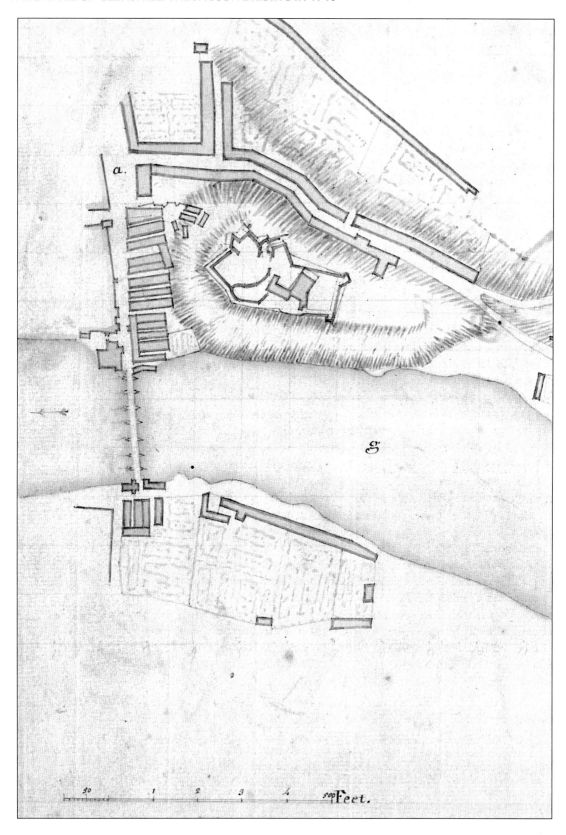

45. (left) Detail of the 1719 Board of Ordnance survey plan of the castle at Inverness. Showing the position of the castle hill commanding both the town and bridge spanning the River Ness. (Reproduced by permission of the National Library of Scotland)

volunteers based in and around Inverness, mostly Grants, Munros and the Earl of Sutherland's people.[29] Preparations for defending Inverness itself had in April involved the formation of a town guard, and agreement among the local authorities to break the bridge over the River Ness on the westerly side of town if Jacobites advanced that way. Fishing boats and inshore craft on the nearby waterways of Loch Ness and the Moray Firth were moored at the town to prevent an enemy making use of them. The work reportedly done to put Inverness Castle 'into a good posture of defence' was more or less complete by 10 May. The defences involved the emplacement of several cannon behind freshly thrown up pallisaded earthworks. Manned by Colonel Clayton's regiment these fortifications would probably have been sufficient to repel a Jacobite assault had it come, although, as already mentioned, Inverness Castle was unprepared to withstand a siege.[30]

The defensive posture of Inverness was strengthened on 4 May with the arrival in the Moray Firth of Captain Edward Gregory's 20-gun HMS *Bideford* – and it seems likely the cannon positioned in the castle were some of her 6-pdrs. On 7 May the garrison was supplied with gunpowder, cannon shot and musket ball from *Bideford*'s stores.[31] Nine days later *Bideford* was joined by the 40-gun HMS *Gosport* under the command of Captain Francis Blake Devall. After sailing from the Nore on 23 April, *Gosport* had cruised northward off the North Sea coast of England and Scotland conducting an uneventful patrol looking out for Jacobite arms runners.[32]

With Inverness more than adequately defended, and with no sign of the Jacobites advancing from Kintail, both warships spent the latter part of May on patrol. While *Gosport* kept watch off the north-east coast, as far northerly as Duncansby Head, and easterly toward Peterhead, *Bideford* sailed further north-westerly, off Orkney, and off the mainland as far as the Kyle of Tongue. As *Gosport*'s sailing master put it, both crews engaged in 'chasing sails'. This involved pursuing and then launching boat parties to question and search vessels suspected of bringing aid for the Jacobites. The traffic in the busy sea-lanes about the north of Scotland involved fishing and merchant vessels sailing between Scandinavia and Ireland, and into and out of Scottish harbours like Aberdeen and Peterhead. While *Bideford* remained on station well into July, *Gosport* in early June completed her mission and sailed southward. During this time neither warship intercepted any arms runners.

---

29 *The Post Man and The Historical Account*, 11–13 June 1719.
30 Atholl, *Chronicles*, vol. 2, pp. 279, 281; *The Weekly Journal or British Gazetteer,* 23 May 1719.
31 TNA, ADM 51/108: Captains' Logs, including HMS *Bideford*, Mar. 1718–Sept. 1720.
32 TNA, ADM 52/184: Sailing Masters' Logs, HMS *Gosport*, Apr. 1719–Dec. 1720.

46. (right) Reconstruction of the appearance of a sergeant of Foot in the British Army, *c*.1719. His polearm, a halberd, was a symbol of rank. Because all infantry wore red coats, regiments were distinguished by the contrasting colour of the lining. These 'facing' colours were displayed on the turned and buttoned back cuffs, and increasingly at the lapels.
(Illustration by Ed Dovey, © Helion & Company Limited)

The Deployment of Regular Troops

Major-General James Wightman, acting commander-in-chief of the British Army in Scotland, was based at Edinburgh Castle. Wightman would manage the land-based response to the Jacobite emergency under the oversight of ministerial and military superiors: respectively, the Duke of Roxburghe, secretary of state for Scotland; secretary at war George Treby; under secretary Charles Delafaye representing the Earl of Stanhope, secretary of state for the Northern Department; and Lieutenant-General George Lord Carpenter, commander-in-chief of Scotland. Carpenter was instructed by secretary Treby on 21 April to go to Scotland to take command, but had been slow to do so. Following a further directive from Treby on 28 April, Carpenter had left London on 3 May.[33]

Sensibly, Treby only offered advice to the capable Wightman in regard to the deployment of the troops in Scotland. He recommended taking standard precautions: to reinforce the garrisons of Dumbarton (where the governor was to gather four months-worth of provisions for the garrison), of Fort William and Inverness, and to concentrate troops at Perth should the Jacobites threaten to advance out of the Highlands.[34] Stirling Castle, a key stronghold, was put on a war footing. Lieutenant-Colonel John Blackader, the deputy-governor there, noted in his journal on 18 April being 'busily employed in the castle ordering things for the defence'.[35] However, with the Spanish invasion threat lifted, on 28 April Treby wrote confidently informing Wightman that 'we are so little apprehensive of any descent in England that the troops are ordered to separate'. On 3 May Treby wrote more directly, for Wightman 'to use your utmost endeavours to dislodge them [i.e. the Jacobites in Kintail] from thence and not suffer them to remain anywhere quiet [...] this is likely to be the only scene of action'.[36]

On paper (and it seems in fact), by May 1719 Wightman had under his command approximately 2,600 soldiers of the British Army in eight marching regiments.[37] Wightman therefore had to deploy across Scotland about 900

---

33 TNA, WO4/22, folios 93, 108, 112; *The Post Boy,* 30 April–2 May 1719.

34 TNA, WO4/22, folio 93; SP 55/8, folio 140: State Papers Scotland, Letter Books, letter book of the Duke of Roxburghe.

35 A. Chrichton (ed.), *The Life and Diary of Lieutenant-Colonel J. Blackader* (1824), p. 234.

36 TNA, WO4/32, folios 108, 112.

37 The source for the marching regiments of the British Army in Scotland is TNA SP41/5/112, 'Quarters of the regiments in North Britain with an account of the detachments and outposts from each garrison May the 9th 1719'. This document provides a snapshot in time, based on recent regimental returns. Comparison with TNA SP54/13/78B: State Papers Scotland Series II, a similar list of regimental returns of Horse and Foot in North Britain in July 1719, indicates that the units available to Major-General Wightman in April, May and June were at established strength.

fewer regulars than, by his own reckoning, had been in the Duke of Argyll's field army at Sheriffmuir in 1715.[38] Together, the four regiments of Foot in Scotland in early May numbered approximately 1,780 officers and men. These were deployed as follows: Lieutenant-General George Macartney's Regiment garrisoned Stirling and had 83 officers and men detached to secure the construction site of the barracks at Inversnaid; Colonel Henry Harrison, apart from a 37-man detachment out-posted to Duart Castle on the Isle of Mull, had brought his regiment to Fort William under overall command of the governor there Colonel Sir Robert Pollock; all or most of Colonel Jasper Clayton's Regiment was mustering at Inverness, and 13 of its men occupied the barracks in building at Kiliwhimen; and Colonel Edward Montague's Regiment, under the command of Lieutenant-Colonel Herbert Lawrence, was marching fully or in part from Perth for Inverness. The cavalry available to Wightman were four regiments of dragoons, numbering 828 officers and men or thereabouts. By May, Lord Cobham's Royal Regiment of Dragoons was described as 'resting', billeted in Edinburgh, at Canongate, and east of the city at Haddington, preparatory to moving northward. This suggests that the regiment had only recently marched into Scotland. Posted across the lowland central belt of Scotland were Lord Carpenter's own Dragoons, with three troops at Linlithgow, a troop at Bathgate, and north of the Firth of Forth, two troops at Dumfermline; and also Colonel James Campbell's North British Royal Dragoons (known later as the Royal Scots Greys), with two troops each billeted at Stirling, Falkirk and nearer Glasgow, at Kilsyth. Further north, three troops of Brigadier John Dalyrmple 1st Earl of Stair's Dragoons were at Perth, and south-west of there, three troops quartered about Auchterader. Advanced detachments from all four regiments numbering 133 officers and men were already in the north-east, occupying outposts about Inverness and Elgin.

With this small and dispersed force Wightman had to secure garrisons and maintain internal security, while concentrating a field army to engage the Jacobites in battle. The lack of regular troops worried government loyalists like the Duke of Atholl. He was concerned that if his sons Tullibardine and Lord George Murray raised forces on the family estates in Perthshire, as they had in 1715, Blair Castle itself would fall to the Jacobites. In later April, Atholl asked Wightman to base some regular Foot at Blair. None, however, could be spared, so Wightman arranged to send patrols of dragoons from Perth to Blair, while reassuring the duke that Dutch reinforcements were on their way.[39]

The government had by then decided to send the Dutch auxiliary battalions to Scotland. On 21 April, secretary at war Treby wrote informing Wightman that both battalions of Brigadier Sturler's Regiment, then billeted about Chelmsford in Essex, were ordered to Edinburgh, with the regiments of Van Huffel, Van Amerongen and Sixmar to follow.[40] The second lift by eight transports carrying across the North Sea the three latter regiments probably left Willemstad around 12 April. After being forced by bad weather

---

38 Wightman in his account of the battle of Sheriffmuir, in Patten's *History of the Rebellion*, pp. 159–61, estimated that Argyll's army numbered 2,500 foot and 1,000 dragoons.
39 Atholl, *Chronicles*, vol. 2, p. 279.
40 TNA, WO 4/22, folio 93.

to shelter off the coast of Yorkshire for a while in Bridlington Bay, the convoy had arrived at Newcastle-upon-Tyne on probably the 18th.[41] From there it seems the regiments marched to Edinburgh; from where on 30 April it was reported 'part of the Dutch forces which landed at Newcastle arrived there that day'.[42] While Sixmar's Regiment remained about Edinburgh, billeted at Canongate and on the coast at Leith, by 7 May eight of 12 companies of Van Amerongen's were, or were soon expected to be, at Perth and two at Dundee. The two other companies were at or on their way to Montrose on the east coast. Meanwhile, all 10 companies of Van Huffel's Regiment were by then expected to be further north at Aberdeen (these 12 latter companies were probably shipped from Edinburgh).[43] The Dutch were a vital reinforcement substantially increasing Wightman's force of regular infantry.

It is unclear when the two Swiss battalions of Brigadier Sturler's Regiment reached Scotland. Major-General Baron van Keppel and his deputy Brigadier-General Walderen, the commanding officers of the Dutch brigade, appear to have left London on the same day as Lieutenant-General Carpenter, 3 May, likely sailing in company. It is assumed that both battalions embarked for Edinburgh around the same time. Lord Carpenter with the commanding Dutch officers probably arrived in Edinburgh on 12 May.[44]

Sturler's Regiment when it reached Scotland was posted to Stirling, and probably also to Perth. It therefore played no part in the forthcoming Highland campaign. By June, Swiss troops formed part of the garrison at Stirling. During their stay there the Swiss officers, described appreciatively by Lieutenant-Colonel Blackader as 'a very civil people', also made a good impression on Stirling's councilors. Accordingly they favoured Keppel and several of his subordinates by making them honorary burgesses and townsmen.[45]

On 11 May King George I made a stately departure from London to attend court in his favoured homeland of Hanover. It was reported how: 'this morning about nine a clock [*sic*] his majesty left St. James's [Palace], passed in his barge from Whitehall to Lambeth, and from thence proceeded by coach to Gravesend, where his majesty embarked for Holland on board the *Caroline Yacht*, which sailed between two and three in the afternoon'.[46] The king confidently set out on his progress to Hanover reassured there was no threat of invasion, and in the expectation that the Jacobite expeditionary force isolated in remote north-west Scotland was contained and soon would be crushed.

---

41 *The Weekly Journal or British Gazetteer*, 18 April 1719; *The Weekly Packet*, 18–25 April 1719; *The Post Boy*, 25–28 April 1719.
42 *The Post Man and The Historical Account*, 5–7 May 1719.
43 TNA SP41/5/112.
44 *The Weekly Journal or British Gazetteer*, 23 May 1719.
45 Chrichton, *Blackader*, p. 235; Renwick, *Royal Burgh of Stirling*, p. 161.
46 *The London Gazette*, 9–12 May 1719.

9

The Jacobite Rising and the Battle of Glenshiel

'Continual fire and hazardous dispute.'

Wider backing for the Jacobite force in Kintail failed to materialise. As already mentioned, some of its leaders had travelled beyond the beachhead attempting to measure and gain support. Furthermore, in early May the Earl Marischal in disguise was said to have visited Inverness. The same correspondent mentioned that Marischal had been seen in Stonehvaven, in Aberdeenshire, not far from the Keith family's crumbling former stronghold at Dunnotar Castle, and this seems more likely. Also during May, Lord George Murray apparently met clandestinely with sympathisers on his familial lands in Perthshire. Murray, however, returned to Kintail with few followers; indeed, in July Lieutenant-General Carpenter wrote reassuring the Duke of Atholl, Lord George's father, that only one noteworthy individual from the Atholl estates fought with the Jacobites at Glenshiel.[1]

The expedition gained the support of the notorious Highland outlaw and sometime Jacobite Robert 'Rob Roy MacGregor'. He had probably been informed well before the landing in Kintail that a Spanish-backed rising was planned.[2] Although Rob Roy, as de facto leader of Clan MacGregor, had joined in the 1715–16 rising, his Jacobitism was self-serving. From the MacGregor heartlands in the Trossachs about Loch Lomond, Rob raided the lands of the government-supporting Marquess of Montrose, with whom he was already feuding, but also supplied (albeit ambiguous) intelligence to the opposing commander-in-chief, the Duke of Argyll. Given this equivocal conduct, at the battle of Sheriffmuir Rob Roy and the MacGregors were not trusted to take position with the Jacobite army. Awaiting the outcome of the battle from the

---

1   Atholl, *Chronicles*, vol. 2, pp. 281–2, 287–8.

2   MacGregor was in effect a pseudonym. In the mid-1690s Robert had adopted the name Campbell when penal laws were enacted against the MacGregors as a notorious cattle-raiding clan. See D. Stevenson, 'MacGregor, Robert [Rob Roy]' (*bap.* 1671, *d.* 1734)', in *ODNB* (2004), online edn., accessed Feb. 2017.

side-lines in any case served Rob's interests. When one of his men asked why they did not intervene, Rob was said to have replied, that 'If they [i.e. Mar's army] could not do it without me, they should not do it with me'.[3]

Remaining outlawed in spring 1719, Rob Roy had little to lose by siding with the Jacobites again. The previous August, his followers had raided the army barracks being built on traditional MacGregor land at Inversnaid, kidnapping workmen despite the site being guarded by regular troops. Rob Roy had by then made an enemy of the Duke of Atholl as well as Montrose. Because of further depredations against the latter's tenants during December, in early March 1719 a royal proclamation demanded the apprehension of 'Robert Campbell alias MacGregor commonly called Rob Roy' for his 'several crimes'.[4] By the third week of April Rob Roy was assumed to have gone northward to join the Jacobites in Kintail. He was also expected to launch another raid against the barracks at Inversnaid, and so Major-General Wightman ordered the garrison strengthened and the building site made defensible.[5]

Other erstwhile Jacobites with much to lose by backing a rising were dissuaded from doing so. On the Isle of Mull, Donald MacLean, third laird of Brolas, had received one of the Duke of Ormond's letters soliciting support for the Earl Marischal's expedition. Because Brolas in 1715 had joined the Jacobite army and fought at Sheriffmuir, in 1719 he was expected to help raise the MacLeans of Mull. There was some optimistic talk of such a gathering, but Brolas was cautioned in no uncertain terms by the deputy-sheriff of Argyllshire, James Campbell, about the likely outcome of engaging in rebel activity. Duly chastened, Brolas gave the Jacobites no further support.[6]

Beyond the Highlands, Jacobite Lowlanders, 'the King's friends [...] on the south side of the Forth', as the Jacobite Scots nationalist George Lockhart described them, sensibly would not engage themselves until knowing for sure that Ormond had landed. Beyond a fragmented network of personal contacts, Lowlanders minded to take up arms for King James III and VIII were in any case disorganised. They lacked armaments, leadership and reliable ways of gaining and communicating intelligence – and in turn feared infiltration by government spies. Moreover, being so distant from the beachhead in Kintail, without further Spanish reinforcements Lowland Jacobites would have no support. Lockhart had received notice of the expedition to Scotland via one of Ormond's messengers. In April, he unenthusiastically penned a communiqué for the Earl Marischal explaining: 'It is not to be desired or expected that they [i.e. Lowlanders] should rise in arms until there be such a number of forces near them, as they can make a stand, and to which they may resort'.[7] Misinformation, however, almost caused some Edinburgh-based Jacobites to do just that.

3   *Ibid.*; quotation from Patten, *History of the Rebellion,* p. 170.
4   TNA, SP 55/8/124.
5   Atholl, *Chronicles,* vol. 2, p. 280; TNA, SP 55/8/146–7.
6   Dickson, *Jacobite Attempt,* p. 70.
7   Aufnere, *Lockhart Papers,* vol. 2, p. 20; D. Szechi, *George Lockhart of Carnwath, 1689–1727: A Study in Jacobitism* (2002), p. 124.

Probably during the second week in May, an informant claiming to be a servant of John Cameron of Lochiel told that Ormond's fleet had been sighted off south-west Scotland. A coinciding letter from a Border Jacobite appeared to corroborate the news, and so a number of gentlemen led by the Earl of Dalhousie excitedly rode from Edinburgh to attempt to effect a rising. Lockhart (by his own account), however, recognized Lochiel's supposed servant's story was bogus, and that he was probably in government pay. Lockhart sent timely warnings after Dalhousie's party which they received and heeded before taking any action. Lockhart was an influential Jacobite, but would not risk supporting a rising without substantial foreign backing. This caution was shaped by his own arrest and imprisonment during the 1715–16 rising, and because his brother, having surrendered with the Jacobite army at Preston, was executed for treason. The product of Lockhart's understandable wariness was to undermine the chances of success for the expedition in Kintail.[8]

The Rising Gets Underway

It seems similar unreliable intelligence that almost triggered a Lowland rising of sorts compelled Tullibardine finally to take action. Before decamping from Glen Elchaig for Strath Croe on 23 May, the Jacobites received encouraging news. One correspondent optimistically cited a report in a London newspaper in early May of word from Spain, that Ormond's expedition was re-formed and so Tullibardine's force should remain prepared. This encouraged Tullibardine to write afresh to Lochiel and Clanranald to keep their followers on standby. On 23 May, as his force prepared to march to Strath Croe, Tullibardine received a letter from Edinburgh dated the 11th. This told it seemed certain the reorganised Spanish fleet was probably already underway with Ormond's army aboard. Tullibardine hurriedly rescinded his earlier instructions and ordered a gathering of forces; having, as he later explained for the Earl of Mar, resolved to 'keep life in the affair till we should have some certain accounts of the expedition from Spain, or else the king's commands, which would enliven everybody and make things go right'.[9] The general rising of clans was at last underway.

On 4 June, Lochiel leading about 150 Camerons was first to arrive at the rendezvous at Glenshiel. Tullibardine joined them next day with the Spanish troops and some clansmen, bringing the munitions from Strath Croe. The weather that early June was seasonably, although somewhat untypically for the western Highlands, very sunny and hot; to the extent that during the march into Glenshiel one of the Spanish soldiers collapsed and died from heatstroke.[10]

Tullibardine's force camped some way into the westerly reaches of the glen. This was probably in the vicinity of a now long-abandoned settlement in the area known in Gaelic as Achadh nan Seilach, not far westward of the present farmstead at Achnangart. In early September 1773 Dr Samuel Johnson and

---

8   Aufnere, *Lockhart Papers*, pp. 22–3; Szechi, *Lockhart*, p. 125.
9   Oliphant, 'Distinct Abridgment', *Jacobite Lairds of Gask*, pp. 460–1; quotation from Dickson, *Jacobite Attempt*, pp. 269–70: Tullibardine's account of the battle of Glenshiel, written for the Earl of Mar on 16 June 1719.
10   Dickson, *Jacobite Attempt*, p. 296.

47. View eastward towards the head of Loch Duich. Showing, far middle distance, Strath Croe, and, right, the north Glenshiel ridge and its peaks known as the Five Sisters of Kintail. The pass of Glenshiel is in the far-right distance.

his friend James Boswell had paused here for refreshment as they rode as tourists through Glenshiel. As Boswell described: 'We came to a rich green valley, comparatively speaking, and stopped at Auchnashiel, a kind of rural village, a number of cottages being built together, as we saw all along in the Highlands'. Boswell mentioned how the companions had 'passed through Glen Shiel, with prodigious mountains on each side. We saw where the battle was in the year 1719. Mr. Johnson owned he was now in a scene of as wild nature as he could see. [One particular] mountain I called immense. "No", said he, "but 'tis a considerable protuberance".[11]

Glenshiel, the glen of the River Shiel, from its seaward opening at the head of Loch Duich, at present Shiel Bridge, to the point inland where the glen broadens towards Loch Cluanie, reaches north-westerly to south-easterly for approximately nine miles (14.5 km) by the present A87 road. This mostly follows and overlies the route of the later 18th century military road linking Fort Augustus to the barracks at Bernera. This in turn had engineered and metalled the ancient grassy drove way track that traversed the glen in 1719.[12] The pass of Glenshiel provides a routeway through a huge tract of mountainous country that otherwise remains impenetrable other than on foot. The northerly Glenshiel ridge forms a series of summits rising increasingly steeply from sea level to 3,500 feet (1,060 metres). The most prominent of these peaks, dominating the westerly stretch of the glen, are the adjoining so-called Five Sisters of Kintail. These together form a challenging traverse for present-day hill-walkers. The slopes of the southerly Glenshiel ridge, bounding the glen southward, climb a little more gradually then progressively steeply to about 3,300 feet (1,000 metres). Glenshiel is sometimes described as being uniformly precipitous and gorge-like, but in fact the floor of much of the northerly reach of the pass is one third of a mile

11 J. Boswell, *Boswell's Journal of A Tour to the Hebrides with Samuel Johnson*, (eds.) F.A. Pottle and C.H. Bennett (1936), p. 107.

12 The Fort Augustus to Bernera military road was constructed in the later 1750s and early 1760s under the direction of Major William Caulfied. As Inspector of Roads, Caulfied was the successor to Major-General George Wade in charge of the military road-building programme in the Highlands: W. Taylor, *The Military Roads in Scotland* (1996), pp. 80–1.

48. Glenshiel viewed westward from the River Shiel, at the narrowing in the pass known at the time of the battle as 'the little glen'. The bluff, centre middle distance, rising steeply right (northward), was fortified and held as the centre of the Jacobite lines.

or more in breadth. Watered by the River Shiel, Glenshiel made a suitable camping ground for the gathering Jacobite forces. It was also known to be the most defensible 'strongest ground in those parts'.[13]

Reports reached the Jacobite camp that government forces were marching from Inverness. On 7 June this was confirmed by a message from Roderick Chisholm, the 22-year-old head of Clan Chisholm, sent from his clan's heartland in Strathglass, south-west of Inverness. The British government had proscribed Chisholm for being both a Roman Catholic and a militant Jacobite. Because of his military involvement in the 1715–16 rising most of his lands had been forfeited to the crown. Nevertheless, Chisholm had attended the Jacobite council of war at the beachhead at Eilean Donan on 20 April, and now requested arms and ammunition for 100 of his own followers and those of John Grant, the laird of nearby Glenmoriston. Grant was another attainted Jacobite whose estates were managed by the Forfeited Estates Commission. With their clansmen Chisholm and Grant, or so they wrote, meant to shadow the enemy column before joining the forces at Glenshiel. Accordingly, Tullibardine sent muskets and ammunition to them. However, for reasons that remain unclear, in the event neither they nor their men joined in the battle at Glenshiel.[14]

On 5 June Tullibardine and Lochiel reconnoitered the 'narrow passes in the little glen' as a suitable defensive position.[15] This was the narrowest point

13   Oliphant, 'Distinct Abridgment', *Jacobite Lairds of Gask*, p. 461.
14   A. MacKenzie, *History of the Chisholms* (1881), pp. 59–60; Oliphant, 'Distinct Abridgment', *Jacobite Lairds of Gask*, p. 461.
15   Dickson, *Jacobite Attempt*, p. 270, Tullibardine's account.

in the pass of Glenshiel, about five and a half miles (8 km) from the westward entrance. Here, rocky bluffs projecting from the lower slopes of the lofty ridges on both sides of the glen constrict the pass. The spot was a natural bottleneck, commanding the drove road where it crossed the River Shiel by the nearby ford. It was agreed to be 'the properest [sic] place for defence'. On 7 June Seaforth with 500 clansmen came to the Croe of Kintail from the Loch Carron area. They shifted to the camp in Glenshiel early on the 9th. On the 8th, one of Rob Roy's sons arrived with 80 MacGregors and other volunteers (Rob Roy himself, true to form, came sometime later in time to join in the battle).[16] On 9 June, given warning of the enemy's approach, the Jacobite army broke camp and set about occupying positions about the little glen.

49. Remains of the dry stone wall livestock enclosure on the summit of the fortified bluff the Jacobites used as a final defensive position. The distant summits are the westerly reaches of the south Glenshiel ridge.

Wightman's Preparations

Major-General Wightman had left Edinburgh for Inverness on 18 or 19 May, beforehand discussing the military situation in Scotland with his superior Lord Carpenter, recently arrived from London. Rather than lead field operations against the Jacobites Carpenter delegated command to Wightman. While Carpenter therefore trusted his deputy's professionalism, a reading between the lines of the sources suggests the two generals had a difficult relationship. Wightman would complain in his post-battle dispatch from Glenshiel to the Earl Cadogan, of 'all the difficulties' encountered in preparing for the Highland campaign without the full support of 'people

---

16 Oliphant, 'Distinct Abridgment', *Jacobite Lairds of Gask*, p. 461; Dickson, *Jacobite Attempt*, p. 270, Tullibardine's account.

in power', and furthermore that Cadogan would recognise the blame: 'Your Lordship will determine […] who was in the right and who was in the wrong', Wightman wrote indignantly.[17]

Wightman's 'difficulties' were fiscal and logistical. Having to purchase provisions, in particular supplies of bread and biscuit, for his troops on credit, Wightman had issued promissory notes in the commander-in-chief's name. This provoked an irritable rebuke from Carpenter, who, while Wightman was on campaign in the Highlands, complained from his headquarters at Edinburgh to London, to Charles Delafaye in the Northern Department, recommending that Wightman should be reproached 'not to draw more than is absolutely necessary'.[18] So Wightman did not enjoy his superior's unequivocal support, and in turn chose not to write to Carpenter about the battle of Glenshiel until a week afterwards, on 17 June. This calculated breach of military etiquette offended Carpenter considerably, and he complained about it to the Lord's Justices – the London-based council governing the kingdom during King George's stay in Hanover. Under-secretary Delafaye wrote upbraiding Wightman for his conduct, but the matter did not end there. The Lords Justices referred Carpenter's complaint to Lord Stanhope accompanying the king in Hanover. Writing in reply to Delafaye on 3 July, Stanhope noted that while his majesty applauded Wightman's victory at Glenshiel, he also approved of Delafaye's reprimand of him: for 'being more subordinate and respectful to his superior officers was very requisite and necessary'.[19]

Wightman arrived at Inverness as his operational base on 24 May, joining his colleague and friend Colonel Jasper Clayton.[20] Having put Inverness in a state of defence, Clayton was then organising Lord Strathnaver's quarrelsome loyalist militia. Wightman wrote later warmly commending Clayton, for 'his judgement as a good officer', and 'as a sincere friend in all the difficulties we have gone through'.[21] In 1715, at the battle of Sheriffmuir Clayton had been brigadier and second-in-command to Wightman of the infantry; now Wightman made him brigadier and deputy in command of the troops mustering at Inverness. Clayton's first commission in the British Army dated to 1696. In the War of the Spanish Succession he had served in Flanders and Spain, and in 1712 held the governorship of Dunkirk. In June 1713 Clayton secured the colonelcy of a regiment of Foot that had spent most of the war in garrison duty in Ireland. In October 1715 Clayton's Regiment was shipped from Ireland to reinforce the Duke of Argyll's forces in Scotland and had fought at Sheriffmuir.[22] In spring 1716 Clayton, like Wightman, led mopping-up counter insurgency operations in the Highlands under Lord Cadogan's direction. Based at Fort William, he took troops as far afield as the Isle of Skye enforcing the submission and disarmament of rebellious clans,

---

17 TNA, SP 43/61, folio 93: Papers of under-secretary Charles Delafaye, copy of Wightman's dispatch to Lord Cadogan reporting the battle of Glenshiel, written from there on 11 June 1719.
18 TNA, SP 54/13/56, Carpenter to Delafaye, 13 June 1719.
19 Cited by Dalton, *George The First's Army*, vol. 1, p. 53.
20 *The London Gazette*, 2–6 June 1719.
21 TNA, SP 43/61, folio 93.
22 Dalton, *Army Lists and Commission Registers*, vol. 6, pp. 339–40; Rae, *History of the Rebellion*, p. 300.

including the Camerons of Lochaber.[23] Clayton had since remained with his regiment on garrison duty in Scotland.

Wightman and Clayton recognised the particular challenges of conducting regular military operations in the Highlands. In order to bring the Jacobites in Kintail to battle, a force projected from Inverness would have to be self-supporting. It would be campaigning in ostensibly enemy territory, where the prevailing subsistence economy made rations for soldiers and fodder for horses in bulk hard to find. Wightman therefore waited on completion of logistical arrangements Clayton already had in hand. As the Jacobite James Keith acknowledged, 'The enemy was by this time within three days march of us […] and waited only for the provisions which was necessary to be carried along (into a country full of mountains and possessed by the enemy)'.[24] Wightman, as already mentioned, making use of credit for essential purchases, had stocks of bread baked and other provisions gathered at Inverness. From there local boatmen hired at generous rates ferried supplies down Loch Ness to Kiliwhimen, where an advanced depot was established in the barracks in building there under the command of one Captain Douglas, the superintending commissary officer.[25]

Wightman meanwhile became frustrated by, as he found them, unhelpful local officials. On 4 June he impatiently complained: 'had the gentlemen of the civil power performed their parts in the least proportion to my actions, I should have been ashamed to have dated this letter from Inverness'.[26] Transport was a pressing concern. Away from the coast and inland waterways, in the Highlands bulky loads were shifted by packhorse. Lacking its own logistical corps, the Georgian army on campaign hired horses and civilian handlers as and when required. Therefore, while operating from Inverness in April 1716 Wightman had issued warrants via the lord lieutenancy for Inverness-shire to contribute 100 packhorses with drivers, in the proportion of one handler to three horses, along with suitable pack saddles with sacks for holding supplies. Three years later, Wightman now called upon the region to provide a larger number of horseflesh and handlers.[27] However, the quotas were not met, creating difficulties during the forthcoming campaign. Indeed, shortage of packhorses may have caused Wightman to march with fewer troops than he originally intended.

So what was the size of the army Wightman organised at Inverness to do battle with the Jacobites in Kintail? Wightman's post-battle dispatches (in which he did not clearly differentiate between units at his disposal about Inverness, and those actually engaged at Glenshiel) mentioned three regiments of infantry – the British regiments of Clayton and Montagu, and the Dutch regiment Van Huffel; elements of two other regiments of Foot – 50 men of Colonel Henry Harrison's Regiment, and four companies of the

---

23   *The London Gazette*, 10–14 April 1716; *The London Gazette*, 1–5 May 1716.

24   Keith, *Fragment of a Memoir*, p. 51.

25   Warrand, *More Culloden Papers*, p. 200.

26   Cited by Michael, *England under George I*, p. 199.

27   Daniell, *Calendar of Stuart Papers*, vol. 2, pp. 65–6; *The Post Man and The Historical Account*, 11–13 June 1719.

Dutch regiment Van Amerongen; and a mounted contingent of 150 dragoons. Of these, according to Wightman, 'besides the dragoons', about 850 infantry were engaged at Glenshiel, while a detail guarded the packhorse train and field hospital during the battle. There were in addition approximately 150 loyalist Highland militiamen.[28] *The London Gazette* for 16–20 June 1719 ran a detailed account of the battle, drawing on news from Edinburgh including from Wightman. This confirmed the number of 850 Foot, quoted a lower figure of 136 militiamen, and stated 120 dragoons were engaged. The edition of the London newspaper *The Evening Post* for 20–23 June made mention that the baggage guard had numbered 100 Foot and 10 dragoons. By the addition of these troops to the number in *The London Gazette*, plus a few artillerymen, it seems Wightman's army at Glenshiel numbered about 1,230 officers and men; a figure in agreement with the Marquess of Tullibardine's estimation, that the enemy marched 'from Inverness with above twelve hundred Horse and Foot'.[29]

The order of battle of Wightman's army can be reconstructed in further detail. In regard to the regular infantry, as already mentioned, by early May Clayton's and Montagu's regiments were then at or marching for Inverness. However, it remains uncertain whether the combined likely strength of 890 officers and men fully arrived there, or whether detachments were stationed elsewhere. It must be assumed, for example, that when the part-built barracks at Kiliwhimen became a depot for the forthcoming campaign Wightman reinforced the 13-men first out-posted there. From a report mentioning the withdrawal of the Dutch regiments at the end of June 1719, it seems that four companies of Amerongen's and all of Huffel's Regiment arrived at Inverness during May.[30] Wightman mentioned four companies of Amerongen's at Glenshiel, while a newspaper ran news from Edinburgh dated 6 June mentioning that four Dutch companies (therefore from the 10 forming Huffel's Regiment) remained at Inverness when Wightman took the offensive.[31] These companies were probably near the established strength of 44 men of all ranks when leaving the Low Countries. Allowing for sick and other absentees, then, the 10 companies of Dutch infantry at Glenshiel together likely numbered 390 officers and men. Deducting the Dutch from the total of 950 regular infantry present leaves the three British regiments between them with 560 men of all ranks. 50, Wightman stated, were detached from Colonel Henry Harrison's Regiment based at Fort William.

---

28 Wightman's fullest account of the battle of Glenshiel appears to be the dispatch begun 11 and completed 13 June for the attention of Lord Cadogan. At this time Wightman also wrote summaries of the action for James Craggs, secretary of state for the Southern Department, and for the Duke of Roxburghe, secretary of state for Scotland; his dispatch to the latter, written from Glenshiel on the morning of 11 June and received at Whitehall eight days later, was published in *The London Gazette* for 16–20 June 1719. Referenced here is TNA, SP 43/61, folio 93, from under-secretary of state Charles Delayfaye's papers; and TNA, SP 43/61, folio 96, Delafaye's copy of Wightman's supplementary letter to Craggs, 'Giving an account of the disposition of the forces when they attacked the rebels and a list of the killed and wounded'.

29 Dickson, *Jacobite Attempt*, p. 270, Tullibardine's account.

30 Warrand, *More Culloden Papers*, p. 202.

31 *The Post Man and The Historical Account*, 11–13 June 1719.

Harrison had taken command of the regiment from the Earl of Hertford in February 1715. During the War of the Spanish Succession it had campaigned in Flanders under Marlborough, and was the last of three regiments of Foot to remain there under the Peace of Utrecht until returning to England in probably November 1715.[32] Of Colonel Jasper Clayton's Regiment, only four platoons are mentioned as having fought at Glenshiel. But, as will be argued here, the grenadier company was also present. Given that battalions on the current English establishment had 10 companies, each at full strength numbering 44 officers and men, it seems likely that for tactical purposes the companies acted as platoons. If so, and allowing for the inevitable absentees, then the five companies of Clayton's Regiment may have numbered 210 men. By this reckoning, the balance of Wightman's regular infantry came from Montagu's Regiment – so about 300 officers and men in seven companies. During the War of the Spanish Succession this unit had served very far afield, in Spain, in Flanders, and in 1711 in Canada, in the expedition against French-held Quebec. Colonel Edward Montagu, brother of George Montagu, Earl of Halifax, had taken command from his predecessor Colonel John Hill in July 1715, prior to the regiment being transferred from the Irish to the British establishment that August. The following November Montagu's Foot fought at Sheriffmuir and had remained in Scotland since.[33]

The Highland militia reinforcing Wightman's regular infantry were 80 Munro clansmen, led by Captain George Munro of Culcairn, and 56 men of Clan Sutherland, under the command of Lieutenant Hugh MacKay, an ex-regular officer on half-pay.[34] The involvement of his followers at the battle of Glenshiel would delight the Earl of Sutherland. Writing from his London residence on 19 June about the engagement to the Earl of Stanhope, Sutherland crowed that 'there were no Highlanders with the regular troops but some of mine and some of the Munros. My folks were upon the right of the regular forces and behaved themselves as if I had inspired them'.[35]

Together with most of the loyalist militia, 30 of 150 dragoons under Wightman's immediate command remained based about Inverness.[36] The 120 officers and men at Glenshiel were detached from the four dragoon regiments in Scotland at the time, brought under the command of Major Patrick Robertson of Campbell's North British Royal Dragoons. This was the first time regular cavalry had deployed so far into the western Highlands, terrain that was considered wholly unsuitable for them. Later Wightman proudly mentioned this achievement: 'It will be almost impossible to persuade the world that Horse were brought this length, and not to have any out of order'. This, he continued, 'in a great measure is owing to Major Robinson [sic] of the Grey Dragoons,

32 Dalton, *Army Lists and Commission Registers,* vol. 1, p. 154, vol. 6, p. 302; W.A. Shaw and F.H. Slingsby (eds.), *Calendar of Treasury Books, Volume 29, 1714-1715* (1957), p. cxvii.

33 Dalton, *Army Lists and Commission Registers*, vol. 1, p. 148, vol. 6, p. 106; Shaw and Slingsby, *Calendar of Treasury Books, Volume 29*, p. cxvii.

34 TNA, SP 55/8/183, Lord Roxburghe to Earl Stanhope, 23 June 1719.

35 W. Fraser (ed.), *The Sutherland Book,* 3 vols. (1892), vol. 1, p. 224.

36 *The Post Man and The Historical Account*, 11–13 June 1719; *The Weekly Journal or British Gazetteer*, 23 May 1719.

50. Designed as siege weapons, Coehoorn mortars with Wightman's army at Glenshiel also proved highly effective as battlefield artillery. (Illustration by Ed Dovey, © Helion & Company Limited)

whose zeal has been remarkable'.[37] At a time when officers regularly sought to gain promotion by exchanging between regiments, Robertson was unusual for having spent his career so far with one. He was commissioned as a cornet into the then Royal Scots Dragoons in 1692 (when the unit was becoming known for having grey horses). During the War of the Spanish Succession Campbell served with the 'Grey Dragoons' throughout Marlborough's campaigns. He was promoted lieutenant in 1702, captain-lieutenant by 1704, and full troop captain in 1707. In 1715 the regiment, then the Earl of Portmore's Dragoons, fought at the battle of Sheriffmuir, where Campbell was wounded. He was promoted major in May 1717.[38]

Artillery as well as cavalry was difficult to deploy on Highland terrain. Nonetheless, while it was impracticable to take wheeled cannon Wightman's army carried with it a battery of four so-called Coehoorn mortars. Firing hollow shells, known as bombs or grenades, these portable anti-personnel weapons had been invented in the 1670s by the Dutch military engineer Menno van Coehoorn as trench mortars for siege-work. They were described in 1704 by Vauban, the renowned French military engineer, and Coehoorn's contemporary and great rival, as 'small, portable grenade-launching mortars carried by two men, with which they [i.e. Dutch and allied forces] provide a tremendous weight of fire'.[39] Designed for use *en masse* in siege-work, the Coehoorn mortars deployed at Glenshiel demonstrated the weapon could have significant effect in a field engagement. The mortars came from storage, either from Edinburgh, Stirling or Fort William. Nationally at this time there was a plethora of artillery (although serviceable carriages and mounts for the weapons were in short supply), kept at the forts and castles of the garrisons of Great Britain. In 1716 there were probably more than 3,200 pieces of cast iron and brass ordnance of all sorts, cannon, howitzers and mortars included.[40]

Bombardiers to serve the Coehoorn mortars (each required just a two-man crew) came from among the dozen garrison artillerymen in Scotland at the time, and from the Field Train in North Britain based at Edinburgh. Formed by the Board of Ordnance in December 1708 during the War of the Spanish Succession, the role of the Field Train in North Britain was, like other trains with British land forces, similarly formed during wartime on an ad hoc basis, to provide mobile artillery support. However, the poor performance of the artillery train in Scotland during the 1715–16 rising had been the main reason for the formation in May 1716 of a 'new establishment'; of the first two 'marching companies' of what became the Royal Regiment of Artillery. Henceforth, the Board of Ordnance's 'old establishment' of artillery trains, including that in North Britain, would be wound down as a cost-saving measure to be replaced by marching companies on the new establishment. Accordingly, the North British Establishment for 1717 of 26 officers, gunners

---

37 TNA, SP 43/61, folio 93.

38 Dalton, *Army Lists and Commission Registers*, vol. 5, part 2, pp. 24–5.

39 Vauban, from *Traité de l'attaque des places* (c.1704), cited in J. Ostwald, *Vauban under Siege: Engineering Efficiency and Martial Vigor in the War if the Spanish Succession* (2007), p. 289.

40 Chandler, *Warfare in the Age of Marlborough*, p. 148.

and bombardiers was reduced to 21 the following year.[41] By 1725, the 'old military establishment in North Britain' had dwindled to 12 officers and men, while the 'new military branch' of the Royal Artillery grew in strength.[42] The Coehoorn mortars would be carried by packhorse into the Highlands, the separate barrel and wooden bed (firing platform), the bombs and equipment for each piece broken down into loads; rather as in the later 19th century light field artillery known as screw guns, designed to be dismantled into mule-borne loads, were deployed by the British Army on campaign in the mountainous north-west frontier of India.

Wightman's Advance and Jacobite Preparations

Early on Friday 5 June, Wightman's column marched southwestward from Inverness heading for Kiliwhimen; a distance of about 28 miles (45 km) by the present B8682 road. This follows approximately the course of the trackway Wightman took that led further to Fort William. This easier way, crossing moorland and areas of cultivated ground, ran more or less parallel with but a couple of miles inland of the southerly shore of Loch Ness. It avoided the higher hills that fell steeply and heavily wooded to the shore of the loch.[43]

Wightman reached Kiliwhimen late on Saturday and rested his men there all next day. They also waited for fresh packhorses to carry the additional stores at Kiliwhimen brought by boat from Inverness. However, the expected horses did not arrive, so Wightman resumed the advance taking fewer supplies than intended: 'little more than the men could carry with them', as he put it.[44] An unnamed soldier correspondent mentioned the shortage and loss of packhorses, either by injury to the animals or desertion of their civilian handlers. He was reported as saying: 'Often wanting provisions [...] we have lost a great many horses in the mountains that were to carry our baggage'.[45] It was at Kiliwhimen that Colonel Henry Harrison joined Wightman with 50 men of his regiment from Fort William. Harrison seems to have been another of Wightman's associates; after the battle of Glenshiel he wrote to the Earl Cadogan that Harrison deserved 'a just recommendation for his good behaviour'.[46]

On the morning of Monday 8 June Wightman's army left Kiliwhimen. After fording the River Oich near the barracks, the column took a trackway heading north-easterly (leading eventually back to Inverness) beside the shoreline of Loch Ness. After several miles they turned westward, away from the loch and into Glen Moriston. From here onward there was no clear routeway. A few years later a military cartographer mapped this as a region

41   *Ibid.*, pp. 161–2, 169; W.A. Shaw and F.H. Slingsby (eds.), *Calendar of Treasury Books, Volume 31, 1717* (1960), pp. clxxxiv–clxxxv; W.A. Shaw and F.H. Slingsby (eds.), *Calendar of Treasury Books, Volume 32, 1718* (1962), p. clxciii.

42   R.A. Cleaveland, *Notes on the Early History of the Royal Regiment of Artillery* (undated), p. 205.

43   This route was depicted on a Board of Ordnance survey map of *c.*1727, titled 'To his Excellency General Wade [...] Plan containing Lochness, Lochoych, Lochlochey [*sic*] & all the rivers and strips of water that runs in & set out from the same [...]', NLS, Military Maps of Scotland (18th century), MS.1648 Z.03/21.

44   TNA, SP 43/61 folio 93.

45   *The Post Man and The Historical Account*, 2–4 July 1719.

46   TNA, SP 43/61 folio 93.

of 'barren hills', with no tracks worthy of depiction. When in later June the aforementioned correspondent with the column returned to Inverness, he wrote of 'having marched above 100 miles through rocks, mountains and bogs', and of 'so many difficulties that some days we could not march above three miles in 12 hours, and up such ascents and down through such steep rocks, that it is almost incredible we could pass through that difficult country'.[47] Notwithstanding the challenging terrain, Wightman's army made steady progress, following the south-westerly course through the glen of the River Moriston to its confluence with Loch Cluanie. Having marched the length of Glen Cluanie, the army camped in its westerly reaches on Tuesday evening. This was probably in Strathloan, not far from the present Cluanie Inn.[48] Measured by today's roads, Wightman troops had marched about 26 miles (42 km) from Kiliwhimen. They were now within five miles (8 km) of the Jacobite positions in Glenshiel.

The arrival of the government army came as no surprise to the Jacobites; their scouts and informants had monitored the column's progress since leaving Inverness. On the evening of 9 June, lookouts under the charge of Lord George Murray posted at the easterly entrance to Glenshiel watched Wightman's men setting up camp beside Loch Cluanie and reported back to the main body further up the glen.[49]

The Jacobites had by then strengthened the naturally strong defensive position on the foothills in the little glen by building fieldworks in the form of dry stone walls, remains of which are still visible. These walls, or breastworks, are shown on contemporary depictions of the battle, on the maps drawn by Lieutenant Jean Henri Bastide, as an officer in Montagu's Regiment an eyewitness, and on the panorama of the engagement painted by the Dutch artist Peter Tillemans.[50]

51. View eastward into Glen Cluanie, along which Wightman's army advanced on 9 May 1719. Although Loch Cluanie, centre, far middle distance, has expanded since being dammed in the 1950s, it was a substantial expanse of water in the 18th century.

---

47   NLS, MS.1648 Z.03/21; *The Post Man and The Historical Account*, 2–4 July 1719.
48   Dickson, *Jacobite Attempt*, p. xlix.
49   *Ibid.*, p. 270, Tullibardine's account.
50   Bastide drew four detailed, near identical battle maps in manuscript form (one annotated in French), depicting from a southerly perspective the deployments and movements of both armies. That referenced here (and reproduced as Plate D in the colour section) is: NLS, MS 1648 Z.03/22a,

52. Tumbled remains (foreground) of one of the dry stone wall breastworks the Jacobites constructed on the fortified bluff. The Jacobites retreated up the mountainous slopes in the far distance.

On the bluff rising north of the River Shiel overlooking the drove road, the Jacobites constructed a discontinuous line of breastworks at vantage points commanding the approaches. Although perhaps not much more than waist high, given the advantage of higher ground these made effective firing positions against attackers scrambling up the steep hillside. On the summit of the bluff (although this about 500 foot – 150 metre – high hilltop is only the lower reach of a ridgeline rising increasingly steeply to the peak Sgur na Ciste Dubhe at 3,370 feet – 1027 metres) a pentagonal dry stone wall enclosure formed a final defence. This breastwork was defensively not well situated, in a hollow overlooked by surrounding ground. However, this tactical oversight is explainable in that the Jacobites adapted a pre-standing livestock enclosure.[51] At the southerly foot of the bluff a further breastwork blocked the drove road and reached to the River Shiel.[52] This marked the

A Plan of the Field of Battle that was fought on the 10th June 1719, at the Pass of Glenshiels [sic] in North Britain with ye Dispositions of his Majtys. Forces under ye Command of Majr. Genl. Wightman & those of the Rebels. An engraved plan of the battle from an easterly perspective also attributed to Bastide is reproduced here as Colour Plate E: NLS, EMS.s 163, *A Disposition of his Majesties Forces Commanded by Majr. Gen. Wightman & of ye Rebels at ye Pass of Glenshiels [sic] in Kintail in North Britain where ye Battle was Fought on ye 10th of June 1719.* Bastide's maps included an alphanumeric key identifying the units engaged and their movements. These annotations are very useful in reconstructing the likely course of the battle. The Tillemans painting of *c.*1719, now in the collection of the Scottish National Portrait Gallery, is also reproduced here as Colour Plate E.

51 On a terrace below the enclosure are remains of associated sheilings, the stone huts providing accommodation for herdsmen during the summer grazing season on mountain pastures. See Anon., 'Battlefield Remains', *The National Trust for Scotland Archaeology Bulletin*, 9 (1997), p. 1. One such hut is depicted on the Tillemans painting.

52 Because of later road building and widening no noticeable remains of this breastwork appear to have survived to the present.

53. View eastward into Glenshiel, on the line of the later 18th century military road traversing the glen. This is likely the vicinity of Strathloan, where Wightman's army first encountered Jacobite outposts on 10 June 1719.

right of the centre of the Jacobite line. The fieldworks strengthened a position naturally protected by the river to the right, and to the front by a stream-fed valley separating the fortified bluff from an approximately parallel rockier ridge some 400 yards (370 metres) eastward. It was towards the centre the Jacobites 'supposed and believed the regular troops would chiefly attack, being the most open and the best and common passage and road'.[53]

The Battle of Glenshiel

Wightman was determined as a symbolic gesture to bring the Jacobites to battle on Charles Francis Edward Stuart's thirty-first birthday. However, that morning, 10 June, his troops unhurriedly broke camp. When the vanguard eventually advanced from Strathloan towards Glenshiel Lord George Murray's outposts fell back before them, keeping distance by about half a mile. Intelligence reports led Wightman to expect the Jacobites to deploy in the wide expanse of the easterly mouth of the glen, where the ground appeared to suit the Highlanders' favoured tactic of a massed charge. At one point Murray's men stood for a while as if intending to provoke an engagement. But whether or not this was a ploy to delay the enemy advance, Murray withdrew to the main position in the narrowing glen. From there the Jacobites watched Wightman's army come into view at about two o'clock in the afternoon.[54]

The size of the Jacobite army remains debatable. Later next day Wightman understood that 1,640 Highlanders had joined in the battle, while 500 more gathered on the higher slopes of Glenshiel had remained onlookers. Also writing on 11 June, Captain James Abercrombie, wounded during the engagement, agreed that 'we attacked the rebels when they were celebrating the Pretender's birthday [...] and [there] were sixteen hundred Highlanders and

---

53   A.H. Millar (ed.), 'The Battle of Glenshiel. Note upon an unpublished letter in the possession of C.S. Home-Drummond-Moray Esq. of Abercairnet', *Proceedings of The Society of Antiquaries of Scotland,* 19 (1884–5), p. 65.

54   Dickson, *Jacobite Attempt,* p. 270, Tullibardine's account; *The London Gazette* for 16–20 June 1719, citing Wightman's dispatch to the Duke of Roxburghe.

three hundred Spaniards'.[55] In early July, Wightman provided Lord Carpenter and King George's ministers with more detailed estimates. 'The names and numbers of those who were in the rebellion and engaged at Glenshiel' included a total 'in action' of 1,595 Highlanders – for the most part, 950 of the Earl of Seaforth's men, 300 Camerons, and 150 MacDonalds of Glengarry – as well as 274 Spanish foot. The report further mentioned the Jacobites had expected reinforcements. 500 MacDonalds of Clanranald, from Knoydart, Morar, Arisaig and Moidart, the areas westward of Fort William known collectively as the 'Rough Bounds', were expected at Glenshiel late on 10 June or early next day, while from the east Chisholm of Strathglass and Grant of Glenmoriston were believed to be on their way with at least 120 followers.[56]

Other sources indicate, however, that there were fewer Jacobites than the British Army officers had been led to believe. Tullibardine's dispatch written for the Earl of Mar on 16 June (and the similar copy included in 'The Distinct Abridgement' transcribed by Oliphant), and an anonymous account penned on 15 June by an informed Jacobite sympathiser, mentioned the Jacobite positions were held by about 1,100 Highlanders.[57] Furthermore, James Keith recollected that 'we ordered the gentlemen who were nearest us to assemble their vassals, but [...] not above a thousand men appeared, and even those seemed not very fond of the enterprise'.[58] It must be assumed that Tullibardine as commander-in-chief, and Keith as a fellow senior officer and brother to the de facto second-in-command, knew fairly well the number of men (and while Keith was a critical observer, had he wished to cast aspersions on Tullibardine had more reason to exaggerate than underestimate the size of the Jacobite army).

The discrepancy of up to 500 Highlanders between Jacobite and government sources can be accounted for as representing those clansmen in the vicinity of the battle who did not fight. In the statistics presented in July, Wightman omitted the 'five hundred on the hills' mentioned in June, and instead included them among the 1,595 all told 'in the rebellion and engagement'. Lieutenant Bastide's annotated maps also noted the 'straggling number of Highlanders' at the periphery of the battle. Tullibardine mentioned the 'several men that were to [have] been with us on the top of the mountains on each side, yet they did not descend to incorporate with the rest'.[59] During the battle Wightman was concerned these uncommitted Highlanders would encircle his force and attack the packhorse train, but in fact they were not under Tullibardine's command. James Keith mentioned that even the clansmen in the Jacobite battle line were unenthusiastic. They had come in obedience at the behest of their chiefs, especially the powerful Earl of Seaforth, but, as events would show, their support was half-hearted. Those Highlanders who watched from higher ground were even more doubtful of the outcome, and waited on the turn of events before committing themselves.

55   TNA, SP 43/61 folio 93, folio 97.
56   Atholl, *Chronicles*, vol. 2, p. 288.
57   Dickson, *Jacobite Attempt*, p. 270; Oliphant, 'Distinct Abridgment', *Jacobite Lairds of Gask*, pp. 462–4; Millar, 'Battle of Glenshiel. Note upon an unpublished letter', pp. 64–6.
58   Keith, *Fragment of a Memoir*, p. 51.
59   Dickson, *Jacobite Attempt*, p. 270.

Taking this evidence into account, the best estimate would be that few more than 1,100 clansmen and other Scots serving as volunteers were in the Jacobite battle line. Of the 274 or so Spanish infantry, about 30 of them, with some sick comrades, during the battle remained at the camp at Achadh nan Seilach guarding the baggage and remaining munitions. About 230 Spanish soldiers therefore helped defend the little glen. Including also the supernumerary officers and adventurers with the expedition, the Jacobite army probably numbered 1,400 men in all.

They deployed under the direction of Brigadier Colin Campbell of Ormidale. A council of war had unanimously agreed that Ormidale should make 'all the dispositions for defending the pass and receiving the regular forces'.[60] South of the River Shiel, in an advanced position about 550 yards (500 metres) forward of the fortified bluff, the right of the Jacobite line rested on a prominent 750 foot (230 metre) high conical foothill of the lower slopes of the south Glenshiel ridge. Left undefended by field works, the hilltop was held by about 150 Highlanders, mostly Seaforth's men. They were commanded by Lord George Murray, assisted by John MacKenzie of Avoch, and John MacDougall of Dunollie (with his 10 followers). They were meant to be reinforced by another 80 clansmen, 'who were to have come from the top of the mountain above them, but 'tho [sic] they sent twice that they were coming yet they only beheld the scuffle at a distance'.[61] Across the river, the Spanish Foot manned the breastworks at the drove road and on the fortified bluff above. Reinforcing them was Lochiel with 150 Camerons, and next in line 150 Glengarry MacDonalds, led, in the apparent absence of Alasdair Dubh MacDonnell, 11th chief of Glengarry (who had fought at Sheriffmuir) by John MacDonald of Shian and the young Donald MacDonald, 5th Baronet of the Skye MacDonalds of Sleat. Next in position as the extended Jacobite line curved uphill was a body of 150 men from the Kintail region, including 50 MacLeods from Glenelg, then the 80 MacGregors and volunteers led by Rob Roy. To their left were about 80 men of Clan MacKinnon from Skye (probably led by John MacKinnon), then 200 of Seaforth's clansmen under the command of Sir John MacKenzie of Coul. Furthest left, 'at some distance', Seaforth himself held the end of the Jacobite line with as many as 250 'of his best men, upon a steep rock'.[62]

The Jacobite position extended for more than a mile (1.6 km) across the hillsides and narrow floor of the glen. The line curved in the form of a horseshoe, with its opening facing east. One tip of the horseshoe represented Murray's position on the conical hill south of the river, the other marked Seaforth's northerly position high on the rocky ridgeline forward of the fortified bluff. The mid-point of the horseshoe's inner curve was the fortified bluff and centre of the position. It was a 'post, which', as James Keith recollected, 'by the situation, was strong enough had it been well defended; our right was covered by a rivulet [the River Shiel] which was difficult to pass, and our left by a ravine, and in the front the ground was so rugged and

60 Millar, 'Battle of Glenshiel. Note upon an unpublished letter', p. 65.
61 Oliphant, 'Distinct Abridgment', *Jacobite Lairds of Gask*, p. 462
62 *Ibid.*

54. Panorama of Glenshiel, looking eastward from the summit of the fortified bluff at the Jacobite centre. This gives an impression of the horseshoe-shaped Jacobite lines; with, far left middle distance, the rising outcrop MacKenzies occupied as the Jacobite left; and, centre right, middle distance, the conical hill held by Lord George Murray's men.

55. View westward into Glenshiel, from the approximate position of the British start line. Note at right steep slopes traversed by Clayton's right wing. Partly visible far left is one of the glacial drumlins that obstructed the advance of the British left.

steep it was almost impossible to come at us'.[63] The open horseshoe invited a frontal attack westward across the narrowing floor of the glen. Perhaps Campbell of Ormidale made his dispositions with this in mind, assuming regular officers would be wary of committing to manoeuvre across the higher rocky slopes. While the rugged hillsides were in turn not ideal ground for launching a massed Highland charge, if the enemy attacked uphill they would be vulnerable to localised counter-attack by rushes of clansmen. The Jacobites were well-placed for an offensive or a defensive action. However, because of uncertainty over the battle readiness of many clansmen the latter course of action ensued. But if setbacks for the government forces stiffened the Highlanders' resolve, then a charge might prove decisive.

Senior Jacobites without their own followers took position to assist in the direction of the expected engagement. Marischal and Campbell of Ormidale accompanied Seaforth on the left. Brigadier Mackintosh of Borlum accompanied Lieutenant-Colonel Bolaño on the fortified bluff, with Campbell of Glendaruel, Tullibardine, Lochiel and Rob Roy elsewhere in the centre; 'where all imagined the main attack would happen, it being by far the easiest ground, beside the only way through the glen'.[64]

'Their dispositions for defence were extraordinary', Wightman acknowledged, 'with the advantage of rocks, mountains and entrenchments'.[65] He rode ahead escorted by dragoons and took some time to view and assess the enemy position. A detachment of six dragoons served as lookouts on a low hillock several hundred yards in front of the government army as it deployed. It took position across the glen floor a mile or so from the Jacobite centre and largely hidden from it, at a place known in Gaelic as Luban Eorna – the barley fields beside the bending river.

63 Keith, *Fragment of a Memoir*, p. 51.
64 Oliphant, 'Distinct Abridgment', *Jacobite Lairds of Gask*, p. 462
65 *The London Gazette*, 16–20 June 1719.

Wightman's line of battle formed in 10 divisions. Some way up the northerly hill slopes, Lieutenant Mackay's 56 Sutherland militiamen occupied the far right of the line. Next on the right flank were the grenadier companies of the regiments of Montagu, Clayton, Huffel and Amerongen, combined as an independent tactical battalion. They took the honoured position on the right of the regular infantry as was customary for these elite troops. There were three detachments – two, at the far right a sergeant and 12 grenadiers, then an officer and 24 grenadiers, in close support of the militia, then the 120-strong main body. The 158 grenadiers were under the overall command of Major Richard Milburn of Montagu's Regiment. Milburn was another veteran of the War of the Spanish Succession in Flanders and Spain. As brevet colonel in Montagu's absence, in 1715 he had led the regiment at Sheriffmuir.[66] To the left of the grenadiers were the line infantry. First was Montagu's Regiment, led by its second-in-command Lieutenant-Colonel Herbert Lawrence (another long-serving regimental officer), next was Colonel Henry Harrison's detached battalion. Wightman mentioned that 'out of the two battalions with me [i.e. Montagu's and Clayton's regiments], together with the detachment [the 50 men of Harrison's Regiment] I made up three', by placing some of Montagu's men under Harrison's command. These three ad hoc tactical battalions each numbered about 160 men. Next in line after Harrison's battalion were the Dutch Foot, elements of Huffel's and Amerongen's regiments, together perhaps 210 men (assuming that the remaining 100 Dutch infantrymen guarded the baggage). The Highlanders, grenadiers, and Anglo-Dutch Foot formed a strong right wing under acting Brigadier Jasper Clayton. The main body of dragoons, the Coehoorn mortar parties, and the packhorse train guarded by 10 dragoons and 100 (probably Dutch) Foot formed the centre of Wightman's line, straddling the drove road and nearest the River Shiel. A small detachment of infantry probably helped guard and handle the mortars. Across and drawn up south of the River Shiel were the 160 men in four platoons of Clayton's Regiment. Alongside them the 80 Munro clansmen led by Captain Munro of Culcairn held the army's far left flank. This much smaller left wing was commanded by Lieutenant-Colonel John Reading, second-in-command of Clayton's Regiment and another veteran of the War of the Spanish Succession.

Major-General Wightman 'was posted in the centre where everyone had free access to him for orders'.[67] Contrary to Jacobite expectations, instead of a frontal assault Wightman planned to make the main attack by his strong right wing against the enemy left, notwithstanding the difficulties of advancing steeply uphill. He intended 'to gain the tops of the mountains and attack the left of the rebels, who were drawn up in a half circle'.[68]

The battle of Glenshiel began at approximately five o'clock in the afternoon, when the government army commenced a general advance along the glen. Given continued fine weather, there were still more than five hours of

---

66 The deployment of the grenadiers is mentioned in Lieutenant Bastide's map, NLS, MS 1648 Z.03/22a. For Milburn, see Dalton, *Army Lists and Commission Registers*, vol. 5, pp. 66, 168, 237.
67 *The London Gazette*, 16–20 June 1719.
68 TNA, SP 43/61 folio 96, summary appended to Wightman's report.

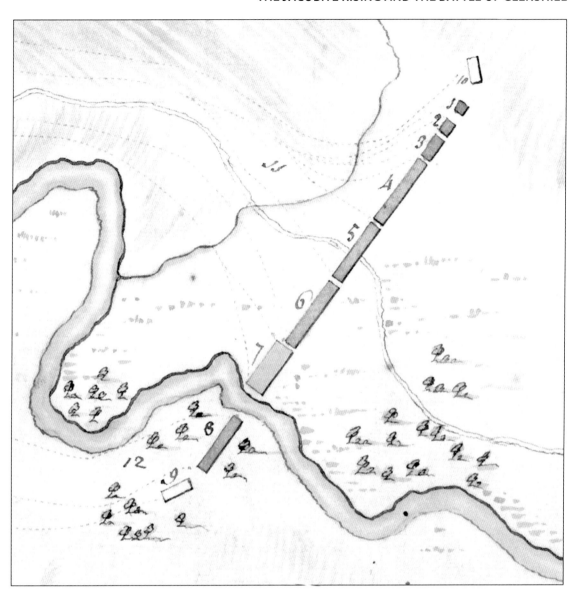

56. Starting line of battle of the British army. Detail from Lieutenant John Bastide's 'Plan of the Field of Battle that was fought on ye 10th of June 1719, at the Pass of Glenshiels [*sic*]'. The numbered references were described in Bastide's key as follows (spellings as per original): '10 The Sutherland Highl[anders]; 1 A serjt and twelve granadiers; 2 An officer & 24 granadiers; 3 Main body of granadiers 120 in number; 4 Col. Montague's regimt; 5 Col. Harrison's detatcht Battalion; 6 Huffel's Regiment and four Companys of ameronce; 7 Dragoons; 8 Col. Clayton's Regiment; 9 The Monro's Highlanders'; 12 Clayton's march by the left'.
(Reproduced by permission of the National Library of Scotland)

57. The conical hill held as the Jacobite right, photographed from the central fortified bluff.

daylight to decide the outcome. The encounter, as Wightman later put it, would be decided by 'continual fire and hazardous dispute'.[69]

The first engagement developed south of the River Shiel. Lieutenant-Colonel Reading's left wing set out to storm Lord George Murray's hilltop position, with the support of a preparatory mortar bombardment. This may have been an early adjustment of Wightman's battle plan; 'finding it more necessary to begin the attack on the enemy's right with the left of his line'.[70] The troops advancing south of the river were slowed by a series of hillocks; these were drumlins, mounds of soil, clay and fragmented rock deposited in the glen floor after the last Ice Age. While the Munros and Clayton's platoons moved into attacking positions, shielded by a screen of dragoons the four Coehoorn mortars were brought into range opposite the conical hill. Bombs following a high curving trajectory began to fall among or near Murray's men, as the Munros and two of Clayton's platoons began to ascend the steep slopes. In doing so they were shot at from a distance by Highlanders on the higher ground to their left, and by a few others who had worked their way behind them. These sharpshooters took cover behind rocks and the trees of the open woodland then covering parts of the glen.

The Tillemans painting (see Colour Plate C) provides an interesting representation at this point in the battle of the platoon as a mobile tactical formation, rather than as a sub-division of a battalion's firing line. While one platoon of Clayton's Regiment is depicted advancing beside the river on level ground in close-order column four ranks deep, others ahead are shown breaking into irregular groups or knots of men due to the difficulty of keeping in rank on the steepening rocky ground. A company-size platoon of 42 men deployed in the customary close order firing line three ranks deep occupied a frontage of about 16 yards (approximately 15 metres); a tight formation difficult to maintain on sloping rough ground.[71]

Both sides were said to have 'fired several times on [each] other without doing much damage'.[72] The limitations of the combatants' musketry came to characterise the battle. The rugged terrain made concentrated platoon fire hard to achieve, and the regulars were not proficient in aimed firing. At Glenshiel this resulted in the expenditure by government troops of a great

---

69 TNA, SP 43/61 folio 93.
70 TNA, SP 43/61 folio 96.
71 Guy, 'Army of the Georges', p. 103, depicting the 'British platoon firing system c.1709'.
72 Oliphant, 'Distinct Abridgment', *Jacobite Lairds of Gask*, p. 463

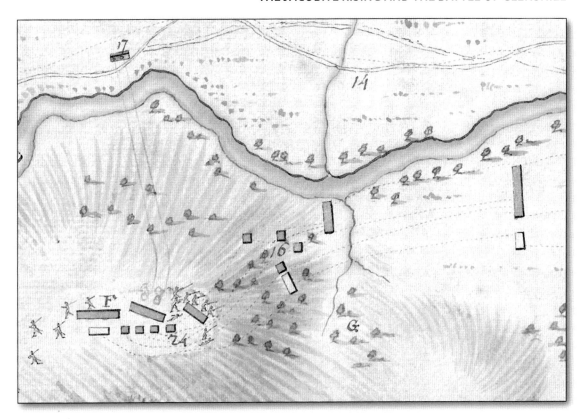

deal of ammunition for very few enemy casualties inflicted. Four and a half years later, Major-General George Wade attributed this outcome to:

> The great disadvantages regular troops are under when they engage with those who inhabit mountainous situations […]. They are unacquainted with the passages by which the mountains are traversed, exposed to frequent ambuscades, and shots from the tops of the hills which they return without effect, as it happened at the affair of Glenshiel […] [where] a considerable number of your majesty's troops were killed and wounded.[73]

Highlanders, on the other hand, while adept at individual marksmanship lacked training to direct their shots to inflict heavy casualties in a firefight. Leading his men in the first attack against the hilltop position, George Munro of Culcairn was shot in the thigh: 'from a party of the rebel Highlanders posted upon the declivity of a mountain, who kept on firing at him after he was down, *according to their want of discipline, in spending much fire upon one single officer, which, distributed among the body, might thin the ranks of their enemy*' [author's emphasis].[74] Some Jacobites rushed forward apparently intent on finishing off Munro, but he was protected by one of his militiamen while a sergeant led a detachment that drove the enemy back.

58. Developing assault by Wightman's left upon the Jacobite right occupying the conical hill. Detail from Lieutenant Bastide's 'Plan of the Field of Battle'. Refence number 16 refers to: 'Clayton's four plottoons & the Monro's making ye first attack on the rebells right' (spelling as per original). For explanation of reference letters F and G, and numbers 17 and 24, see commentary for Colour Plate D. (Reproduced by permission of the National Library of Scotland)

73 Allardyce, *Historical Papers*, vol. 1, pp. 139–40.
74 Jamieson, *Letters from a Gentleman,* vol. 2, p. 13.

With the government troops pinned down by the Highlanders' fire, the assault faltered and lost momentum for some time. But the Munro's local counter attack may have coincided with the scrambling, outflanking advance further round the hill by the two other platoons of Clayton's Regiment. In the face of this renewed assault, the Jacobites began abandoning the hilltop before it came to hand-to-hand fighting. The clansmen retreated westward across a steep ravine in which tumbled a mountain stream. Lord George Murray, MacKenzie of Avoch and MacDougall of Dunollie bravely attempted to encourage the remaining men to hold their ground. However, when Murray was wounded in the leg – shot by the advancing government troops, or struck by a fragment of exploding mortar bomb – they too abandoned the summit and joined those of their comrades rallied on the far side of the ravine. Murray's shaken detachment would occupy this position for the remainder of the battle, but played no further active part. Their defeat had been due largely to the accuracy and demoralising effect of the fire of the Coehoorn mortar crews in the glen below. An unanticipated side effect of which had been to set alight undergrowth turned tinder-dry by the recent hot weather: 'The grenades thrown from the cannons [i.e. meaning mortars] among the enemy did not only surprise the Highlanders and gall them, but fired the long heather where they were lying, and was among the first things that brought them in disorder'.[75]

Wightman had waited to commit Clayton's wing fully against the enemy's left in case Reading needed reinforcement. Once it appeared that Murray's force had been dislodged, the advance began up the steepening hillsides on the right. Lieutenant Bastide's maps and the Tillemans painting show that the British and Dutch units adopted both narrower column and more extended line formations in approaching their objective, the rocky ridgeline forward of the Jacobite centre (the northerly tip of the 'horseshoe'). The broken ground (and probable warmth of the evening?) inevitably made their advance slow and deliberate. Standing orders of the British Army of the period in any case tended to stress that advancing infantry should proceed unhurriedly, so as to maintain formation and ensure the men were not breathless when they closed with the enemy.[76]

Furthest uphill leading as a skirmishing screen were the Sutherland militia, with both smaller detachments of grenadiers in close support. They were first to notice further up the ridge the Earl of Seaforth's detached battalion. From here the MacKenzie's threatened to outflank Clayton's wing. To counter this, screened by the grenadiers and militia the British and Dutch battalions wheeled to the right to force Seaforth's position. Meanwhile two advanced platoons pressed forward to outflank the MacKenzies to the south.

On the hillside a firefight broke out as the government troops closed in. This exchange of musketry at long range caused few casualties, but probably brought Clayton's advance to an awkward halt. The reluctance of Lord George Murray's men on the right to engage at close quarters, however, had given notice that many clansmen were not committed to the fight. As Sir John

---

75 Graham, *Annals and Correspondence of the [...] Earls of Stair*, vol. 1, p. 120, Sir David Dalrymple to Stair, July 1719.

76 See Blackmore, *Destructive and Formidable,* pp. 92–3, citing orders issued in 1712 by Major-General Lord Cobham in command of the British garrison of Ghent.

59. Foreground, the (now partly forest covered) rocky ridgeline held by MacKenzies high on the Jacobite left.

MacKenzie of Coul hurried up his 200 men in Seaforth's support, some held back or turned away as the enemy came in sight. Nonetheless, the engagement intensified as Coul's men came up. The Anglo-Dutch units responded by extending and thickening their firing line further up the mountainside.

Seaforth sent to the centre for reinforcements, but soon after Brigadier Campbell of Ormidale arrived there in person. Attempting to exert some control and direction over the situation, Ormidale, believing the enemy still intended to shift the weight of their attack against the centre, delayed the 80 MacGregors and volunteers with the MacKinnons from going to reinforce the left.[77] Worryingly, however, clansmen could already be seen retiring across the mountainside from the firefight on the left, and so Rob Roy took it upon himself to lead his men and the MacKinnons that way. Before nearing the enemy, they found an increasing number of MacKenzies falling back in the face of the Anglo-Dutch platoon fire. Seaforth had been wounded in the arm and was being helped away, further dampening the fighting spirit of his men. He was said to have 'behaved gallantly, but his friends were backward. In so far that it was with difficulty he had men to support him retiring to the top of the hill'.[78] Seaforth himself later admitted that few of his men were engaged, 'tho' [sic] a great many standing by'.[79]

Rob Roy's detachment now also fell back in what was fast becoming a general retreat, joined by the body of Kintail men led from the centre by Campbell of Glendaruel. They too had gone to shore up the collapsing left wing; 'but seeing everybody retire before them, occasioned their doing also

---

77   Dickson, *Jacobite Attempt*, p. 272, Tullibardine's account.
78   Millar, 'Battle of Glenshiel. Note upon an unpublished letter', p. 65.
79   Dickson, *Jacobite Attempt*, p. 274, Seaforth to James Francis Edward Stuart, 10 Aug. 1719.

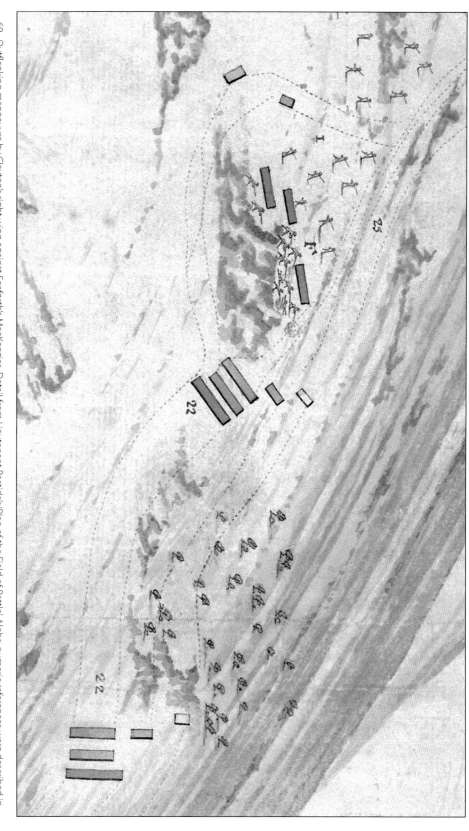

60 Outflanking manoeuvre by Clayton's right wing against Seaforth's Mackenzies. Detail from Lieutenant Bastide's 'Plan of the Field of Battle'. Alpha-numeric references were described in Bastide's key as follows: 'F the Highlanders drawn up before the attack; 22 Our march in line of battle to the rock where the attack began under the command of Col. Clayton; 23 Our right pursue the rebels'. (Reproduced by permission of the National Library of Scotland)

the same'.[80] The Anglo-Dutch had by now overrun the rocky ridgeline the MacKenzies had occupied, and so threatened to cut off the uphill way of retreat of the remaining Jacobites holding the centre. The last reinforcements to arrive on the left were some Camerons led by Lochiel. Together with clansmen rallied by Glendaruel, the Earl Marischal and Campbell of Ormidale they formed a firing line. For a while this ad hoc rearguard appears to have slowed the approaching Anglo-Dutch Foot.

Since Lord George Murray's detachment had been driven from the conical hill, fighting south of the River Shiel had petered out. There was a stalemate of desultory exchanges of musketry fire at long range. Lieutenant-Colonel Reading was content to hold position on the hill to anchor the army's left, rather than launch the Munros and Clayton's platoons in a tricky attack across the ravine overlooked by Lord George Murray's remaining men. A small party of probably Cameron Highlanders sent across the river from the roadside barricade and fortified bluff arrived as reinforcements. However, they too did no more than hold position on the right of the Jacobite line.

With the left secured and Clayton's attack on the right increasingly gaining ground, Wightman launched his final assault against the Jacobite centre. As the battle developed, the advance of the troops remaining on the floor of the glen north of the river had been coordinated with the shifting positions of the units pressing forward on the high ground to left and right. Wightman had taken particular care to move the packhorse train and the field hospital forward in pace with the attack. He was mindful that advancing further into the little glen risked envelopment by the uncommitted Highlanders seen on the mountainsides.

While the main body of mounted dragoons stood by to discourage an enemy counter attack, the mortars were shifted and brought forward to a firing position facing the fortified bluff. Probably within 250 yards (228 metres) of the Spanish positions the four Coehoorn's opened fire. While a platoon, or more, of Clayton's Regiment, so at least 40 men, gathered on the south bank of the river, Wightman himself organised an assault party of 35 dismounted dragoons. While doing so, at one point he came under fire from Spanish troops manning the breastworks. Under cover of the mortar bombardment the men of Clayton's Regiment crossed the river and attacked the roadside barricade. At the same time the dragoons made a frontal assault on the fortified bluff. There were by now probably few clansmen manning the barricades, and the Spanish infantry had already begun to abandon their positions with the retreat of the rest of the Jacobite army. The falling mortar bombs bursting in the air or on the ground further disconcerted the remaining defenders. Clayton's Foot quickly overran the barricade in the glen and joined the dragoons attacking the hilltop positions. Wightman reckoned that within 10 minutes of starting the attack the British troops gained the summit of the bluff, on the way taking prisoner a Spanish captain in charge of the rearguard.

Led by Tullibardine and Lieutenant-Colonel Bolaño, the main body of Spanish Foot maintaining formation pulled back uphill in the footsteps

---

80 Oliphant, 'Distinct Abridgment', *Jacobite Lairds of Gask*, p. 463.

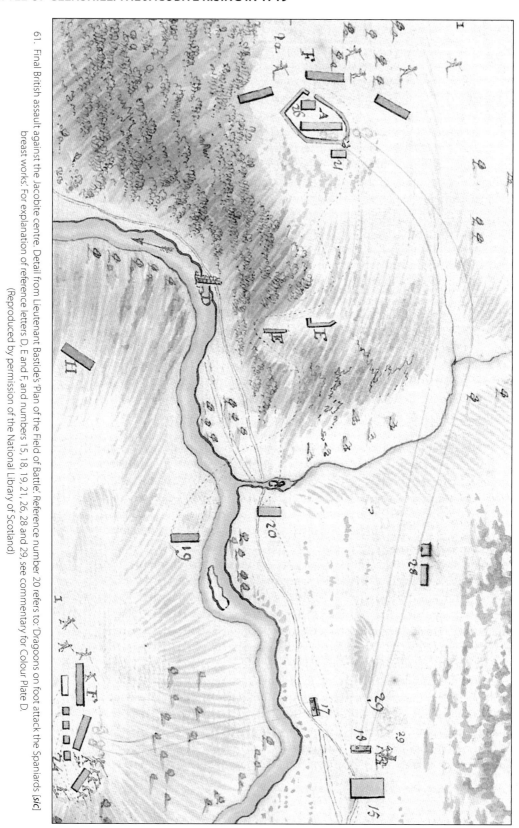

61. Final British assault against the Jacobite centre. Detail from Lieutenant Bastide's 'Plan of the Field of Battle'. Reference number 20 refers to: 'Dragoons on foot attack the Spaniards [sic] breast works'. For explanation of reference letters D, E and F, and numbers 15, 18, 19, 21, 26, 28 and 29, see commentary for Colour Plate D. (Reproduced by permission of the National Library of Scotland)

of the retreating Highlanders. The skirmish line organised by Glendaruel, Marischal, Ormidale and Lochiel had gained enough time to allow their withdrawal. The Spanish became the Jacobite rearguard, pausing from time to time to form a firing line against the Anglo-Dutch troops approaching across the mountainsides. The Highlanders were now in full flight. 'At last the Spaniards […] likewise', Tullibardine recollected, 'were obliged':

> To draw up the hill on our left, where at last all began to run, tho' [sic] half had never once an opportunity to fire on the enemy, who were heartened on seeing some of ours once give way, and our own people as much discouraged, so that they could never be again brought to anything. But all went off over the mountains.[81]

The Spanish were thus the last formed Jacobite unit to leave the area of the battlefield.[82] It was now after eight o'clock, and as the evening drew on they continued much further up the north Glenshiel ridge towards the summit of Sgur na Ciste Dubhe. Fugitives of the defeat, senior figures including Tullibardine, Marischal and Lochiel, and a few clansmen rallying to them, joined the Spanish infantry. Together they spent the short summer night at a height of about 2,600 feet (800 metres) bivouacked in a hollow or shallow valley on the mountainside. In time, the Gaelic-speaking locals came to know the place as Bealach nan Spainteach – the 'Pass of the Spaniards'.[83]

Victorious, Wightman was pleased to report next day that 'we beat them from all corners over all the mountains and rocks', but admitted: 'They were better at climbing the rocks than we at their retreat, so that we have few or no prisoners of the rebels'.[84] The slowness of the pursuit of the government troops was probably due to fatigue as much as the rough ground. Nonetheless, on the Jacobite left the Anglo-Dutch advanced across the mountainside after the defeated enemy to a height of about 1,650 feet (500 metres) – where, if Lieutenant Bastide's maps are taken at face value, they halted in semblance of line of battle order.

That night Wightman's men camped on the battlefield in the little glen to allow time to bring down their wounded from the hillsides before nightfall.

The casualties were carefully recorded by unit.[85] In Montagu's Regiment, two officers, one sergeant and seven sentinels (i.e. private soldiers, corporals included) killed, two officers, one sergeant and 38 sentinels wounded; in Clayton's Regiment, two sergeants and one sentinel killed, two officers, one sergeant and 23 sentinels wounded; in Harrison's Regiment, three sentinels killed, and three officers and 14 sentinels wounded; among the Dutch companies of Huffel and Amerongen, one officer, one sergeant and four sentinels killed, three officers, two sergeants and 35 sentinels wounded; in the

---

81 Dickson, *Jacobite Attempt*, p. 272, Tullibardine's account.
82 It must be assumed the remaining Highlanders on the Jacobite right south of the River Shiel, those under Lord George Murray's command and the few reinforcements, left the battlefield once the Spanish withdrew and British troops occupied the fortified bluff.
83 The Spanish soldiers were also memorialised by the naming after them in the native tongue of a nearby 3,250 feet (990 metre) high summit as Sgurr nan Spanteach – 'The Spaniard's Peak'.
84 TNA, SP 43/61 folio 93.
85 TNA, SP 43/61 folio 93, casualty list appended to Wightman's report.

Sutherland militia, one sentinel killed and three wounded; in the Munro militia, three sentinels killed, two officers and 13 sentinels wounded. The dragoons suffered no casualties. In all, 25 officers and rank and file were killed, and 139 wounded (of whom some would have died later of injuries). Thus Wightman's army suffered about 14 percent casualties; a significant loss for so small a force.

Jacobite losses remain incalculable, but seem to have been remarkably light. Wightman found it 'impossible to give an account' of enemy casualties, except that Lord George Murray and the Earl of Seaforth were wounded. Several years later, Major-General Wade was led to understand that the 'Rebels lost but one man'.[86] 'There was very little loss on either side', recollected George Keith, 'after a skirmish of about three hours, in which not above a hundred were killed or wounded on both sides, and of distinction only the Marquess of Seaforth wounded'.[87] An informed Jacobite reckoned that no more than 10 Highlanders were killed and wounded.[88] There must have been many more walking wounded, who alone or assisted by comrades escaped the battlefield. However, it remains curious why Wightman did not mention the body count had the number of Jacobite fatalities been significant.

The disparity in losses was an outcome of the difficulty regular troops had attacking uphill to target an enemy taking advantage of cover. Moreover, regulars were not accustomed in their small arms training to aimed firing, which would have inflicted greater casualties in the skirmishing at Glenshiel. However, the psychological effect of platoon volley fire, even when not effectively delivered, should not be underestimated as having had demoralising effect on the clansmen. Wightman mentioned his relief not to have to fight again next day, because his men had expended most of their ammunition.[89] A Whig loyalist was told that by the end of the battle most government soldiers had just two of eighteen rounds left in their cartridge boxes.[90] If only half the 950 regular Foot had used so many, then that expenditure of ammunition would have resulted in some 7,600 rounds having being fired!

The battle of Glenshiel showed that contemporaries such as George Wade tended to underestimate the capability of experienced regular troops to adapt to the unusual tactical circumstances of battle in the Highlands of Scotland. Major-General Wightman and his deputy Colonel Clayton had both led operations in the Highlands in 1716, and many British troops at Glenshiel were accustomed to serving in Scotland. In 1715 Montagu's and Clayton's regiments and some of the dragoons had fought Highlanders at Sheriffmuir. There remained War of the Spanish Succession veterans in the British and Dutch units. The Dutch infantry appear to have been as reliable troops as was expected. For their part, 'Lord Strathnaver's and Culcairn's Highlanders', Clayton mentioned, 'behaved perfectly well'.[91]

86 TNA, SP 43/61 folio 93; Allardyce, *Historical Papers*, vol. 1, p. 140.
87 Keith, *Fragment of a Memoir*, pp. 51–2.
88 Millar, 'Battle of Glenshiel. Note upon an unpublished letter', p. 66.
89 TNA, SP 43/61 folio 93.
90 Warrand, *More Culloden Papers*, p. 201, Anon. to Duncan Forbes of Culloden, 25 June 1719.
91 *Ibid.*, p. 200, Clayton writing from Glenshiel to one Dr. Thomas, 11 June 1719.

Wightman's generalship seems beyond reproach, and his subordinates as professional in their conduct. The use of cavalry was effective as well as notable, in reconnaissance, in screening other units, and in deterring counter attack. Wightman's deployment of ordnance was also novel and productive. Mortars could target troops on higher ground hidden from view and in cover. The clansmen were unaccustomed to artillery and the falling bombs had a powerful shock effect, although apparently causing few casualties. The effect of mortar fire against Highlanders at Glenshiel confirmed a Jacobite officer's view, that 'nor will the wit of man bring them to stand cannon, which has an astonishing influence over them'.[92] Moreover, Wightman believed his army to be quite heavily outnumbered but remained committed to the attack, notwithstanding the strength of the enemy position. He concentrated sufficient force to each assault in turn to achieve local superiority and breakthroughs, while pinning the enemy down elsewhere.

Jacobite leadership was far less effective. Tullibardine was commander-in-chief but lacked confidence as a field commander, so responsibility for pre-battle deployment passed to Brigadier Campbell of Ormidale. It is unclear whether Ormidale was meant to direct the battle, but at the height of the fighting he was at crossed-purposes with the Earl of Seaforth over reinforcements, so his sole command was perhaps not respected. The other notable Jacobites attempted to lead bravely by example, but on the whole their men remained uninspired. The Jacobite position was naturally formidable, but too lengthy to be held strongly by the number of men available. Units posted thinly around the hills and across the glen were vulnerable to concentrated attack. Despite the Highlanders' familiarity with the ground, the distance and unforgiving terrain slowed the movement of reinforcements from one section of the line to another.

Their marksmanship enabled the Highlanders to engage defensively for a while, but they lacked the discipline of good regular troops to hold position for long. The charge was their characteristic and most effective tactic. In certain circumstances it gave clansmen as occasional soldiers a decisive advantage over regular troops. But as a contemporary commentator pointed out, 'not a sword [was] drawn in the action'.[93] No charges were attempted at Glenshiel, and no hand-to-hand fighting occurred in which clansmen would have been advantaged. On this occasion they lacked motivation that bred courage to commit to the attack. The view from the 1740s that Highlanders lost 'their ardour' when passively holding position was true in 1719.[94] James Keith remembered the lack-lustre morale of the Highlanders at Glenshiel. He recollected how the night after the battle, leading Jacobites reflecting on the defeat accepted 'the few troops they had behaved in a manner not to give encouragement to try a second action'.[95] Because most clansmen had decided not to stand and fight, in less than three hours both the battle and the rising were lost.

---

92 Sinclair, *Memoirs of the Insurrection*, p. 130.
93 Warrand, *More Culloden Papers*, p. 201.
94 Johnstone, *Memoirs of the Rebellion*, p. 115.
95 Keith, *Fragment of a Memoir*, pp. 51–2.

10

Aftermath and Impact

'All things in these parts remain perfectly quiet.'

Overnight, the defeated Jacobites gathered on the heights above Glenshiel contemplated their plight. The enemy's clear-cut victory on the battlefield became decisive with the dispersal of most of the Jacobite army. The Highlanders had suffered remarkably few casualties, and their retreat was more a voluntary withdrawal than a total rout. But most clansmen had shown little fighting spirit. They took it upon themselves to disperse under cover of darkness rather than rally and join forces next day. The historic difficulty of keeping a clan army together was again apparent. The anticipated reinforcements of Clanranald's MacDonalds, the Chisholms of Strathglass and the Grants of Glenmoriston had taken no part. They either reached Glenshiel too late in the evening or were still on their way, and so turned back on news of the defeat, or were among those Highlanders on the mountainsides waiting on which way the battle turned. Hopes that 'they would all join next day and make a second trial' proved false, although part of the army kept together overnight.[1] With the Spanish infantry were some Camerons, MacKenzies and MacGregors, a few other stray clansmen, and a number of supernumerary officers and volunteers – probably few more than 400 men altogether.

The Rising Collapses
They 'should keep in a body with the Spaniards', Tullibardine recollected having said at this point, in one of his occasional bouts of fatalistic determination, 'and march through the Highlands for some time till we could gather again in case of a landing, or else should the king send instructions, the Highlanders would then rise and soon make up all that was past'.[2] However, the decision of the final Jacobite council of war held early in the morning of 11 June, with Seaforth, Lochiel, the Earl Marischal, James

---

1 Millar, 'Battle of Glenshiel. Note upon an unpublished letter', p. 65.
2 Dickson, *Jacobite Attempt*, p. 272, Tullibardine's account.

Keith, and Campbell of Ormidale also known to have been present, was that further action would be in vain, and instead they should straightaway disband and disperse. Lieutenant-Colonel Bolaño was apparently prepared to fight on, but it was acknowledged the Spanish regulars lacked tents for shelter and adequate provisions. Tullibardine therefore reluctantly granted their officers leave to surrender.[3] In effect putting an end to the rising, he instructed Rob Roy to destroy the remaining stores at the camp at Achadh nan Seilach. Then 'everybody else went off to shift for themselves'. Ormidale and the Keith brothers were the first to head off, according to Tullibardine, 'without any more ado or so much as taking leave'.[4]

The completeness of his victory was unclear to Major-General Wightman first-thing that Thursday morning, as his men broke camp and advanced further along Glenshiel. Some armed Highlanders hung around the area, and not until two days later did Wightman consider it safe for couriers to leave with dispatches. Government troops reached the settlement at Achadh nan Seilach at about seven o'clock, to find that Rob Roy had got their first and taken or destroyed the supplies.[5] As the rest of the army arrived, at around eight o'clock a Spanish captain appeared bearing a letter requesting terms of surrender. The only condition Wightman was prepared to grant was that his men would not rob the Spaniards. Accordingly, at about two o'clock in the afternoon the Spaniards wearily trooped into Achadh nan Seilach, where Wightman accepted the capitulation of Lieutenant-Colonel Bolaño and his 273 officers and men.[6]

Later that morning the sound of distant gunfire was heard. Wightman hoped this 'great firing from our men of war' was directed against rebels, but in fact Captain George Clinton aboard HMS *Success* anchored in Loch Alsh upon hearing of the victory had ordered a 13-gun salute fired in celebration.[7] Later on the 12th or early the next day Wightman left the camp at Achadh nan Seilach and met with Clinton. They arranged for the troops to be resupplied from *Success*'s stores, including much-needed gunpowder and ammunition. The navy also assisted in the evacuation of the wounded. As the anonymous soldier-correspondent among Wightman's troops pointed out: 'it being [*sic*] impossible to have brought them with us'.[8] With commendable foresight, Major James Cunningham, the lieutenant-governor of Fort William, had chartered a bark to sail from Mary Burgh carrying provisions for Wightman's column.[9] The bark had probably joined *Success* in Loch Alsh shortly before the battle. The supplies were offloaded from the bark in Loch Duich and the wounded taken aboard. *Success* also took on some of the casualties, and on 15 June sailed in company with the bark for Fort William.

---

3   Millar, 'Battle of Glenshiel. Note upon an unpublished letter', p. 65.

4   Dickson, *Jacobite Attempt,* p. 273, quotes from Tullibardine's account.

5   Warrand, *More Culloden Papers,* p. 200.

6   TNA, SP 43/61 folio 93; Warrand, *More Culloden Papers,* p. 200; *The London Gazette,* 16–20 June 1719.

7   *The London Gazette,* 16–20 June 1719; TNA, ADM 51/938, no folio.

8   *The Post Man and The Historical Account,* 2–4 July 1719.

9   J. Reddington (ed.), *Calendar of Treasury Papers, 1720–1728* (1889), p. 96.

The progress of Wightman's army over following days remains uncertain. He wrote to Lord Carpenter 'from the camp at Aderhanan' on 17 June that 'I have the Spaniards with me, the whole number, officers included, is 274':

> And am taking a tour through all the difficult parts of Seaforth's country, to terrify the rebels, by burning the houses of the guilty, and preserving those of the honest. I hope to be in Saturday with the troops at Inverness [...]. There are no bodies of the rebels together, unless stealing parties in [places?] up and down the mountains. Seaforth, Tullibardine, Marischal etc. are gone off to the Lewis Islands, as is given out, but we rather apprehend to the Orkneys and no number with them; and it is believed they will go to Spain as soon as they can.[10]

Dickson made a convincing case for 'Aderhanan' being a phonetic misspelling of Edracharon, an area in southerly Strathcarron where there certainly was a settlement in the mid-18th century.[11] Strathcarron, opening from the head of Loch Carron, seems a likely spot for Wightman's campsite. It lay amid the Earl of Seaforth's country and was well situated for the eastward return march to Inverness via Seaforth's seat at Brahan, which Wightman intended to inspect. While in the area Wightman executed long-standing governmental policy of suppressing Roman Catholic and Episcopalian ministers suspected of Jacobitism. His men terrorised the Episcopalian minister in Loch Carron by looting his manse, or house, and probably burnt the Catholic church of St. Duthac nearby Castle Donan. Alasdair Dubh MacDonnell of Glengarry was suspected of involvement in the rising. On 2 July his house at Invergarry north-east of Fort William was ransacked by a company of Foot from Inverness acting under Wightman's orders. The soldiers also set alight the manse of the local Episcopalian minister, causing Glengarry angrily to complain that:

> If the Highlanders will ever rise in arms they have got a good example to become robbers and destroy ministers' churches and others, and give the regular troops as their teachers and masters, of whose doctrine and learning I dare promise they will not be short, if not exceed it, and so General Wightman must have the blame of such barbarity, begun and committed by him.[12]

Whatever the actual extent Wightman's punitive actions did not last long, and he brought the army back to Inverness on 25 June.[13]

In military terms the victory by government forces at Glenshiel crushed the 1719 rising. From Inverness at the end of June, Wightman wrote assuring under-secretary Delafaye that the Jacobites had dispersed completely. In early July a government loyalist agreed that 'all things are quiet in the Highlands',

---

10 *The Weekly Journal or British Gazetteer*, 4 July 1719.
11 Dickson, *Jacobite Attempt*, p. liii. Spelt 'Edracharran', the settlement is depicted on William Roy's military mapping undertaken 1747–55.
12 Sinclair, *Statistical Account of Scotland*, vol. 6, p. 250; Atholl, *Chronicles*, vol. 2 pp. 289–90, quotation from the latter.
13 *The Weekly Journal or Saturday's Post*, 27 June 1719.

but added: 'thieves are swarming in the hills carrying off cows, which the troops cannot prevent'. The rising had failed, but for a while an upsurge of lawlessness followed in its wake, a consequence of the gathering of groups of armed Highlanders. Before returning to their homelands some clansmen took the opportunity to settle old scores by indulging in a spate of cattle raiding. Toward the end of July, however, the banditry had lessened; the Whig Munros, at least, were no longer complaining about cattle rustling.[14]

Other than localised policing actions such as that against MacDonnell of Glengarry, unlike the aftermath of the 1715–16 rising there were no further counter-insurgency operations, or attempts made to track down the leaders of the rising. While the Highlands were not demilitarised, Wightman scaled down troop numbers and rotated units. The Dutch Foot for the rest of the summer were billeted along the easterly Anglo-Scottish border. Harrison's and Clayton's regiments also marched south, replaced as the garrisons of Inverness and Fort William respectively by Montagu's and Colonel Cholmondeley's regiments of Foot. By July, the overall number of British regulars in Scotland had, however, increased since May by 500 men to just over 3,100 effectives – 2,534 Foot in six regiments, and 580 dragoons in three regiments (Lord Cobham's Regiment of Dragoons had by then returned to England).[15] Wightman left Inverness for army headquarters at Edinburgh, on his way reaching Aberdeen on Wednesday 8 July. Local officials and 'the best inhabitants of the borough' congratulated Wightman on his victory and he enjoyed their entertainment for several days. Aberdeen hosted a civic reception the following Saturday, when:

> [Wightman] with several officers came to the townhouse [town hall] about four a clock [sic] in the afternoon, where they drank the king's health, with that of the

62. The imposing hilltop remains of Ruthven Barracks, near Kingussie. It is by far the most well preserved of the four infantry barracks planned from 1717 by the Georgian government to impose military authority in the Highlands. Ruthven Barracks was finally completed in 1724. It saw action, and sustained permanent damage, during the Jacobite rising of 1745–46.

---

14 TNA, SP 54/13/60, Wightman to Delafaye, 30 June 1719; Warrand, *More Culloden Papers,* p. 202, Reverend Robert Baillie to Duncan Forbes, 10 July 1719; TNA, SP 54/13/65, Carpenter to Delafaye, 21 July 1719.

15 Warrand, *More Culloden Papers,* p. 202; TNA, SP 54/13/78B, 'Return of all the Regiments of Foot in North Brittain [sic] for the Month of July 1719, Return of all the Regiments of Dragoons in North Brittain [sic] for the Month of July 1719'. It is worth noting that although there were 580 'effective' dragoons of all ranks between Campbell's, Carpenter's and Stair's regiments, only 482 horses were considered fit for service.

prince and princess, Prince Frederick and the royal family, the lords justices, and many other health's of those well affected to the government, both civil and military, under the discharge of small arms by a detachment, consisting of one hundred men of Huffell's Regiment, all the foresaid time the waterworks played at the [market] cross fountain'.[16]

By the time Wightman reached Edinburgh, the London government had already tasked Lord Carpenter with formulating a strategy for securing the Highlands; for 'making dispositions for preventing robberies, seizing rebels, and disarming the Highlanders'.[17] Accordingly, in later June at Edinburgh Carpenter held a meeting of a committee of leading military and judicial figures to discuss policy. They included Brigadier-General George Preston, deputy governor of Edinburgh Castle; Adam Cockburn, the lord justice clerk; Lord Ormiston, the second most senior judge in Scotland after the lord advocate Sir David Dalrymple; and Robert Dundas, the solicitor-general of Scotland representing secretary of state Lord Roxburghe. It was agreed a proclamation should be issued offering, in effect, an amnesty for (low-ranking) rebels who surrendered their arms and returned home peaceably. Obdurate rebels, on the other hand, would have their homes burnt and livestock driven off in punishment. It was accepted that those who disarmed deserved the government's protection from those who did not, but therein lay the rub of the difficulty of policing the Highlands. As Carpenter admitted to under-secretary Delafaye: 'we could not form any scheme that would answer those ends. It is impossible to catch any rebel Highlanders with parties of regular troops, and any sort of orders from the civil or military here to bring in their arms would signify nothing'. While Carpenter advocated launching winter-time raids upon settlements of the Jacobite clans, during the summer months 'they are on the mountains with their cattle, and will be able easily to avoid any parties of troops that might be sent to take them or their cattle'.[18] In later July, Carpenter opined that a further Act of parliament was needed making unauthorised ownership of arms a criminal offence in the Highlands, but only the full cooperation of chiefs would make it workable.[19] The limitations of the 1716 Act for securing the peace were clear.

Wightman had also advised Delafaye of the difficulty of identifying and naming rebels, and obtaining hard evidence against them; as 'most of the gentlemen of this country who profess to be in his majesty's interest, think their ties of affinity and consanguinity such obligations that they will not bear the evidence their excellencies expect'.[20] This inclination among Whigs towards honourable accommodation with their Jacobite neighbours and acquaintances was an outcome of the social inter-relationships of the northerly Scottish elite. It seems that in turn rehabilitated Jacobites, sharing a

---

16   *The Weekly Journal or British Gazetteer*, 1 Aug. 1719.
17   TNA, SP 54/13/63, Carpenter to Delafaye, 6 July 1719.
18   TNA, SP 54/13/63, Carpenter to Delafaye, 7 July 1719.
19   TNA, SP 54/13/65, Carpenter to Delafaye, 21 July 1719.
20   TNA, SP 54/13/60.

63. The remains of the stable block at Ruthven Barracks, added on the orders of Major-General Wade in 1734. It provided stabling for 30 horses, enabling dragoons to patrol the military road network.

sense of obligation, held it dishonourable to betray a trust, a service accepted or an act of patronage received from former opponents. Their engagement with the Whig regime in this way would in time serve to weaken the active Jacobite community.[21]

Traditional Highland ties of kinship also protected the chief figures of the rising from capture, notwithstanding the government's proclamation issued on 21 July encouraging their betrayal; a £2,000 reward (and, if requested, a free pardon) was offered for the apprehension of either Tullibardine, Marischal or Seaforth.[22]

Given the clandestine nature of their movements after the battle of Glenshiel, there seems little evidence of the whereabouts of the leading Jacobites over coming months, although all eventually escaped to the Continent. James Keith recollected how he 'lurked some months in the mountains' with the Earl Marischal, until in September they took passage from Peterhead to the Texel in northern Holland. Helped by the Spanish ambassador at The Hague the brothers then went to Paris.[23] Tullibardine, Seaforth and others kept together, or at least in contact, while shifting southward to the region of Lochaber and the Rough Bounds under Cameron and MacDonald protection. Tullibardine after the battle had gone southward into Glen Garry, intending with 'some others with the clans concerned' to 'endeavour to keep private till we know how affairs are like to go'.[24]

Tullibardine for a while hoped to re-kindle the rising. In mid-August, he met with Seaforth and a small handful of other chiefs, among them MacDonnell of Glengarry, somewhere in the Jacobite fastness of Knoydart.

---

21 See Sankey and Szechi, 'Elite Culture and the Decline of Scottish Jacobitism', pp. 90–128, *passim*.
22 *The London Gazette*, 21–25 July 1719.
23 Keith, *Fragment of a Memoir*, pp. 52–3.
24 Dickson, *Jacobite Attempt*, p. 273, Tullibardine's account.

They debated fresh news that Ormond's re-fitted expeditionary force was heading for England. However, although as many as 200 clansmen may have turned up, no course of action was agreed and the gathering dispersed. At the end of August, a well-informed correspondent advised Lord Carpenter that while 'these misfortunate people wants not encouragement', their hopes and support were 'slightly grounded'; and that notwithstanding, the leading rebels were 'endeavouring to get abroad, which against next post I believe I shall give your lordship more particular accounts of'.[25] Tullibardine was probably the last to leave Scotland. At the end of October 1719 he was continuing to write to supporters as commander-in-chief of the forces of King James III and VIII, from a refuge near the westerly coast of the Rough Bounds on one of the wooded islands in remote Loch Morar.[26]

The Problematic Spanish Prisoners

The repatriation of most of the Spanish troops who had served dutifully under Tullibardine took several months. In June, the short-standing garrison of Castle Donan were sent on their way, shipped from Edinburgh for Spain aboard the British transport *Anne*. On the 19th the *Anne* put into Falmouth in Cornwall to re-provision for the voyage to Corunna.[27] On 27 June, the 274 Spaniards who surrendered at Glenshiel marched from Inverness for Edinburgh guarded by dragoons. On the morning of 10 July Swiss troops of Sturler's Dutch Regiment escorted them to confinement in Edinburgh Castle. The Spanish arrived in the city without causing public disturbance, the precautions taken by Edinburgh's magistracy to ensure the populace did not abuse them proving unnecessary. Quite the contrary in fact, the Spanish officers allowed under parole to visit the city were respectfully entertained by Edinburgh's inhabitants, including local Jacobites.[28] However, no one in authority knew what to do with the captives next. Wightman assumed they would be shipped to Plymouth and onward to Spain. However, some officials suggested the Spaniards should be marched to an embarkation port via London, so as to mute conspiracy theorists believing the rising in Scotland had been a self-serving invention of government ministers.[29]

Instead the Spanish troops remained in Edinburgh Castle. There was no treaty arrangement between Great Britain and Spain regarding fiscal responsibility for the long-term subsistence of prisoners of war. Therefore, the Spanish officers had somehow to pay their own way and for their men or obtain credit. Over summer and into autumn the situation grew awkward for the British government. Monies advanced by Lord Carpenter, against promissory notes in the name of Lieutenant-Colonel Bolaño to be reimbursed by the Marquess de Bereti Landi, the Spanish Ambassador to the United Provinces, ran out. Wightman too had to advance £50 for the Spaniards'

---

25 TNA, SP 54/13/79C, Earl of Findlater to Lord Carpenter, 24 Aug. 1719; TNA, SP 54/13/79D, Gordon of Glenbucket to Carpenter, 29 Aug. 1719. Quotation from the latter.
26 Atholl, *Chronicles*, vol. 2, p. 294.
27 *The Weekly Journal or Saturday's Post*, 20 June 1719.
28 Atholl, *Chronicles*, vol. 2, p. 290; Aufnere, *Lockhart Papers*, vol. 2, p. 23.
29 Michael, *England under George I*, p. 204.

subsistence, apparently 'to keep their men from starving'.[30] Edinburgh Jacobites clubbed together to provide Bolaño with clandestine credit, on the promise of reimbursement by Ambassador Landi (which apparently he eventually fulfilled). Nonetheless, by September the Spanish were falling sick, complaining of the dampness of the vaulted chambers where they were held, and demanding more habitable quarters before winter's onset. The situation worsened at the end of the month, when the Spanish officers rejected a bond obliging their government to repay all subsistence and transportation costs. Wightman suggested to Delafaye that Lieutenant-Colonel Bolaño should be held hostage until the Spanish authorities paid up.[31] By mid-October Brigadier Preston, in charge of the prisoners, intended to keep them in close confinement on a diet of bread and water. However, the thirteen lords justice in London, ruling in King George's absence in Hanover, finally took charge of the situation. During September they arranged with the Admiralty to ship the Spaniards home. A transport that left the Thames on 9 October was delayed reaching Edinburgh, but at the end of the month the Spaniards finally sailed from Leith for Spain.[32] It transpired that they got home sooner than the Dutch auxiliary troops brought to Britain to oppose them. By autumn the Dutch regiments were based in north-east England, about Durham and Newcastle-upon-Tyne. They were eventually shipped from the port of Harwich in Essex to the Netherlands in early January 1720.[33]

64. George Wade (*b*. 1673, *d*. 1748). Major-General Wade's insightful reconnoitering of the Highlands in 1724 gained him the command-in-chief in north Britain, a post he held until 1740. Wade is best known to history for directing the Highland military road and bridge-building programme begun in the mid-1720s. Portrait attributed to Johan van Diest. Oil on canvas, *c*.1731. (© National Portrait Gallery, London)

The Failed Rising and the Wider War of the Quadruple Alliance

On 1 September 1719 Major-General Wightman, requesting a period of leave from duty in Scotland, pointed out to under-secretary Delafaye that 'All things in these parts remain perfectly quiet'.[34] From the viewpoint of the Georgian government, the Protestant succession had withstood another Jacobite insurrection and foiled the ambitions of the Pretender. The victory at Glenshiel and collapse of the Highland rising was reported with satisfaction in the English press. The edition of *The Weekly Journal or British Gazetteer* for 27 June, for example, declared with robust Whiggish patriotism:

30 TNA, SP 54/13/80, Wightman to Delafaye, 17 Sept. 1719.
31 Aufnere, *Lockhart Papers*, vol. 2, p. 23; TNA, WO 4/22, folio 17, folio 258; SP 54/13/78A; TNA, SP 54/13/82.
32 TNA, SP 54/13/84, Preston to Delafaye, 22 Oct. 1719; Dickson, *Jacobite Attempt*, pp. 295–6.
33 TNA, W04/22, folio 300; *The Post Man and The Historical Account*, 5–7 January 1720.
34 TNA, SP 54/13/78A, Wightman to Delafaye, 1 Sept. 1719.

> Were not our Jacobites under a judicial infatuation, they would certainly denounce their treasonable principles, and become good subjects. They might observe, among many other remarkable providences which have been against them ever since the late happy Revolution [i.e. the Glorious Revolution of 1688], that their cause in Great Britain has received a finishing blow on the 10th of June, the supposed anniversary of the Pretender's birth. They may henceforth leave off their white roses on that day,[35] since they must always remember, to their grief, that they were dyed red by the blood of the rebels at the battle of Glenshiel.

There had been little backing for the short-lived rising in Scotland, and no clear support shown in England. Militant English Jacobites compromised by the alliance with Catholic Spain never had the duplicitous task of attempting to rally support for Ormond's invasion of the West Country. In any case, the deployment of troops to the region and the close watch kept on suspect Tories such as Sir William Wyndham and George Granville, baron Lansdowne, influential landowners in Somerset and Cornwall respectively, allowed Jacobite conspirators no opportunity.[36] Nonetheless, given the Spanish invasion scare and fear of Jacobite plots, isolated seditious expressions against the Georgian government were made example and severely dealt with. In London in April, a Scots Foot Guardsman convicted of 'using scandalous reflections on his majesty's person and government' was flogged three times in the city's public parks, each time in front of one of the three regiments of Foot Guards paraded for the occasion. Similarly, a Roman Catholic sedan chairman who insulted and spat in the face of the Princess of Wales as she was carried by chair to St. James's Palace was whipped through London's streets by the city executioner, who reportedly 'made him cry God bless King George before he had done with him.'[37]

Provincial authorities mindful to follow the government's lead remained vigilant against displays of support for the Stuart dynasty, and suspicious of gatherings that might mask Jacobite conspiracy. Pockets of Jacobite support were suspected in northerly Wales and its borderlands, where the Tory–Jacobite magnate Sir Watkins William Wynne was the greatest landowner. Wynne's landholdings and influence spanned the English border into Shropshire, a county that throughout the period of Jacobitism produced Tory parliamentarians sympathetic to the cause.[38] In May 1719, dragoons billeted at Ludlow in south Shropshire were involved in disturbances on the 29th when the bells of the parish church were rung to mark Restoration Day, celebrating the return from exile of the Stuart King Charles II in 1660. In June, dragoons came to Shrewsbury, Shropshire's county town, at the request of local Whig gentlemen worried that 'some dangerous work' might be encouraged

---

35 The white bush rose is a shrub native to Scotland the Jacobites took as their emblem. It was symbolised and worn as a cloth or paper pleated badge known as the 'White Cockade'.

36 Lord, *Stuarts' Secret Army*, pp. 124–5.

37 *The Weekly Packet*, 11–18 Apr. 1719; *The Weekly Journal or British Gazetteer*, 18 Apr. 1719.

38 K. Feilding, *A History of the Tory Party, 1640–1714* (1924), pp 495–6; Lord, *Stuarts' Secret Army*, pp. 258, 262; P.D.G. Thomas, 'Wynn, Sir Watkin Williams, third baronet (1693?–1749)', in *ODNB* (2004) online edn. (available June 2018).

by Jacobites among the crowds in town come to watch a cock-fighting competition.[39] Not-well documented Anti-Whig demonstrations in northern England, at Halifax, Yorkshire, around this time, in which several persons were injured, may also have been fueled by local Jacobites.[40]

In the autumn, the British mounted a retaliatory amphibious raid upon the Spanish coast. The operation was in reprisal for Spanish actions that year, and to support Britain's allies in the continuing War of the Quadruple Alliance. A 4,000-strong expeditionary force was organised under the command of Lieutenant-General Richard Temple, Lord Cobham, with Vice-Admiral James Mighels in command of the fleet. In April, Mighels, scouting ahead of Lord Berkeley's fleet covering the Western Approaches, had provided the first accurate reports of the dispersal of the Spanish armada.

Instead of Corunna, judged too well defended to take by seaborne assault, the expedition instead targeted the naval base at Vigo in south-west Galicia. With a Royal Navy squadron already supporting French operations in the region of San Sebastian, at the end of September Mighels's fleet approached the harbour at Vigo. The Spanish defenders were taken by surprise, and troops and artillery soon landed. After a short siege by land and sea, on 10 October the citadel commanding the town and defences was surrendered. The British then occupied Vigo, seizing or destroying supplies from Ormond's invasion force found stockpiled there, and taking over or burning several merchantmen and privateers at anchor. A detachment sent inland briefly occupied unopposed the city of Pontevedra and wrecked the arsenal there. The British also exacted a humiliating punitive fine on the city of Santiago de Compostela, the provincial capital. The expedition withdrew unopposed from Vigo on 27 October. It returned to England in the second week of November with acceptable casualties, mostly from sickness, of about 300 men. The conspicuous success of the Vigo raid stood in marked contrast to the failed Hispano-Jacobite alliance.[41]

This and Spanish military reverses elsewhere resulted in December in the political downfall and exile of Cardinal Alberoni and the end of the War of the Quadruple Alliance. In February 1720 Spain agreed the terms of the Treaty of The Hague, forcing King Phillip to renounce his claims in Italy and Spanish forces to evacuate Sicily and Sardinia. The failed rising in Scotland, the peace between Spain and Great Britain and her allies, together with the humiliation of Alberoni left Jacobite fortunes at a very low ebb. In early January 1720 an English newspaper gloated how: 'We hear […] that the Pretender who is still in Rome, is inconsolable at the approaching peace between the High Allies and Spain'.[42]

By summer 1719, James Francis Edward Stuart's stay in Madrid was an embarrassment to the Spanish crown. As he symbolised a failed foreign and

39 *The Weekly Journal or Saturday's Post,* 13 June 1719; *The Weekly Journal or Saturday's Post,* 20 June 1719.
40 Oates, 'Jacobitism and Popular Disturbances', pp. 119–20, 122.
41 Rodger, *Command of the Ocean,* p. 229; W.M. Clowes, *The Royal Navy, A History from the Earliest Times to the Present,* 5 vols. (1898), vol. 3, pp. 261–2; Black, *Politics and Policy,* p. 117.
42 *The Weekly Journal or British Gazetteer,* 9 Jan. 1720.

military policy, James was politely encouraged to return to Rome and did so in August. In early January 1720 he wrote from there to one of his Scots followers. James gloomily reflected on Spain's imminent peace accord with Great Britain, and expressed concern for the safety of Tullibardine and others involved in the late rising, of whose whereabouts he was still unsure. He added:

> In the last expedition, neither Ormond nor I had the entire disposition of matters, it was on other people's money and help that we depended, so that we were not masters neither of the time nor the beginning, nor dispositions to be previously made; but with all this, had I or Ormond landed, I doubt not but the matter had succeeded, 'tho [sic] that not happening, it was lucky the whole country did not rise. The zeal of those who were for taking that part ought not to be blamed, but the prudence of the others certainly deserves the approbation of all men of sense, as it meets with mine entirely.[43]

James's was perhaps a realistic appraisal of the 1719 rising, when luck and mischance had shaped events. Because so few Spanish troops went to Scotland, prudent men remained unconvinced the time was right to rise with the risks entailed, while the zealous lacked necessary force. Coordinating a rising in the Highlands with Spanish landings in the west of England was a high-risk strategy dependant more on luck than judgement. But had the Spanish armada been lucky with the weather at sea, a strategy that ended looking desperate and foolhardy could have been bold and opportune. Between them Ormond and Alberoni erred by not committing more Spanish military resources to Scotland; where less than four years before as many as 20,000 men may at one time or another have appeared in arms in the Stuart cause.[44] Even as events turned out, victory at Glenshiel by a better led and motivated Jacobite army could have triggered a wider rising government forces would have been hard pressed to subdue.

Jacobitism and Government Policy in the Highlands after the '19

For the best part of a generation the Highlands of Scotland remained at the centre of Jacobite plans, as the most dependable source of armed manpower in the British Isles. The 1719 rising did not result in the pacification of clans considered most troublesome by the British government. The influx of arms had in fact left them quite well equipped. When Major-General Wade reconnoitered the Highlands in summer 1724, he reckoned the hardline Jacobite clans had at least 6,000 modern muskets. Many of these were identified as Spanish, 'from their peculiar make and fashion of their locks'.[45] Sporadic clashes with government troops attempting policing operations continued to occur. In November 1720, for example, a 17-man detachment from the barracks at Kiliwhimen, who had

---

43 Oliphant, *Jacobite Lairds of Gask*, p. 467.
44 Contemporary and recent estimations vary of the fluctuating size of Jacobite forces in the 1715–16 rising. Pittock, in *Myth of the Jacobite Clans*, pp. 50–1, posited a wide-ranging estimate of 12,000 to 20,000 men, while Szechi, in *Jacobites*, p. 77, reckoned that up to 20,000 Scots rose in arms for the Jacobites, although many did so only for a short while.
45 Allardyce, *Historical Papers*, vol. 1, p. 137.

seized cattle in reprisal from some Camerons suspected of stealing horses from a local laird, fought a fierce skirmish with losses on both sides when a party of 20 Camerons attempted to retake the beasts. In another incident reported in September 1722, MacKenzies fired upon a party of troops 'going too far into the Highlands', leaving one soldier killed and another wounded.[46] The MacKenzies remained especially recalcitrant, hampering attempts by agents of the Commissioners of Forfeited Estates to collect rent from Seaforth's tenants. Most revenue was instead collected by the Earl's factor and sent annually to him in France. In 1723 the factor, one Donald Murcheson, stayed openly in Edinburgh while arranging the transfer of money abroad. In 1721, Murcheson with a large body of armed clansmen had prevented a government factor and his military escort from entering MacKenzie territory.[47]

In 1724 Simon Fraser, 11th Lord Lovat, brought the disquiet about the continuing undercurrent of unrest in the Highlands to the attention of the London government. Lovat had been a Jacobite intriguer, but in 1715 raised the Frasers in support of King George and in Inverness-shire opposed the Earl of Seaforth's MacKenzies. In 1716 he received the King's approbation, a full pardon, and captaincy of one of the Independent Companies of Highlanders. Eight years later, Lovat composed a 'Memorial, addressed to His Majesty George I Concerning the State of the Highlands'. The memorandum served Lovat's interests, particularly the axe he had to grind over the loss of his command and associated prestige at the disbandment of the Independent Companies in 1717, and struck a chord with ministers easily disturbed by worrisome news from the Highlands. Lovat painted a detailed and for the government alarming picture of widespread lawlessness, of the continuation of blood feuds, blackmail and cattle rustling:

65. Clothing and equipment of the Highland Companies of Foot raised in 1725 was similar to that of the Royal Highland Regiment in *c.*1740, depicted here. (New York Picture Library Digital Collection)

> The law has never had its due course and authority in many parts of the Highlands, neither in criminal nor civil matters. […]. The families in the Highlands are divided (besides the disputes arising among themselves) in principles between the Whigs and the Jacobites. The use of arms in the Highlands will hardly ever be laid aside, till, by degrees, they begin to find they have nothing to do with them. […]. One of the evils which furnishes the most matter of complaint at present is the continual robberies and depredations in the Highlands, and the country adjacent. […]. The bad consequences of those robberies are not the only oppression which the people suffer in the loss of their cattle and other goods but by the habitual practices of

---

46 *The Weekly Journal or Saturday's Post,* 17 Dec. 1720; *St. James's Journal,* 20 Sept. 1722.
47 Allardyce, *Historical Papers,* vol. 1, p. 139.

> violences [*sic*] and illegal exactions. The Highlanders [...] constantly practice their
> use of arms, they increase their numbers, by drawing many into their gang who
> would otherwise be good subjects, and they remain ready and proper materials for
> disturbing the government upon the first occasion.[48]

Lovat pointed to the failings of the 1716 Act for securing the peace, and,
unsurprisingly, advocated re-forming the Independent Companies. The
garrisons of the recently completed Highland barracks, Lovat reckoned, were
ineffective: 'The regular troops were never used to such marches, with their
usual arms and accoutrements; were not able to pursue the Highlanders;
their very dress was a signal to the robbers to avoid them; and the troops,
who were strangers to the language, and often reviled by others, could never
get any useful intelligence'.[49]

Lovat's assertions carried sufficient weight to prompt a governmental
enquiry. In early July 1724 Major-General George Wade was tasked with making
a tour of inspection in the Highlands. He had King George's commission to:

> Go into the Highlands of Scotland, and narrowly to inspect the present situation of
> the Highlanders, their customs, manners and the state of the country in regard to
> the robberies and depredations said to be committed in that part of your majesty's
> dominions [...] and how far the memorial delivered to your majesty by Simon Lord
> Lovat and his remarks thereupon are founded on facts.[50]

Wade had served with distinction in Spain during the War of Succession,
and in 1719 as second in command of the land forces in the expedition to
Vigo. He was a loyal servant of the Georgian government, with a reputation
for intelligence work countering Jacobite intrigue. In autumn 1715 Wade
broke a conspiracy in Bath in the West Country, and in January 1717 exposed
the Swedish Gyllenborg plot.[51]

Wade's assessment of the state of the Highlands submitted to the
government in early December 1724 largely upheld Lovat's view of the
situation. The clans that had risen in 1715 and 1719 were 'ready, whenever
encouraged by their superiors or chiefs of clans, to create new troubles
and rise in arms in favour of the Pretender', meanwhile living 'in a state of
anarchy and confusion'.[52] Wade was critical of current military organisation
in the Highlands, finding two of the new barracks poorly sited and all four
undermanned and unprovisioned. He made a number of recommendations
to pacify the Highlands, including re-establishing independent companies
under full military regulation, improvements to the Highland forts, and
imposing disarmament more forcefully. In recognition of his workmanlike
approach, just before Christmas Wade was appointed commander-in-chief
in North Britain. In the New Year, with appreciative government backing

---

48   Birt, *Letters from a Gentleman*, vol. 2, pp. 256–8.
49   *Ibid.*, p. 264.
50   Allardyce, *Historical Papers*, vol. 1, p. 131.
51   J.B. Salmond, *Wade in Scotland* (1934), pp. 21–2.
52   Allardyce, *Historical Papers*, vol. 1, pp. 132, 137.

Wade shaped a strategy for the pacification of the Highlands that became official policy in April 1725.

Wade arrived in Edinburgh in mid-June to put his plans into effect. He was further empowered by a new statute, 'For more Effectual Disarming the Highlands in that Part of Great Britain called Scotland'. The 1725 Disarming Act supplanted that of 1716 for securing the peace, by going beyond prohibiting wearing arms in public to imposing actual disarmament. The army and the lord lieutenancy could summons the surrender of weapons at a certain place and time, and gained arbitrary powers to conduct searches. Strict penalties could be imposed. Men who concealed or defaulted to surrender arms faced arrest and summary enlistment into the army for service overseas. Women who aided and abetted could be imprisoned for two years. Although stringent, the 1725 Act was a watered down version of a bill that in its earlier form had advocated in the Highlands the death penalty for keeping arms, prohibition of traditional dress and the suppression of the Gaelic tongue.[53]

66. Likeness of Duncan Forbes of Culloden (*b*. 1685, *d*. 1747), Whig politician and judge. A devout Presbyterian and strong supporter of the Hanoverian succession, Forbes acted against Jacobite risings in 1715–16, 1719 and 1745–46. In 1725 he became lord advocate, the chief legal officer of the crown in Scotland. (New York Picture Library Digital Collection)

Wade intended to base a taskforce at Inverness to impose the Disarming Act on the Highlands during the summer, and made logistical arrangements to do so. However, he was delayed having to deploy troops in support of the civil powers, under the new lord advocate Duncan Forbes, to police serious, Jacobite-inflamed rioting in Glasgow over the introduction of a heavy-handed tax on malt.[54]

Wade eventually arrived at Inverness on 10 August. There he took command of three regiments of Foot, two troops of dragoons, and the 550 men of the six new Highland Companies of Foot. These had been formed in April by recruiting from Whig clans. There were three companies of Campbells, and one each of Frasers (captained by Lord Lovat), Munros and loyalist Grants. In time the Highland Companies became known as the Black Watch, from the sombre regulation colour of their plaids.

Wade's declarations of clemency coupled to this impressive show of force encouraged as many as 150 gentlemen of the MacKenzies and aligned clans to meet him at Inverness on 12 August, expressing willingness to make their peace. At Brahan Castle at the end of August the MacKenzies led the surrender of almost 800 items of proscribed weaponry (Wade tactfully deploying regular dragoons rather than Highland Companies to oversee this act of submission). The combination of summonses and troop movements inclined the Camerons

53 D. Pickering (ed.), *The Statutes at Large from the Ninth Year of King George I to the Second Year of King George II* (London, 1765), pp. 246–52; Aufnere, *Lockhart Papers*, vol. 2, pp. 142, 159–60
54 Ferguson, *Scotland*, pp. 141–2; Szechi, *Lockhart*, pp. 133–4.

of Lochaber, the MacDonalds of Glengarry, the MacLeouds of Glenelg, the Chisholms of Strathglass and the Grants of Glenmoriston to deliver up arms to Wade at Kiliwhimen barracks on 15 September. Other clans, including from the isles of Skye and Mull, handed in weapons to the garrisons at Bernera and Ruthven, and at Fort William and Inverness. The Disarming Act was enforced northward as far afield as Braemar, on the Earl of Mar's forfeited estates, and southward in Perthshire and Dumbartonshire. By the time Wade's taskforce withdrew to winter quarters (with just ten fatalities between the three regiments of Foot involved in the operations), in all 2,685 weapons had been surrendered. This was an impressive but, as Wade admitted, indifferent haul, including far more blade weapons than firearms. For their part, Jacobite agents reckoned the clans had concealed their best weaponry, and that Wade had only accepted their 'trash' to 'make himself pass as an [sic] useful man and fit to be continued in Scotland with a good salary'.[55]

Having at least tacitly complied with the Disarming Act, several chiefs involved or implicated in the 1719 rising were encouraged by Wade to make submissions for King George's clemency. They included Roderick Chisholm of Strathglass ('I had not attained to the years of manhood, when I unnaturally allowed myself to be led to bear arms against his majesty King George'); John Grant of Glenmoriston; John Mackinnon, Laird of Mackinnon ('I am heartily sorry for being ever engaged in rebellion against so good and gracious a prince'); John MacDougall of Dunollie, and even Rob Roy ('I was forced to take action with the adherents of the Pretender; for […] it was neither safe, nor indeed possible, to stand neuter').[56] Reporting with justifiable self-satisfaction his work in the Highlands to King George in January 1726, Wade wrote:

> When the news came that your majesty was graciously pleased to accept their submission and had given the proper orders for preparing their pardons, it was received with great joy and satisfaction throughout the Highlands, which occasioned the Jacobites at Edinburgh to say (by way of reproach), that I had not only defrauded the Highlanders of their arms, but had also debauched them from their loyalty and allegiance.[57]

Wade's attempted pacification of the Highlands was for the Georgian government an act of unfinished business from the 1719 rising. Wade's strategy was pursued into the 1730s, by building new and improving existing strongholds, and, with the start of construction in summer 1726 of an arterial road through the Great Glen linking Fort William, Kiliwhimen and Inverness Castle (rebuilt as the first Fort George), by building military roads to hasten troop deployments. In September 1726 Duncan Forbes of Culloden, then an MP and as lord advocate Scotland's chief law officer, who in spring 1719 had organised loyalist militia against the Jacobites, wrote to a friend that due to Wade's activity: 'The Highlands are at present in full rest.

---

55 Salmond, *Wade in Scotland*, pp. 41–2; Burt, *Letters from a Gentleman*, vol. 2, pp. 289–335, *passim*; Aufnere, *Lockhart Papers*, vol. 2, pp. 191, 197, quotation from p. 195.
56 Burt, *Letters from a Gentleman*, vol.2, pp. 334–5.
57 *Ibid.*, p. 314.

There is not the least complaint of robberies or depredations, and a great stick is become as fashionable an instrument in a Highlander's hand as a broadsword or pistol by his side used formerly to be'.[58]

Forbes optimistically reflected the view that perhaps times had changed for good. Positive signs of the demilitarisation of the clans coupled to the pardon and rehabilitation of notable Jacobites such as the Earl of Seaforth and Lord George Murray signified that Jacobitism in arms in the Highlands had run its course. While Scottish Jacobitism certainly receded into the background, it lingered with the potential to inflame antagonisms between Scots and English, and among Scots.[59] Within 20 years the western Highlands were the springboard for the militarily often successful, although ultimately failing, Jacobite rising of 1745–46. Ironically, the 24-year-old 'Bonnie Prince Charlie' landed in the Western Isles in July 1745 without foreign troops, accompanied by far fewer followers, and bringing a much smaller quantity of military supplies than the Marquess of Tullibardine and the Earl Marischal had arrived with in 1719.

58 J.H. Burton, *Lives of Simon Lord Lovat and Duncan Forbes of Culloden from Original Sources* (1847), pp. 329–30.
59 Ferguson, *Scotland,* p. 140.

Colour Plate Commentaries

Plate A: 'Plann of the Castle of Island Dounan [*sic*]; Profile of the Front of the Castle of Island Dounan markt [*sic*] ABCD'
Board of Ordnance plan and perspective elevation of Castle Eilean Donan. Drawn *c.*1714 by the engineer Brigadier Louis Petit, who surveyed in Scotland for the Board intermittently from 1713 to 1716.[1] The structure was mainly 15th-century build, forming a tighter defensive enclosure than the more expansive 13th-century castle it replaced. The dominant feature was the rebuilt 14th-century keep or tower house, shown by Petit as apparently roofless and missing its southerly gable. Note the only entrance was a raised gap in the south curtain wall, reached by a removable ladder. This at first obstructed Royal Navy landing parties when they seized Castle Donan on 10 May 1719.

Plate B: 'Attack on Eilean Donan Castle'
Ted Walker's reconstruction depicts His Majesty King George I's Ships *Worcester*, *Enterprise* and *Flamborough* bombarding Castle Donan on the morning of 10 May 1719. *Flamborough* is furthest distant, partly obscured by clouds of gun smoke.

Plate C: The Battle of Glenshiel 1719
This lively depiction of the battle is work of the Dutch painter and draughtsman Peter Tillemans (*b. c.*1684, *d.* 1734), active in England from 1708. The painting is assumed to date from 1719, but may in fact be a little later. The dominant landscape reflects both the nature of the battlefield and Tillemans's specialism as a topographical artist.[2] The composition closely resembles Lieutenant Bastide's contemporary engraved battle plan (see Colour Plate E), which seems to have been Tillemans's main reference. Tillemans depicted all phases of combat concurrently, a narrative device also resembling Bastide's cartography. Thus, Colonel Reading's left wing is shown in action against the Jacobite right, at the same time as Clayton's wing, depicted right, engages the Jacobite left. In the far middle distance British troops deploy to attack the Jacobite centre, supported by Coehoorn mortar

---

1   C.J. Anderson, *Constructing the Military Landscape: The Board of Ordnance Maps and Plans of Scotland, 1689–1815* (PhD Thesis, 2009), pp. 259, 261–2.
2   E. Bottoms, 'Tillemans, Peter (*c.*1684–1734)', in (eds.) C.G. Matthew and B. Harrison, *Oxford Dictionary of National Biography* (Oxford, 2004), online edition (available June 2018).

fire. The breastworks on the fortified bluff, manned by white-coated Spanish Foot, are clearly visible, further echoing Bastide's map-work.

The equestrian figure in blue coat prominent centre foreground is Major-General Joseph Wightman, with the mounted red-coated officer to his right assumed to be acting Brigadier Jasper Clayton. Tillemans appears to have taken particular care depicting the government troops and their uniforms. In a hollow behind and to Wightman's left, a body of dragoons include a detachment of North British Royal Dragoons wearing the unit's distinctive mitre caps. These so-called 'Grey Dragoons' are mounted on suitably coloured horses. Visible (far right foreground) are the column's pack horses, their civilian handlers and other camp followers; at least one woman is shown. Advancing uphill in column behind the dragoons are Dutch Foot, a body of white coats followed (and mostly obscured behind the dragoons) by bluecoats, representing the regiments of Huffel and Amerongen; although which was uniformed light blue and which in white is unclear. Halfway upslope far right the composite grenadier battalion can be identified by their mitre caps; including, but mostly hidden by a fold in the ground, white and blue coated Dutch grenadiers.

Tillemans included for dramatic effect on the mountainsides at left and right scenes of bitter hand-to-hand fighting that in reality did not occur. Jacobites are but sketchily depicted: apart from a light-blue clad figure prominent on the conical hill, left, assumed to be Lord George Murray; a corresponding figure, on the bluff right middle distance, wielding broadsword and targe, may be the Earl of Seaforth.

Plate D: 'A Plan of the Field of Battle that was fought on ye 10th of June 1719, at the Pass of Glenshiels [sic] in Kintail North Britain with ye Disposition of his Majtys [sic] Forces under ye Command of Majr. Genl. Wightman, & of those of ye Rebels'

One of four, near identical, Board of Ordnance manuscript maps made by Lieutenant Jean Henri Bastide; draughtsman, and, as an officer in Montagu's regiment, present at the battle. Drawn in ink and wash, Bastide's 'Plan' topographically very accurately views the engagement in the glen from the south. Like Bastide's other, engraved, plan of the battle, and the Tillemans painting, the action is shown occurring concurrently. Thus, the British army start line is shown far right (east), and the mountain slopes depicted left (west) are dotted with figures representing the fleeing Jacobite army.

The map combines both plan and perspective view. Opposing units, their deployment, and movements are indicated, respectively, by a combination of shaded symbols, letters and numbers, and dotted lines. But Bastide departed from contemporary military cartographic convention by depicted loose and retreating bodies of Highlanders as musket-armed stick men.[3]

The accompanying alpha-numeric key of 'References' is in its own right an important source, and is worth citing fully (spellings as per the original):

---

3   Anderson, *Constructing the Military Landscape*, p. 133.

References to His Majtys Forces

1 A serjt and twelve granadiers; 2 An officer & 24 granadiers; 3 Main body of granadiers 120 in number; 4 Col. Montague's regimt; 5 Col. Harrison's detatcht Battalion; 6 Huffel's Regiment and four Companys of ameronce; 7 Dragoons; 8 Col. Clayton's Regiment; 9 The Monro's Highlanders; 10 The Sutherlands High1[anders]; 11 The first march by the Right; 12 Clayton's march by the left; 13 The Dragoons march to the plain; 14 The Dragoons halt; 15 The Dragoons advances to the middle of the plain; 16 Clayton's four plottoons & the Monro's making ye first attack on the rebells right; 17 Cohorn mortars throwing grenades at the rebells where the first attack was orderd; 18 Cohorn mortars throw granades att the Spaniards in their intrenchments; 19 Part of Claytons attacks the barricade of the pass; 20 Dragoons on foot attack the Spaniards breast works; 21 The Dragoons mount the hill; 22 Our march in line of battle to the rock where the attack began under the command of Col. Clayton; 23 Our right pursue the rebels; 24 The plotooons and the Monro's halt upon the hill having put the ennemy to the flight; 25 Our right halts upon the mountain; 26 Part of Clayton's takes possession of the hill that commanded ye pass; 27 Guard for the Baggage and place for the Hospitall; 28 The baggage advanc'd with the wounded men for their security; 29 Maj. Genll Whightman giving his directions during the battle.

References to the Ennemy.

A Spanish Regiment posted on the Hill that commanded the plain and the pass; B Spaniards march to the mount and halt; C The Spaniards retire to the top of the mountain; D The Barricade that defended the pass on the River Side; E The Breastworks on the side of the Hill; F The Highlanders drawn up before the attack; G A straggling number of Highlandrs fires upon the plottoons of Claytons & the Monros behind them in the time of the attack; H A body of Highlanders going to sustain their right; ii the flight of the rebels; M The mount call'd Skururan the Highest in Scotland except Benevis; N.B. That the Ennemy in their flight still fir'd & defended the places of difficult access.

Plate E: 'A Disposition of His Majesty's Forces commanded by Major-General Wightman & of the Rebels at the Pass of Glenshiells in Kintail North Britain where the battle was fought on the 10th of June 1719'.

A birds-eye view reconstruction of the action drawn by Lieutenant Bastide. An eyewitness, Bastide had his drawing engraved and published as this print in London on the following 6 August. The newspaper *The Post Man and the Historical Account,* in the edition for 4–6 August 1719 advertised that: 'A plan of the Battel of Glenshell [*sic*] near Kintail in North Britain […] by John Bastide, a lieutenant in the honourable Colonel Montague's Regiment of Foot' was on sale from two city outlets priced six pence.

The starting position of the British army is shown at the foot of the print, with the fortified bluff held by the Jacobites prominently depicted off centre. The drawing provides a good impression of the horseshoe-shaped Jacobite lines. Bastide's accompanying 'References' are again worth citing in full (spellings as per the original):

'References for the Enemy

1. The Enfred[?] hill for ye defence of ye Pass; 2. The Spaniards; 3. Their intrenchments defended by the Highlanders; 4. Breastworks defended by ye Spaniards; 5. The Pass; 6. Detachment from their right commanded by Ld. George Murray; 7. Body of 400 Highlanders commanded by Ld. Seaforth; 8. Other body of men to sustain the First; 9. Woods from whence they Fir'd hid behind rocks; 10. Highlandrs going to sustain their Right; 11. Spaniards marching up ye Hill to retreat; 12. Top of ye Hill where they fled to after ye action; 13. Highlandrs Sculking about the Hills; 14. Highlanders broke and running away.

References for his Majtys. Forces

A. Ground where we drew up before ye battle; B. The 3 Battalions and Granadrs for ye attack of their Left & My.d [i.e. My Lord] Strathnever's Highlanders; C. Battalion and our Highlanders for the attack of the Right; D. A Plotton and Highlandrs marching up the Hill to attack Ld. Ge. Murray; E. 2 Plottons of Reinforcement; F. Dragoons advanc'd on Horseback; G. Foot and Dragoons dismounted for the attack of the Fortified hill; H. Our March in line of Battle to ye rock where we wheel'd to ye right at I to attack the Enemy at 7; L. Our army drawn up after the action; M. Guard for ye Baggage & place for ye Hospitall; N. Cohorn mortars'.

Bibliography

Manuscript Sources

Edinburgh, The National Library of Scotland

Military Maps of Scotland (18th century), digitally available online (June 2018) at <https://maps.nls.uk/military/info.html>

London, The National Archives

Admiralty Records
ADM 2, Admiralty Out-Letters
ADM 51, Captains' Logs
ADM 52, Sailing Masters' Logs

Records of the Auditors of the Imprest, Commissioners of Audit, Exchequer and Audit Department, National Audit Office and related bodies
AO 1/2310/26

State Papers Domestic
SP 41, Secretaries of State: State Papers Military, 1702–1782
SP 43, Secretaries of State:State Papers Regencies, George I and George II
SP 54, Secretaries of State: State Papers Scotland Series II
SP 55, Secretaries of State: State Papers Scotland: Letter Books

War Office
WO 4, War Office: Secretary-at-War, Out-Letters
WO 24, War Office: Papers concerning Establishments
WO 47, Ordnance Office: Board of Ordnance: Minutes

London, The National Maritime Museum

Admiralty Collection
ADM/L, Navy Board, Lieutenants' Logs

Published Primary Sources

Early 18th Century English Newspapers

St. James's Journal

The Daily Currant

The Evening Post

The Exeter Mercury, or Weekly Intelligencer

The London Gazette

The Post Boy

The Post Man and The Historical Account

The Weekly Journal or British Gazetteer

The Weekly Journal or Saturday's Post

The Weekly Packet

The Whitehall Evening Post

Books and Edited Collections of Documents

Anon., *The Political State of Great Britain, Volume XIV* (London, 1717)

Anon., *The Political State of Britain, Volume XV* (London, 1718)

Anon., *The Historical Register, Containing An Impartial Relation of all Transactions, Foreign and Domestic* (London, 1719)

Anon., *The Political State of Britain, Volume XVI* (London, 1719)

Anon., *The Journals of The House of Commons of the Kingdom of Ireland, Volume IV* (Dublin, 1763)

Anon., *A Collection of all the Treaties of Peace, Alliance and Commerce, between Great-Britain and other Powers, from the Revolution in 1688, to the Present Time*, 2 vols. (London, 1772)

Anon., *Journals of the House of Commons*, volume 18, August 1714 to September 1718 (London, 1803)

Anon., *Journals of the House of Commons*, volume 19, November 1718 to March 1721 (London, 1803)

Anon., *Journals of the House of Lords*, volume 21, November 1718 to March 1721 (London, undated, 1767–1830)

Allardyce, J. (ed.), *Historical Papers relating to the Jacobite Period 1699–1750*, 2 vols. (Aberdeen, 1895)

Atholl, J., 7th Duke of (ed.), *Chronicles of the Atholl and Tullibardine Families*, 5 vols. (Edinburgh, 1908)

Aufnere, A. (ed.), *The Lockhart Papers: Containing a Memoir and Commentaries upon the Affairs in Scotland from 1702–1715 by George Lockhart*, 2 vols. (London, 1817)

Boswell, J., *Boswell's Journal of a Tour to the Hebrides with Samuel Johnson*, (eds.) F.A. Pottle and C.H. Bennett (London, 1936)

Browning, A. (ed.), *English Historical Documents, Volume VI, 1660–1714* (London, 1966)

Burton, J.H., *Lives of Simon Lord Lovat and Duncan Forbes of Culloden from Original Sources* (London, 1847)

Chamberlayne, J., *Magna Britannia Notitia: Or the Present State of Great-Britain* (London, 1718)

Charteris, E. (ed.), *A Short Account of the Affairs of Scotland in the Years 1744, 1745, 1746 By David, Lord Elcho* (Edinburgh, 1907)

Chrichton, A. (ed.), *The Life and Diary of Lieutenant-Colonel J. Blackader* (Edinburgh, 1824)

Dalton, C. (ed.), *English Army Lists and Commission Registers, 1661–1714*, 6 vols. (London, 1892–1904)

Daniell, F.H.B. (ed.), *Calendar of the Stuart Papers belonging to His Majesty The King Preserved at Windsor Castle*, 7 vols. (London, 1902–23)

Defoe, D., *What if the Swedes should come? With some thoughts about keeping the Army on foot, whether they come or not* (London, 1717)

Dickson, W.K., *The Jacobite Attempt of 1719* (Edinburgh, 1895)

Farquhar, G., *The Recruiting Officer. A Comedy. As it was Acted at the Theatre Royal in Drury Lane* (London, *c.*1706)

Fraser, W. (ed.), *The Sutherland Book,* 3 vols. (Edinburgh, 1892)

Graham, J.M. (ed.), *Annals and Correspondence of the First and Second Earls of Stair,* 2 vols. (Edinburgh and London, 1875)

Horn, D.B. (ed.), *English Historical Documents, Volume X, 1714–1783* (London, 1966)

Jamieson, R. (ed.), *Letters from a Gentleman in the North of Scotland to His Friend in London,* 2 vols. (London, 1822)

Johnstone, J., *Memoirs of the Rebellion in 1745 and 1746 by the Chevalier De Johnstone,* (ed.) Anon. (1821, second edition)

Keith, J., *A Fragment of a Memoir of Field-Marshal James Keith, Written by Himself,* (ed.) T. Constable (Edinburgh, 1863)

Lang, A. (ed.), *The Highlands of Scotland in 1750. From Manuscript 104 in the King's Library, British Museum* (Edinburgh and London, 1898)

Macky, J., *A Journey through Scotland. In Familiar Letters from a Gentleman Here, to His Friend Abroad* (London, 1729)

Martin, M., *A Description of the Western Islands of Scotland* (London, 1703)

Millar, A.H. (ed.), 'The Battle of Glenshiel. Note upon an unpublished letter in the possession of C.S. Home-Drummond-Moray Esq. of Abercairnet', *Proceedings of The Society of Antiquaries of Scotland,* 19 (1884–5), pp. 64–6.

Murray, G. (ed.), *The Letters and Dispatches of John Churchill, first Duke of Marlborough, from 1702 to 1712,* 5 vols. (London, 1845)

Oliphant, K.T.L. (ed.), *The Jacobite Lairds of Gask* (London, 1870)

Pickering, D. (ed.), *The Statutes at Large from the Twelfth Year of Queen Anne to the Fifth Year of King George I* (1764)

Pickering, D. (ed.), *The Statutes at Large from the Ninth Year of King George I to the Second Year of King George II* (London, 1765)

Reddington, J., (ed.), *Calendar of Treasury Papers, 1714–1719* (London, 1883)

Reddington, J. (ed.), *Calendar of Treasury Papers, 1720–1728* (London, 1889)

Renwick, R. (ed.), *Extracts from the records of the Royal Burgh of Stirling, AD 1667–1752* (Glasgow, 1889)

Shaw, W.A. and F.H. Slingsby (eds.), *Calendar of Treasury Books, Volume 29, 1714–1715* (London, 1957)

Shaw, W.A. and F.H. Slingsby (eds.), *Calendar of Treasury Books, Volume 31, 1717* (London, 1960)

Shaw, W.A. and F.H. Slingsby (eds.), *Calendar of Treasury Books, Volume 32, 1718* (London, 1962)

Sinclair, J. (ed.), *The Statistical Account of Scotland,* 21 vols. (Edinburgh, 1791–99)

Sinclair, J., *Memoirs of the Insurrection in Scotland in 1715. By John, Master of Sinclair,* (ed.) Anon. (Edinburgh, 1858)

Warrand, D. (ed.), *More Culloden Papers* (Inverness, 1925)

Secondary Sources

Anon., *The Life and Character of James Butler, late Duke, Marquis and Earl of Ormond* (London, 1739)

Anon., *Biographica Britannica, or the lives of the most eminent persons who have flourished in Great Britain and Ireland,* 6 vols. (London, 1847 reprint)

Anon., *The Hutchinson Illustrated Encyclopedia of British History* (Oxford, 1995)

Anon., 'Battlefield Remains', *The National Trust for Scotland Archaeology Bulletin,* 9 (1997)

Anon. (for Historic Environment Scotland's 'Inventory of Historic Battlefields'), 'Inventory Battlefield, Battle of Glenshiel, Reference: BTL10, Date of Battle 10 June 1719', available (June 2018) at <http://portal.historic-scotland.gov.uk>

Anderson, C.J., *Constructing the Military Landscape: The Board of Ordnance Maps and Plans of Scotland, 1689-1815* (PhD Thesis, The University of Edinburgh, 2009)

Atkinson, C.T., *Marlborough and the Rise of the British Army* (London and New York, 1921)

Backscheider, P.R., 'Defoe, Daniel (1660?-1731)', in (eds.) C.G. Matthew and B. Harrison, *Oxford Dictionary of National Biography* (Oxford, 2004), online edition (available June 2018)

Balestrino, I., *The Coehorn Mortar* (Gibraltar, undated). Article available March 2017 on the website of the Office of the Governor of Gibraltar, but by June 2018 no longer accessible

Barnett, C., *Britain and Her Army: A Military, Political and Social History of the British Army, 1509-1970* (London, 1970), 2013 reprint

Barratt, J., *Battles for the Three Kingdoms: The Campaigns for England, Scotland and Ireland 1689–92* (Stroud, 2007)

Barthorp, M., *The Jacobite Rebellions, 1689-1745* (London, 1982)

Bennett, G.V., 'English Jacobitism, 1710–1715; Myth and Reality', *Transactions of the Royal Historical Society,* 32 (1982), pp. 137–51

Bennett, H., 'A murder victim discovered: clothing and other finds from an early 18th century grave on Arnish Moor, Lewis', *Proceedings of the Society of Antiquaries of Scotland*, 106 (1974), pp. 172–82

Black. J., *Politics and Foreign Policy in the Age of George I, 1714-1727* (Farnham, 2014)

Blackmore, D., *Destructive and Formidable: British Infantry Firepower, 1642-1765* (Barnsley, 2014)

Bottoms, E., 'Tillemans, Peter (*c.*1684–1734)', in (eds.) C.G. Matthew and B. Harrison, *Oxford Dictionary of National Biography* (Oxford, 2004), online edition (available June 2018).

Brooks, R., *Cassell's Battlefields of Britain* (London, 2005)

Brown, K.M., 'Reformation to Union, 1560-1707', in R.A. Houston and W.W.J. Knox (eds.), *The New Penguin History of Scotland: From the Earliest Times to the Present Day* (London, 2002), pp. 182–275

Burton, J.H., *Lives of Simon Lord Lovat and Duncan Forbes of Culloden from Original Sources* (London, 1847).

Carpenter, S.D.M., 'The British Army', in *A Companion to Eighteenth Century Britain,* (ed.) H.T. Dickinson (Oxford, 2000), pp. 473–80

Chandler, D., *The Art of Warfare in the Age of Marlborough* (Staplehurst, 1990)

Chandler, D., 'The Great Captain General, 1702–1714', in *The Oxford History of the British Army,* (eds.) D. Chandler and I. Beckett (Oxford, 1994)

Charles, G., *History of the Transactions in Scotland, in the Years 1715-16 and 1745-46,* 2 vols. (Stirling, 1816)

Childs, J., 'The Restoration Army 1660-1702', in D. Chandler and I. Beckett (eds.), *The Oxford History of the British Army* (Oxford, 1994), pp. 46–66

Childs, J., *The Williamite Wars in Ireland 1688-1691* (London, 2007)

Childs, J., 'Marlborough's Wars and the Act of Union, 1702–14', in *A Military History of Scotland,* (eds.), J.A. Crane, E.M. Spiers and M.J. Strickland (Edinburgh, 2012), pp. 326–47

Claydon, T., 'William III and II (1650-1702)', in (eds.) C.G. Matthew and B. Harrison, *Oxford Dictionary of National Biography* (Oxford, 2004), online edition (available June 2018)

Cleaveland, R.A., *Notes on the Early History of the Royal Regiment of Artillery* (London, undated).

Clowes, W.M., *The Royal Navy, A History from the Earliest Times to the Present,* 5 vols. (London, 1898).

Cockayne, G.E. (ed.), *Complete Peerage of England, Scotland, Ireland, Great Britain and The United Kingdom,* 8 vols. (London, 1887–98)

Colledge, J.J., *Ships of the Royal Navy: The Complete Record of all the Fighting Ships of the Royal Navy* (Oxford, 2010, revised edition)

Cruden, S., *The Scottish Castle* (Edinburgh and London, 1960)

Cuthell, E.E., *The Scottish Friend of Frederick the Great, the last Earl Marischal,* 2 vols. (London, 1915)

Dalton, C., *George The First's Army, 1714–1727,* 2 vols. (London, 1910)

Duffy, C., 'The Jacobite Wars, 1708–46', in *A Military History of Scotland,* (eds.), J.A. Crane, E.M. Spiers and M.J. Strickland (Edinburgh, 2012), pp. 348–79

Dunlop, R., revised H. Murtagh, 'Schomberg, Frederick Herman de, first duke of Schomberg (1615–1690)', in (eds.) C.G. Matthew and B. Harrison, *Oxford Dictionary of National Biography* (Oxford, 2004), online edition (available June 2018)

Dwelly, E., *The Illustrated Gaelic Dictionary,* 2 vols. (Fleet, 1918)

Ehrenstein, C.V., 'Erskine, John, styled twenty-second or sixth earl of Mar and Jacobite duke of Mar (*bap.* 1675, *d.* 1732)', in (eds.) C.G. Matthew and B. Harrison, *Oxford Dictionary of National Biography* (Oxford, 2004), online edition (available June 2018)

Evans, E., (ed.), *British History, A Source Book* (London, 2006)

Falkner, J., 'Wightman, Joseph (d. 1722)', in (eds.) C.G. Matthew and B. Harrison, *Oxford Dictionary of National Biography* (Oxford, 2004), online edition (available June 2018)

Feilding, K., *A History of the Tory Party, 1640–1714* (Oxford, 1924)

Ferguson, W., *Scotland 1689 to the Present. The Edinburgh History of Scotland, Volume 4* (Edinburgh, 1978)

Fritz, P.S., 'The Anti-Jacobite Intelligence System of the English Ministers, 1715–1745', *The Historical Journal,* 16 (1973), pp. 265–89

Fritz, P. S., *The English Ministers and Jacobitism between the Rebellions of 1715 and 1745* (1975)

Furgol, E.M., 'Cameron, Sir Ewen, of Lochiel (1629–1719)', in (eds.) C.G. Matthew and B. Harrison, *Oxford Dictionary of National Biography* (Oxford, 2004), online edition (available June 2018)

Furgol, E.M., 'Keith, George, styled tenth Earl Marischal (1692/3?–1778)', in (eds.) C.G. Matthew and B. Harrison, *Oxford Dictionary of National Biography* (Oxford, 2004), online edition (available June 2018)

Galbraith, J.J., 'The Battle of Glenshiel, 1719', *Transactions of the Gaelic Society of Inverness,* 34 (1927–8), pp. 280–93

Gibbs, G. C., 'George I (1660–1727)', in (eds.) C. G. Matthew and B. Harrison, *Oxford Dictionary of National Biography* (Oxford, 2004), online edition (available June 2018)

Gibson, J.S., 'Cameron, Donald, of Lochiel (*c.*1700–1748)', in (eds.) C.G. Matthew and B. Harrison, *Oxford Dictionary of National Biography* (Oxford, 2004), online edition (available June 2018)

Gregg, E., 'James Francis Edward Stuart (1688–1766)', in (eds.) C.G. Matthew and B. Harrison, *Oxford Dictionary of National Biography* (Oxford, 2004), online edition (available June 2018)

Guy, J., 'The Army of the Georges, 1714–1783', in (eds.) D. Chandler and I. Beckett, *The Oxford History of the British Army* (Oxford, 1994), pp. 92–111

Handley, S., 'Butler, James, second duke of Ormond (1665–1745)', in (eds.) C.G. Matthew and B. Harrison, *Oxford Dictionary of National Biography* (2004) online edition (available June 2018)

Harding, N., *Hanover and the British Empire, 1700–1837* (Woodbridge, 2007)

Harding, R., *Seapower and Naval Warfare, 1650–1830* (Abingdon, 1999)

Hattendorf, J.B., 'English Governmental Machinery and the Conduct of War, 1702–1713, *War & Society,* 3 (1985), pp. 1–22

Haythornthwaite, P.J., 'The First Highland Regiment', *Military Illustrated Past and Present,* 10 (1988), pp. 23–30

Hayton, D.W., 'Grant, Alexander (aft. 1673–1719), of Castle Grant, Elgin', in *The History of Parliament* online (available June 2018)

Henshaw, V., *Scotland and the British Army c.1700–c.1750* (PhD Thesis, The University of Birmingham, 2011)

Hill, J.M., *Celtic Warfare, 1595–1763* (Edinburgh, 1986)

Hill, J.M., 'Killiecrankie and the Evolution of Highland Warfare', *War in History,* 1 (1994), *pp. 125–39*

Horsburgh, D., 'Mackenzie, William, fifth earl of Seaforth (d. 1740)', in (eds.) C.G. Matthew and B. Harrison, *Oxford Dictionary of National Biography* (Oxford, 2004), online edition (available June 2018)

Kemp, A., *Weapons and Equipment of the Marlborough Wars* (Poole, 1980)

Kemp, H., *The Jacobite Rebellion* (London, 1975)

Kennedy, P., *The Rise and Fall of British Naval Mastery* (London, 1976) 2017 revised edition

Klinger, P.J., 'Weather and the Jacobite Rebellion of 1719', *Environment and History,* 23 (2017), *pp. 197–216*

Kohn, G.C., *Dictionary of Wars,* Revised Edition (Abingdon, 1999)

Lenman, B., 'The Jacobite Diaspora 1688–1746: From Despair to Integration', *History Today,* 30 (1980), pp. 7–10

Lenman, B., *Britain's Colonial Wars 1688–1783* (Harlow, 2001)

Lenman, B., 'From the Union of 1707 to the Franchise Reform of 1832', in R.A. Houston and W.W.J. Knox (eds.), *The New Penguin History of Scotland: From the Earliest Times to the Present Day* (London, 2002), pp. 276–354

Lenman, B., *The Jacobite Risings in Britain, 1689–1746* (Dalkeith, 2004)

Lord, E., *The Stuarts' Secret Army, English Jacobites, 1689–1752* (Harlow, 2004)

Lyon, D., *The Sailing Navy List: All the Ships of the Royal Navy, Built, Purchased and Captured, 1688–1860* (London, 1993, revised edition)

MacDonald, A. and A. Macdonald, *The Clan Donald* (Inverness, 1904)

MacGregor, M., 'Warfare in Gaelic Scotland in the later Middle Ages', in J.A. Crane, E.M. Spiers and M.J. Strickland (eds.), *A Military History of Scotland* (Edinburgh, 2012), pp. 209–31

Macinnes, A.I., 'Jacobitism', *History Today,* 34 (1984), pp. 22–8

Mackenzie, A., *History of the Chisholms* (Inverness, 1881)

Mackenzie, A., *The MacDonalds of Glengarry* (Inverness, 1881)

Mackintosh, A.M., *Brigadier Mackintosh of Borlum: Jacobite Hero and Martyr* (Nairn, 1918)

McConnell, D., *British Smooth-Bore Artillery: A Technological Study to support Identification, Acquisition, Restoration, Reproduction, and Interpretation of Artillery at National Historic Parks in Canada* (Ottawa, 1988)

McKay, D. and H.M. Scott, *The Rise of the Great Powers, 1648–1815* (London and New York, 2014)

McKerracher, M., *The Jacobite Dictionary* (Glasgow, 2007)

McLynn, F., *The Jacobites* (London, 1985)

Magnusson, M., *Scotland: The Story of a Nation* (London, 2000)

Mahon, P.S., *History of England from The Peace of Utrecht to the Peace of Aix-la-Chapelle,* 3 vols. (London, 1839)

Michael, W., *England under George I: The Quadruple Alliance* (London, 1939)

Millar, A.H., 'The Battle of Glenshiel, 10th June 1719. Note Upon an Unpublished Document in the Possession of His Grace The Duke of Marlborough', *Proceedings of the Society of Antiquaries of Scotland,* 27 (1882–3), pp. 57–69

Nielsen, C.L., *The Chelsea Out-Pensioners: Image and Reality in Eighteenth-Century and Early Nineteenth-Century Social Care* (PhD Thesis, Newcastle University, 2014)

Oates, J., 'Jacobitism and Popular Disturbances in Northern England, 1714–1719', *Northern History,* 41 (2004), pp. 111–28

Oates, J., 'Dutch Forces in Eighteenth-Century Britain: A British Perspective', *Journal of the Society of Army Historical Research,* 85 (2007), pp. 20–39

Oates, J., *The Jacobite Campaigns: The British State at War – Warfare, Society and Culture* (Abingdon, 2016)

Ordnance Survey Maps – 1:25 000 scale *Explorer* series

OS Explorer 413: Knoydart, Loch Hourn & Loch Duich (Southampton, 2015)

OS Explorer 414: Glenshiel & Kintail Forest (Southampton, 2015)

OS Explorer 415: Glen Affric & Glen Moriston (Southampton, 2015)

OS Explorer 416: Inverness, Loch Ness & Culloden (Southampton, 2015)

OS Explorer 428: Kyle of Lochalsh, Plockton & Applecross (Southampton, 2015)

Ostwald, J., *Vauban under Siege: Engineering Efficiency and Martial Vigor in the War of the Spanish Succession* (Leiden and Boston, 2007)

Paton, H., 'Sutherland, John, sixteenth earl of Sutherland (*bap.* 1661, *d.* 1733)', rev. J. Spain, in (eds.) C.G. Matthew and B. Harrison, *Oxford Dictionary of National Biography* (2004) online edition (available June 2018)

Patten, R., *The History of the Rebellion in the Year 1715* (London, 1745)

Pittock, M.G.H., *The Myth of the Jacobite Clans* (Edinburgh, 1999)

Pittock, M.G.H., 'Murray, Lord George (1694–1760)', in (eds.) C.G. Matthew and B. Harrison, *Oxford Dictionary of National Biography* (2004) online edition (available June 2018)

Pittock, M.G.H., 'Murray, William, styled second duke of Atholl and marquess of Tullibardine (1689–1746)', in (eds.) C. G. Matthew and B. Harrison, *Oxford Dictionary of National Biography* (2004), online edition (available June 2018)

Prebble, J., *Mutiny: Highland Regiments in Revolt 1743–1804* (London, 1977)

Prebble, J., *Glencoe: The Story of the Massacre* (London, 1987)

Rae, P., *The History of the Rebellion raised against His Majesty King George I By the Friends of the Popish Pretender* (London, 1746, second edition)

Randall, A., *Riotous Assemblies: Popular Protest in Hanoverian England* (Oxford, 2006)

Reid, S., *1745 A Military History of the last Jacobite Rising* (Staplehurst, 1996)

Rogers, H.C.B., *The British Army in the Eighteenth Century* (London, 1977)

Rodger, N.A.M., *The Command of the Ocean: A Naval History of Britain, 1649–1815* (London, 2006)

Rowlands, G., 'Foreign Service in the Age of Absolute Monarchy: Louis XIV and His *Forces Étrangères*', *War in History*, 17 (2010), pp. 141–65

Salmond, J.B., *Wade in Scotland* (Edinburgh and London, 1934)

Sankey, M. and D. Szechi, 'Elite Culture and the Decline of Scottish Jacobitism 1716–1745', *Past & Present*, 173 (2001), pp. 90–128

Sharp, D., 'The Battle of Glenshiel', *Military History Magazine* (June 2006), unknown pagination.

Sinclair-Stevenson, C., *Inglorious Rebellion: The Jacobite Risings of 1708, 1715 and 1719* (London, 1971)

Smith, H., 'The Army, Provincial Urban Communities, and Loyalist Culture in England, *c.*1714–50', *Journal of Early Modern History*, 15 (2011), pp. 139–58

Speck, W.A., *Tory & Whig, The Struggle in the Constituencies 1701–1715* (London, 1970)

Stephens, H.M., revised T.H. Place, 'Carpenter, George, first Baron Carpenter of Killaghy (1657–1732)', in (eds.) C.G. Matthew and B. Harrison, *Oxford Dictionary of National Biography* (2004) online edition (available June 2018)

Stephens, H. M., revised W. C. Lowe, 'Dalrymple, John, second earl of Stair (1673–1747)', in (eds.) C.G. Matthew and B. Harrison, *Oxford Dictionary of National Biography* (2004) online edition (available June 2018)

Stevenson, D., 'MacGregor, Robert [Rob Roy] (*bap.* 1671, *d.* 1734)', in (eds.) C.G. Matthew and B. Harrison, *Oxford Dictionary of National Biography* (2004) online edition (available June 2018)

Szechi, D., *The Jacobites: Britain and Europe, 1688–1788* (Manchester, 1994)

Szechi, D., "Cam Ye O'er Frae France?" Exile and the Mind of Scottish Jacobitism, 1716–1727', *Journal of British Studies*, 37 (1998), pp. 357–90

Szechi, D., *1715: The Great Jacobite Rebellion* (New Haven and London, 2000)

Szechi, D., *George Lockhart of Carnwath, 1689–1727: A Study in Jacobitism* (East Linton, 2002)

Szechi, D., *Jacobitism and Tory Politics, 1710–1714* (Edinburgh, 2003)

Tabraham, C. and D. Grove, *Fortress Scotland and the Jacobites* (London, 1995)

Taylor, W., *The Military Roads in Scotland* (Colonsay, 1996)

Terry, C.S., *The Chevalier St. George and the Jacobite Movements in His Favour, 1701–1720* (London, 1901)

Thomas, P.D.G., 'Wynn, Sir Watkin Williams, third baronet (1693?–1749)', in (eds.) C.G. Matthew and B. Harrison, *Oxford Dictionary of National Biography* (2004) online edition (available June 2018)

Thompson, A.L., 'Jacobite Rebellions', *Military Modelling Magazine* (March 1991), pp. 19–21

Wilson, B., *Empire of the Deep: The Rise and Fall of the British Navy* (London, 2014)

Young, J.R., 'Murray, John, first duke of Atholl (1660–1724)', in (eds.) C.G. Matthew and B. Harrison, *Oxford Dictionary of National Biography* (2004) online edition (available June 2018)